THE PROSPERITY SECRETS OF THE AGES

by

Catherine Ponder

DeVorss Publications
Camarillo, California

The Prosperity Secrets of the Ages
Copyright © 1964 by Catherine Ponder
Revised by the Author, 1986

ISBN: 0-87516-567-2
Library of Congress Catalog Card: 64-16436

DeVorss & Company, Publisher
PO Box 1389
Camarillo CA 93011-1389
www.devorss.com

Printed in Canada

CONTENTS

Health, happiness and financial security after having been alone, broke and suicidal. Success attitudes are the secret. Amazing results of success attitudes. Unveil your success!

PART I

BACKGROUND SUCCESS SECRETS FOR YOU

Success is at hand! Dynamic results for the author. Your greatest success book. The search for success. A revolution is needed. A great man's success secrets. Get something going! An exciting interpretation. You are metaphysical. Early Christians taught this interpretation. Symbology in all great literature. You can have everything! Lying down on the job. Business executive chooses success. The secret wisdom of the ages.

Blessing saves marriage. Bless the other woman. Statements of blessing. Sell merchandise through blessing it. Collect money through blessing. Bless when you're tempted to curse. Blessing makes bad check good. Blessing for health. Blessing reduces weight. Blessing improves European trip. More powerful than money or politics. Bless the traffic. Bless every situation. Even bless your income taxes. Use this ancient success secret often.

PART II

THE SUCCESS ALLEGORIES
Their Hidden Meanings For You

You can change your world. Your *first* success attitude. A photographer proved this. This success attitude heals. Your *second* success attitude. A West Berliner proved this. Your *third* success attitude. Imaging saved a grain crop. Your *fourth* success attitude. Lawsuit resolved through this successful secret. Your *fifth* success attitude. Shopping quickly accomplished. Your *sixth* success attitude. How to overcome doubt and fear. No mistakes have been made. Your *final* success attitude. Nothing more to do.

One person can change a situation. Paradise: your choice. Blind to the good. I can hardly wait! A formula for harmony. Evil is nothing. A businessman's success formula. Evil is undeveloped good. Harmony heals heart condition. You are radiant substance. Your words can heal. Lavish abundance. Marriage advice. Your story and mine.

Force causes mental illness. The secret of freedom. Divorced wife discovers release. How to restore your good. A divorcee proves the success law of substitution. When all seems lost. Call on the success law of restoration. A cosmic secret. Businessman rises to greater success. Help others restore their good. A contractor used this success attitude. Healing of cancer. Feeling of loss may cause cancer. What to think about death. Welcome change and call it good.

PART III

THE PROSPEROUS PEOPLE OF GENESIS
Their Success Secrets for You

through imaging. No image, no marriage. The danger of imaging what belongs to another. Adoption of children through imaging. Preparing nursery brings child. Sale of property through imaging. Imaging clothes brings them. Public relations man images foreign travel. Housewife images success for entire family. Our go-kart Christmas. Imaging produces domestic help. Imaging for yourself and others makes dreams come true.

Cause of constant problems. The magic number of increase. The author's experience with this prosperity law. From rags to riches after age 50. Salesman begins to sell again. Professional man proves this prosperity law. Businesswoman saves property. Marriage and prosperity result. Man stops drinking when his wife tithes. Allowance-giving opens way to prosperity. Where you give is important. Charity giving is not tithing. Rich results of consistent giving. A millionaire consciousness.

A success formula for receiving. Get ready for a master demonstration. Attitudes that stop your good. Bitterness causes barrenness. Fear and uncertainty bring wild results. Delay is a time of growth. How to circumcise fear and uncertainty. Demonstration comes in the fullness of time. Great secret of demonstration. Television actress makes her demonstration. Demonstrations bring surprises. There are no mistakes. Demonstrations require changes. Secret of keeping your demonstration. Career woman loses demonstration. Permanent success.

Nothing disrespectful about joy. The attracting power of joy. The healing power of joy. A little-known success secret. Prospering power of fun. One last secret about joy. Your *second* success power: beauty. How to make a start. Personal appearance important to success. Beauty is necessary to spirituality. Beauty is necessary to health. A mystical prosperity formula. Give something beautiful. The magic of giving. Be a good receiver of beauty. Your success powers of joy and beauty.

growth. *Seventh:* Calling on hidden justice makes things right. Do not feel sorry for others. College student proves justice. Justice in state senate. *Eighth:* Justice works in mysterious ways. *Ninth:* Joseph's basic success secret.

Sex is not sinful. Sex is threefold. Sex is more than physical. How to satisfy your deeper longings. You can direct physical desire. Sex is mental. Get rid of extreme notions about sex. Sublimation can produce sublime results. Many people are afraid of sublimation. Dissipation leads to failure. Kindness is sex in expression. How to re-establish sex in marriage. What about frigidity and impotence? Sex is spiritual power.

Success on all levels of life. The author's final message.

Introduction . . . .

YOU CAN HAVE EVERYTHING!

There are many prosperity secrets in this book, but one of the basic ones is this:

You can have everything if you know the power that is within you and then dare to use it!

You have always used this power in some degree— often for failure. Now you can begin deliberately to release it for success; that is, for experiencing greater results of health, happiness and prosperity in your world.

Your success power is released through your mental attitudes and your emotional reactions toward life. You become what you think. Think straight and life becomes straight for you. It's as simple as that.

1

HEALTH, HAPPINESS AND FINANCIAL SECURITY: AFTER HAVING BEEN ALONE, BROKE AND SUICIDAL

A reader from California recently reported:

In 1967 I was alone, broke and suicidal. Five years earlier, I had had a serious accident from which I still experienced severe pain. There had followed such a series of tragedies within my immediate family that we were known as "the crisis-a-week club." Our friends even begged us to stay away from them because they didn't want to hear any more of our troubles.

Then a miracle happened: I got a job as a rehabilitation counselor. One evening my supervisor, a marvelous warm-hearted person who is almost totally blind, said, "Have you ever thought that you can have everything you want in life?" I said I supposed it was possible if a person were willing to pay the price. He answered, "Then I want to lend you a book that will show you how, and the price is well within your reach." The book was *The Prosperity Secrets of the Ages.*

I quickly discovered that the theme of that book is, "You can have everything." When I read it my attitude was, "What have I got to lose? The rules are simple, not hard to follow." The most difficult rule was to decide what I truly wanted out of life. At this point I was a forty-six-year-old widow with three grown children who dreaded visiting me because my constant pain depressed them. So I sat alone in my apartment and analyzed: (1) What I wanted to eliminate from my life and (2) What I wanted to bring into it.

I decided: (1) I wanted to remarry, but only if it were a specific type of man with specific attributes. (2) I wanted the pain to diminish so I could again enjoy living. (3) I wanted an attractive home of my own. (4) I wanted to be employed in an occupation where I could be of real service to others. (5) I wanted to be debt free.

Even though it was a large order, it all came true! As I stopped whining and complaining, my friends all returned. Within six weeks, I met the man to whom I have been happily married since 1968. New treatment brought diminishing health problems. I got a new job in a new field, and was promoted from the entry level in 1969 to the top position in the organization in 1973. We now have a lovely home and are in the process of building an even better one.

My personal net worth has risen from zero in 1967 to well over $100,000, and it is rising all the time. I have given away more than one hundred copies of that book to people who have asked me how I did it.

What my supervisor told me on that eventful evening so long ago is still true: "*You* can have everything if you are willing to 'pay the price,' and that 'price' is well within *your* reach, too!"

SUCCESS ATTITUDES ARE THE SECRET

The secret for thinking straight might be described as "success attitudes." There is a definite place where you can always go to find out how to "think straight" and acquire success attitudes. There are definite reasons why you have a right to believe you can have everything. I will share those dynamic secrets with you in Chapter I.

Meanwhile, let us consider further results still others have experienced by daring to believe they could have everything.

AMAZING RESULTS OF SUCCESS ATTITUDES

I have seen how success attitudes can "lick" every type of problem: inharmony in human relationships, ill health, financial problems, family problems, mental confusion, emotional instability, spiritual uncertainty . . . for people in all types of circumstances.

A business executive was named assistant to the president of his company, and was able to realize long-desired prosperity for paying off a mortgage and bank note. He also experienced improved health and greater happiness in his home life — after he used success attitudes.

Several wives solved the "other woman" problem through success attitudes. Their marriages are now happier than ever, for the "other woman" in each case simply faded out of the picture.

One woman's previously "shiftless" husband first got year-round work and then formed his own gold and silver mining corporation, after his wife began thinking of him as a success instead of a failure.

Another wife's husband received $250 per month in pay raises within a six-month period. He received a promotion and more responsibility in his job and made frequent trips for his company in and out of the United States. As his wife continued to invoke success attitudes, he also inherited a nice sum of money.

A 70-year old retired widower was nearly destitute. Within six months from the time he learned of success attitudes and began to use them faithfully, he inherited a quarter-of-a-million dollars, got married, took his wife abroad on their honeymoon, and then returned to his professional career. A whole new life, from starvation to riches, came to this man when he changed his thinking.

A teenager had been overweight since birth. The diagnosis was "gland trouble — no cure." Diets had not worked. Through success attitudes alone, this young man lost 17 pounds in three months!

A young college student began using success attitudes concerning a piece of property his family owned. They had hoped to "strike gas" on this property, but geologists' tests indicated that there was no gas on this land. This young man held to success attitudes, encouraged his parents to employ other officials to make further tests. Soon they did "strike gas," from which they now receive a prosperous income.

A 17-year-old high school student proved the power of success attitudes during the first weekend he used them on his part-time job at the supermarket. On Thursday, his tips amounted to $2 more than usual for Thursdays. On Friday, his tips amounted to double what he normally made on Fridays. On Saturday, his tips were more than *double* the tips of *all* the other boys at the store combined!

A businesswoman had tried for 25 years to buy a piece of property adjoining her ranch. She needed it for the water it would provide her cattle. After using success attitudes, she learned that the property was again for sale. This time she was able to buy it quickly, harmoniously, and for a lower downpayment than she had expected to pay!

A businessman, informed that his wife had cancer, held to certain success attitudes, and the diagnosis changed! His wife is now enjoying good health again, and has never known about the previous cancer diagnosis.

A career woman had been secretly living with a married man for several years. Her health and financial success declined as her sense of guilt, frustration and confusion mounted. Through success attitudes she found the courage to leave this man and begin a new life for herself. As she did, her health and financial affairs were adjusted nicely. Life has taken on new and satisfying meaning for this woman.

A widow was sustained through the period of bereavement following the sudden death of her husband, and was able to make a quick adjustment to the unexpected changes in her life, after turning to success attitudes.

Another widow met, fell in love with, and happily married a wealthy cattleman after adopting certain success attitudes.

Several people watched lawsuits fade away and be settled out of court as they adopted success attitudes.

Success attitudes helped several other people who were recently divorced to build new lives for themselves.

A 72-year-old man was rehired by his previous employer after adopting success attitudes.

A young couple who had tried unsuccessfully for a number of years to adopt a child were able to quickly do so after employing success attitudes.

A television actress landed a job on a popular network program. She was able to accomplish this after a friend, who was a musician, joined her in using success attitudes.

Along with using success attitudes for your own increased health, wealth and happiness, it is good to know that your success attitudes can and do help others.

The specific success attitudes used by all these people and many more will be shared with you in the pages of this book.

UNVEIL YOUR SUCCESS!

Go quickly to Chapter 1 where you will learn the startling secrets for success which were known and used by the ancient people, long before the time of Genesis. In the chapters following, you will learn the definite secrets taught through the Success Allegories. These were passed from one civilization to another in ancient times. Then, in the latter half of this book, you will learn the definite success secrets used by the prosperous people of Genesis.

You, too, can have everything as you begin applying and sharing these prosperity secrets of the ages!

Catherine Ponder
P.O. Drawer 1278
Palm Desert, California, 92261
U.S.A.

PART I

BACKGROUND SUCCESS SECRETS FOR YOU

STARTLING SUCCESS SECRETS

FROM THE BOOK OF BEGINNINGS

— Chapter 1 —

The startling secret about success is that you've probably searched everywhere for it, when in reality, *it lies within yourself.*

You have the power *within* you, which you can use to experience greater health, happiness and prosperity than you have previously known!

You can begin releasing that power to produce greater good in your life and affairs, when you realize that your mind *is* your world. *When you rule your mind, you rule your world. When you choose your thoughts, you choose results.*

Your world is affected by your thoughts and feelings, your likes and dislikes, more fully than you realize. When your thinking veers, your life veers.

Your thoughts are your greatest power. Better thoughts will bring better conditions to you. That is the miracle of mind power.

The startling secret about success is that there are simple attitudes of mind that can help you choose your thoughts and thereby choose results.

Another startling secret about success is that *it is nearer than you think*. Indeed, it is *what* you think.

A nightclub entertainer heard these words at a time when she and her husband were heavily in debt, after he had undergone a series of operations for cancer. Their combined incomes were far less than the amount needed to pay off the tremendous medical expenses incurred during his illness, although they were grateful that his various operations had apparently been successful.

At the time this woman learned of success attitudes, she was employed as a professional singer and pianist with a combo of her own. As she began to daily practice success attitudes, she suddenly found herself booked into one of the largest nightclubs in a city of more than a million people. Her salary sky-rocketed overnight. With her husband's salary and her own, they were able to begin paying off the many surgeons and hospitals they owed, as well as to again provide adequately for their houseful of small children.

As they continued to deliberately use success attitudes, the woman was soon called to play at another club at over twice her previous salary, which seemed unbelievable. In fact, she found herself one of the highest paid singer-pianists in the nation!

She and her husband agreed that when the medical bills were all paid, she would resume her role as mother and wife only, and would no longer work outside the home. This has now happened—all within two years from the time they faced such tremendous indebtedness. How?

As they continued to declare success attitudes, her husband was offered the best job of his life in another city. He quit his previous job which he had held for twenty years, and they moved. Opportunities kept coming to her husband. Soon he received a promotion in his new job, and they moved to still another city. They bought their "dream house" in that city— a house they would have felt they could never have afforded a few years ago. This woman wrote, "We consistently thank God for our many blessings and for leading us to 'success attitudes.' My husband's health has been fine and there has been no recurrence of the cancer. Furthermore, my husband is now in line for another promotion!"

This couple has proved that success begins with what you think.

SUCCESS IS AT HAND!

The whole world is searching for the secrets of success. The enthusiastic response to my first book proved that to me. I never cease to be amazed at the cross-section of people, both rich and poor, all over the world, who are reading and getting results from *The Dynamic Laws of Prosperity.*[1]

A monk in India recently wrote, "I am one of the members of an ashram, which is a religious hermitage

---

1. Published by DeVorss & Co., Marina del Rey, CA 90294. Rev. ed., 1985.

here in India. For ready reference, I keep your book on my table. I am overjoyed with it. I often meditate, trying to go deep within your writings. I consider your book a valued possession which has led me in understanding the supreme laws of life."

A minister asked me to autograph a copy of the book he had purchased, so that he might give it to a friend. He said, "This man has made more than a million dollars during the last year, using the prosperity laws described in your book. He is now anxious to have a copy of the book so that he may retain that million and go on to his second million."

DYNAMIC RESULTS FOR THE AUTHOR

The happy things that happened to the people around me as I wrote *The Dynamic Laws of Prosperity* proved further the great power for success that is all around us and within us, which we can tap through success thinking.

The steelman who had so strongly encouraged me to write the book, the stockbroker who named it, and the public relations executive who helped locate the publisher for it, all had dynamic success come to them in the process. My secretary resigned, after typing the first half of the book, stating she had learned enough about success thinking in the process to acquire the special things she had gone back to work for: a mink stole and a second car for her family.

While a second secretary typed the latter half of the book, her husband obtained the best job he has ever had, as an engineer in the missile program. Even my housekeeper, who learned about success thinking from me by word-of-mouth as I wrote the book, got results. She then decided that she had the courage and confidence to do something she had long wished to do: go into business for herself as a specialty dressmaker. She soon had more work than she could handle.

Amazingly enough, as I wrote this book, the same thing happened all over again: my new housekeeper learned of the power of success attitudes, used them, and found the courage to do something she had long wanted to do—go to business school and prepare to become a secretary. By the time I finished this book, I was looking for another housekeeper!

There seems to be something electric and exciting that comes alive in the atmosphere where success thinking is employed. Everyone who comes into such an atmosphere seems to become supercharged with it, and to take on its result-getting power.

It can happen to you, too, as you read and use the success attitudes given in this book.

YOUR GREATEST SUCCESS BOOK

There is one great and wonderful place you can always go to find out how to employ success attitudes and think straight—yet it is the last place many people ever think of going—and that is to the Holy Bible.[2]

---

2. See the author's series of books on "The Millionaires of the Bible," all published by DeVorss & Co., Marina del Rey, CA 90294: *The Millionaires of Genesis* (1976), *The Millionaire Moses* (1977), *The Millionaire Joshua* (1978) and *The Millionaire from Nazareth* (1979).

Although the Bible has long been described as a best seller, it has seldom been understood as a book on success. More often, it has been purchased and placed in a conspicuous place at home to ease one's own spiritual conscience, and to impress the preacher when he came to visit. Often, had the visiting preacher dared to inspect the family Bible, he would probably have choked on the dust he found there!

Many fine people have plainly told me that they do not even attempt to read the Bible, because they cannot understand it. A woman in England recently wrote, "I do not read the Bible, it is so full of violence and bloodshed." A Protestant minister confided, "I don't bother to try to interpret the Old Testament for my people, except for some of the Psalms and a few passages from Isaiah. It seems safer to interpret the New Testament."

When evaluated from a literal, moral, or historical standpoint only, the success secrets of the Bible are not always clear. In fact, the word "success" appears literally only twice in the entire Bible (in its usual translations).

Yet, if you look a little deeper, you discover that the beloved stories of the great Biblical characters are filled with "success attitudes" that can help you think straight and make your life straight. You discover that the Bible is the greatest textbook on prosperity ever written! In fact, many of the Bible's great people were millionaires and their success secrets for getting that way are available to you, too.

THE SEARCH FOR SUCCESS

The masses of humanity today are searching for these success secrets. But since they do not realize they can be found in the Bible, they have tried to find them elsewhere.

This is plainly shown in the fact that the Bible is no longer considered the world's best seller. What has taken its place, and why? The Communist writings of Lenin! Since his death in 1924, over 300 million copies of Lenin's books have been printed behind the Iron Curtain, which is six times the number of Bibles distributed by the American Bible Society alone.

If you wonder how this could have happened, it's simple. Lenin based his Communist ideas on the writings of Karl Marx, whose premise was that the rich get richer and the poor get poorer. To eliminate this inequality, Karl Marx, the father of Communism, advocated mass revolution. Lenin followed through on this success and prosperity theme, capturing the imagination of millions of people with such attractive slogans as, "Peace, land and bread." After he came to power he declared, "We have brought peace and killed poverty." In other words, he promised people prosperity and success.

A REVOLUTION IS NEEDED

Mankind has always desired success and always will. It is a universal desire, divinely implanted within each of us. *And a revolution is needed to make success universal.* But that revolution must consist in the use of revolutionary ideas for good that will produce success, not an actual revolution involving soldiers and bloodshed.

The revolutionary ideas that can bring all the blessings that mankind desires are to be found in the success attitudes presented in the Bible. As Horace Greeley wrote, "It is impossible to mentally or socially enslave a Bible-reading people." As you dare to begin realizing and using these success attitudes, you will begin to experience greater health, peace and plenty in your world. You will begin to reap the benefits of the prosperity secrets of the ages.

When enough people have done this, the threat of godless Communism will surely pass from this planet.

A GREAT MAN'S SUCCESS SECRETS

In this book, I wish to share with you the secrets of one of the most successful men who has ever lived. He was a man reared in lavish abundance, who went about in fine garments, who received a royal education, and who was instructed in all the secret teachings of the ancient Egyptians. His sublime strength, faith, and leadership shaped the course of the world. Historians have written that he took one of the greatest steps toward true freedom that the world has ever known. All humanity has been infinitely blessed by his unique achievements.

You can be, too!

His accomplishments include author, prophet, emancipator, lawgiver, warrior, and miracle worker. He was considered a shrewd mathematician, and was the inventor of boats, engines, instruments of war, and hydraulics. He was also considered the author of Egyptian hieroglyphics. He "told off" the most powerful and dangerous political leader of his age, and then rescued some two million people from the clutches of slavery and annihilation.

The man? Moses. His success secrets? They are to be found in the first five books of the Bible. Those books are "loaded" with success attitudes that reveal the prosperity secrets of the ages. But rarely, if ever, have the writings of Moses been understood or interpreted from that standpoint.

I wish to share with you some of his major success secrets found in the Book of Genesis.[3] In future writings, I look forward to sharing with you the success secrets given in his other four books.[4]

GET SOMETHING GOING!

Not by accident does the greatest book on success ever written begin with the powerful allegories, the prosperity secrets, and the success stories found in Genesis. The word Genesis means "to begin, to initiate action, to take the first step, to get something going." Not by accident do six of the world's greatest millionaires appear in the pages of Genesis: Adam, Abraham, Melchizedek, Isaac, Jacob and Joseph. They show you how to take the first steps and the later steps to success.

If you wish to create a new world for yourself of peace, health, and plenty, you can begin immediately initiating action, and getting something going, through applying the success attitudes offered in Genesis. The great truths found in Genesis are so important that they are frequently quoted in many later books in the Bible. The New Testament quotes Genesis 27 times literally and 38 times substantially.

---

3. See also the author's book *The Millionaires of Genesis.*
4. See the author's book *The Millionaire Moses.*

One thing I wish to bring to your attention: The famous old stories found in the first 11 chapters of Genesis—from the Creation story through the Tower of Babel story—were legends universally known to the ancients long before the time of the Hebrews. For instance, the Garden of Eden, the fall of man and the flood allegories appear in many literatures of the world. These old legends are not considered literally true, but they contain great success symbology. That is doubtless why Moses included them in the Book of Genesis, even though these same legends are also found in the sacred writings of Egypt, Chaldea, and other nations which flourished thousands of years before the time of the Hebrews. Not until the twelfth chapter of Genesis, beginning with the story of Abraham, does Biblical history literally begin.

Though part of Genesis is symbolic allegory and part of it literal history, it is surely worth reviewing carefully, because it contains some of the most dynamic prosperity and success secrets ever offered mankind!

AN EXCITING INTERPRETATION

As you read this book, you may wonder how the inner meanings of the names and terms in the Bible are derived. I am sharing with you an exciting interpretation that has been secretly used by occult groups down through the ages, but which has not been generally taught to the masses.

This Bible interpretation is known as "metaphysical," referring to that which is beyond the literal, moral, or historical meaning of Biblical text. Of course, there is nothing wrong with the literal, moral, and historical interpretations of the Bible. In fact, you must know these as a foundation for understanding its metaphysical meaning. However, when viewed only on these levels, the Bible is often confusing and contradictory, so that it is little wonder many people complain that they cannot understand it.

The exciting thing to know is this: The great men of the Bible were master psychologists and metaphysicians, who strove constantly to teach the power of mental attitudes for success or failure. Often they went forth, greatly outnumbered to meet a threatening foe, armed only with their faith in God and their understanding of success attitudes. Over and over again, they were victorious in the face of seemingly impossible odds.

You can be, too, when you understand and use their prosperity secrets and success strategy, which the metaphysical interpretation of the Bible offers you.

YOU ARE METAPHYSICAL

Don't let the word "metaphysical" disturb you. It simply means that which is beyond the physical — it refers to the mental, emotional, and spiritual phases of man's nature. *You are metaphysical.* Every time you use your mind to think and your emotions to feel, you are using that which lies "beyond the physical" realm of your five senses, and you are being metaphysical. Since you are constantly thinking and feeling, both consciously and subconsciously, you are constantly functioning metaphysically.

Some authorities estimate that you are 2% physical and 98% metaphysical. In any event, your inner being is much greater and more powerful than your outer self. Furthermore, your inner being controls your outer self and outer circumstances. When you have learned to master and direct your inner thoughts and feelings through success attitudes, you can transform your outer world, without the usual "blood, sweat, and tears" of human will and human force.

The inner, metaphysical meaning of the Bible gives you the success formulas needed for contacting and releasing the power that lies within your mind, emotions, and spiritual nature, so that you may experience greater good in every phase of your life.

For instance, the characters, places, and events depicted in the Bible are symbolic of those various attitudes for success or failure that you and I use constantly as we strive to get into our Promised Land.

EARLY CHRISTIANS TAUGHT THIS INTERPRETATION

Some of the famous early Christians taught this metaphysical Bible interpretation in the excellent Christian University at Alexandria as early as A.D. 180. Among the early teachers of this exciting interpretation were Pantaenus, Clement, and Origen.

They derived the metaphysical meaning of the Bible simply by tracing significant Bible words and names back to their root meaning, based on the original Hebrew, Greek, and Aramaic words from which they were originally translated. In this book, I am doing likewise.[5]

---

5. The interpretations in this book are based on material from *The Metaphysical Bible Dictionary* and *Mysteries of Genesis*, published by Unity School of Christianity, Unity Village, Missouri. All Biblical references in this book are taken from the

This age-old interpretation surely holds the mental, emotional, and spiritual keys to successful living in our modern world. In this exciting age when many old truths are being rediscovered and used, metaphysical Bible interpretation will again "come into its own," teaching the masses, instead of just a select few, the power of mental attitudes and emotional reactions as keys to one's success or failure in life.

I trust that these inner success explanations of the Book of Genesis will have the same electrifying effect for good in your life as they have had in mine.

SYMBOLOGY IN ALL GREAT LITERATURE

Actually, it is easier to understand why the great teachings of the Bible, in many instances, must be interpreted symbolically, when you understand how the Oriental mind works. In the Orient now, as in biblical times, it is considered impolite to speak in direct terms.

The peoples of the Eastern world shrink from the brash directness and frankness which are typical of Western thought and speech. Instead of approaching a friend directly about a personal matter, they use evasive, impersonal and symbolic terms. That is why Jesus taught in allegory and parable, rather than in direct, literal terms much of the time.

My late husband, from his travels in the Orient as a naval officer, often spoke of observing the rather formal, roundabout way in which most Orientals reply to a direct question.

American Standard Version of the Holy Bible, unless otherwise specified.

All great poetry, drama, literature, indeed fine art of any type, carries a symbolism which tells of beauties and wisdom far beyond the literal meaning. This is one of the first things a college freshman learns from his study of the world's great literature.

If this is true of the world's great literature, we can easily see why it would be even more true of our Holy Bible, which contains much symbolism in allegory and parable that reveals the Oriental viewpoint of truth.

YOU CAN HAVE EVERYTHING!

Along with the success symbology found in the Bible, there are many literal success teachings in its pages, too. For instance, here is a wonderful success attitude which is present over and over in the Bible: a loving Creator bestowed upon you the divine power for making your world as you wish it to be. You do not have to compromise with life. You do not have to settle for less than the best in life. *You can have everything!*

According to the first chapter of Genesis, God created you in His own image of perfection, and endowed you with the power to make your life whatever you wish it to be. Often theologians have overlooked this great success secret as they have blindly stressed the mistakes of Adam and Eve, describing their actions as "original sin."

There is nothing original about sin! I doubt if there ever was, even in the beginning. Neither is there anything original or helpful about brooding over our mistakes. You and I know that it is very hard for a child to be good when we keep telling him that he is bad. Like Adam and Eve, you may have made serious mistakes in life—and who hasn't? But there is a way to get back into Eden. Begin thinking of yourself as you really are—a spiritual being, endowed with power to overcome the sins and mistakes of the past and present.

Remind yourself often that you are not really a "miserable sinner," but a divine being, blessed with sublime power for making your life what you want it to be. *What theology calls a "lost soul" is merely a soul that has lost sight of its divinity.*

I invite you to use often a success attitude that has helped me over the years to free myself of failure and to move forward on the royal road to success: "I CAN HAVE EVERYTHING! THAT IS MY DIVINE HERITAGE."

This one success attitude can make the difference between failure and success in life for you, as it has proved in the lives of many others.

Furthermore, this success attitude will not make you selfish, arrogant, or grasping for your good. It will make you humble, grateful, and better able to help yourself and others to experience life's blessings in orderly, harmonious ways.

Holding to the thought that you can have everything does not necessarily mean that you can realize every desire immediately, of course. Psychologists say that when you are ready for a thing, it will appear. Holding to the thought that you can have everything helps you to get ready mentally to accept more and more of life's blessings. When you prepare mentally and emotionally, those blessings can then appear. You can have them as fast as you can mentally accept them. How soon that will be is up to you.

LYING DOWN ON THE JOB

Your first reaction to the great truth that you are basically a divine being who can have everything may be similar to that of the little boy who had just been so informed by his grandmother. Wanting to believe it was true, but feeling he should be skeptically cautious, he replied, "Well, if I am a divine being and if God is within me, what is He doing? Is He just lying down in there?"

In many instances, that is exactly what seems to have happened! Our God-nature can only do for us what It can do through us. It has been lying down on the job, awaiting our recognition of It. If our divine nature worked with no recognition from us, we would be automatons with no freedom of expression or power of choice. And that's exactly what man was given in the beginning: freedom of choice and dominion over everything in the universe (Genesis 1:26). It has been up to man since the beginning of time to claim and use that freedom and dominion. It is still up to him to do so today.

BUSINESS EXECUTIVE CHOOSES SUCCESS

You can begin using your freedom of choice and dominion from this day forward to choose health, wealth and happiness. Just the act of mentally choosing what you want often starts happy things occurring. For instance, as mentioned in the introduction, a business executive needed a large sum of money to pay off a mortgage and a note at the bank. He also desired more recognition in his work, which had previously been withheld from him.

He learned of success attitudes and began freely choosing mentally that which he wished. He wrote out a list of successful results he wished to experience, which included payment of the mortgage and more recognition in his work. He daily looked at his list and affirmed: "I CAN HAVE EVERYTHING, INCLUDING THESE RESULTS, BECAUSE SUCCESS IS MY DIVINE HERITAGE!" When old fears, doubts, and limited ideas about the availability of these blessings tried to overpower him, he would remind himself, "I CAN HAVE EVERYTHING."

Within a short time, certain of his stocks increased enough in value to take care of over half the amount needed to pay off the mortgage and bank note. Greater harmony and happiness in his home were the next results. Improved health followed, as the strain, tension, and pressure of previous obligations began to subside. Later, the company president named him as his personal assistant, which was the finest position in the company, next to the presidency itself. This was a job he had long hoped for, but he had hardly dared believe it could be his. It was at this point he declared, "These desired blessings came in ways I wouldn't have believed possible a few months ago, and they have all come so quickly!"

THE SECRET WISDOM OF THE AGES

Over and over the greatest success book of all times tries to point out the divine power for success that is within man. David sang about it in the eighth Psalm. Paul described this innate power as the "mystery which has been hid for ages" (Colossians 1:26). Job discovered that, when he dwelled upon the goodness of God and the divinity of man, his health, wealth and happiness were restored to him many-fold, whereas when he had previously dwelled upon his miseries, they had only multiplied.

Those grand people of the ancient world were nobody's fools. They knew and used the secret wisdom of the ages. They had learned the secrets of psychosomatic medicine from the Babylonians. A number of them became millionaires through using the secret teachings on substance[6] known to all the ancient civilizations. They had learned the success power of mental attitudes from the ancient Egyptians, who secretly taught positive thinking thousands of years ago, in an era far advanced over our present age in many ways.

What most people do not realize is that the Book of Genesis is veiled in the secret teachings of the ages that led the early patriarchs to constant victories over life's problems.

You can unveil that secret wisdom of the ages and begin applying it to your own daily affairs with great success here and now!

Proceed now to Chapter 2 where you will learn an ancient secret for happy living. This success attitude can bring a revolution of good in your mind, body, and affairs now — along with the success secrets of the chapters to follow.

---

6. See Chapter 1 of the author's book *The Millionaires of Genesis* (1976) and Chapter 2 of her *Dare to Prosper!* (1983), both published by DeVorss & Co., Marina del Rey, CA 90294.

AN ANCIENT SECRET FOR HAPPY LIVING

THE ART OF BLESSING

— Chapter 2 —

Before launching forth into the specific "success attitudes" of Genesis, you can begin to practice one of the basic secrets for happy living. As you do, that practice can transform your life!

The ancients' secret for happy living was the act of *blessing*. Most of us have heard the terms "blessing," "bless you" or even, "I blessed him out." But seldom have we realized the power we have to experience health, harmony, and prosperity through the ancient practice of blessing.

As presented in the Book of Genesis, *the act of blessing was the Hebrews' favorite method of prayer.* Only twice are other methods of prayer mentioned: once when Abraham prayed for the healing of King Abimelech (Genesis 20:17) and again when Isaac went

forth at eventide to meditate (Genesis 24:63). However, there are numerous instances in which the Hebrews invoked the power of prayer through blessing.

The Hebrews of Genesis loved to voice blessings
and to predict the good that would come to those
whom they blessed. If any Hebrew was to receive a
spoken blessing, he did not want anyone to stand in
his way of accepting that blessing. He considered a
blessing to be a priceless gift.

The ancients felt that a blessing carried great power
to accomplish good. The Lord pointed out the power
of blessing to Abraham, when He advised, "I will
bless thee . . . and be thou a blessing" (Genesis 12:2).
Jacob felt that a blessing was so desirable that he even
stole the blessing which his father intended to bestow
upon his brother, Esau.

The dictionary explains why there is dynamic power
for good in the simple act of blessing. To bless means
"to make holy or whole by spoken words." To bless
means to "ask divine favor for some situation or condition." To bless means "to wish a person or situation
well." To bless means "to make happy or prosperous."
To bless means to "gladden, glorify, praise."

You and I might simply say that to bless means to
"bring forth good in a situation, condition, or personality," whether there seems any good to be brought
forth or not. To bless is to judge not according to
appearances, as Jesus advised, but to judge according
to right judgment—that of beholding the good and
thereby bringing it forth in a condition or person.

How often have you condemned, criticized, or
cursed a situation and only brought forth more problems and unhappy experiences from it? Whereas, if
you had dared to take the opposite view and bless the

situation, you would have activated the omnipresent good within it, and witnessed a happy result.

BLESSING SAVES MARRIAGE

A housewife wrote me in a rage about her "no-good" husband. He was a miner who left home every spring to find work in the gold and silver mines of the northwestern United States. Usually, she did not hear from him again until late fall, when he came home to loaf all winter and to wait for spring and more work. Meanwhile, she was left at home alone to work as a waitress, or to do anything else she could to feed and clothe herself and to pay the bills.

I suggested that, in spite of her husband's "no-good" behavior, she should begin blessing him instead of continuing to condemn him. It was then spring, and he had just left home for another six months in the mines. Alone again to survive the best way she could, this housewife hardly felt like blessing her husband, but she decided to try it anyway if it held the possibility of bringing about a more satisfactory relationship between them.

After she began blessing him, she gained a sense of peace about her marriage that she had not previously had. Next, out of the blue, she received a letter from him, saying he had obtained work and would be sending money when he received his first paycheck. She didn't believe that part of the letter! It just didn't sound like *her* husband, but she kept blessing him anyway. Soon, he *did* send along a portion of his paycheck. As she kept blessing him, he systematically sent home money, and she did not have to work that summer at all, for the first time in many years.

As she continued blessing him, he even began to write her romantic letters, stating his wish to take her on a second honeymoon when he returned from the mines that fall. As she continued to bless him, he was able to get year-round work, rather than just working a few months a year as previously. It was at this point that she read my book *The Dynamic Laws of Prosperity* and began decreeing for her husband the words from the book's introduction, "There's gold dust in the air for you." Believe it or not, he soon went into business for himself, and formed a mining corporation for the sole purpose of mining silver and gold!

How often people have missed the blessings and security of a happy marriage because they have condemned rather than blessed their partner. This housewife proved that when you bless a person or situation, that person or situation just has to bless you.

BLESS THE OTHER WOMAN

An irate housewife had "the other woman" problem in her marriage. She had been to several ministers, counselors, lawyers, relatives, neighbors telling them how terrible it was to have a husband who had become interested in another woman. As she had continued to berate her husband and the other woman, the situation only got worse.

When she finally found her way to me, I explained that all of her critical talk and bids for sympathy were only intensifying the very situation she wanted to be free from. I suggested she get very quiet, stop talking to anyone about the situation, and start blessing her marriage *and* the other woman. If she truly loved her husband, she could bless the other woman right out of her marriage, provided she was willing to stop condemning her. I further explained that the "other woman" is not a cause, but an effect of an unhappy marriage: if the marriage was all it should have been, no third party could have influenced it in any way. Her job was to go within herself, get rid of her critical, cynical, unpleasant attitudes; to start praising her husband for his good points rather than condemning him for his weak points; to start treating him as though nothing had ever happened; and to resume her normal activities as though there was no problem in her marriage.

When her relatives and friends asked for the latest news on the subject for their private entertainment, it was a big challenge for this woman to stop talking about how terrible her husband and the other woman were, and start declaring that everything was fine again. However, as she began the daily act of blessing her marriage, her husband, *and* the other woman; as she began resuming club, church and civic activities as though everything was fine, people began to think so. She again provided a beautiful home, wonderful meals, and a harmonious, appreciative atmosphere for her husband. He began to spend more and more evenings at home, rather than rushing off after dinner, or never coming home from work at all. In due time, the other woman had been blessed right out of the picture! They have also done something they tried for many years to do without success — they have adopted a child, with whom they are very happy. This woman is now using the blessing method to help rear this baby into a healthy, happy child.

STATEMENTS OF BLESSING

The power of blessing is an amazing thing. Begin now to bless and praise everything and everyone that comes into your life! It is just as easy to bless and praise as it is to condemn and complain. When you condemn and complain, you intensify the very unpleasant conditions you wish to be rid of. By blessing such conditions you take the power of evil out of them, and turn on the power of good that is there.

A statement of blessing that I have often used is this: "I BLESS YOU AND BLESS YOU FOR THE GOODNESS OF GOD THAT IS WITHIN YOU." This is a particularly powerful thought to hold for blessing and changing troublesome people.

It will take the "sting" out of unhappy situations and turn on the power of good to declare for them: "I BEGIN NOW TO BLESS EVERYTHING THAT COMES INTO MY LIFE AS GOOD, GOOD, GOOD!"

SELL MERCHANDISE THROUGH BLESSING IT

Merchants can use the power of blessing to cause their merchandise to sell. Several merchants have stated to me that their merchandise began to sell, when it previously had not, after they began declaring for that merchandise: "I BLESS YOU AND BLESS YOU WITH IMMEDIATE, MOVING, SELLING POWER."

A businessman recently spoke of how the power of blessing changed an apparently hopeless business situation. He began to bless his employees and the business conditions involved. As he did, they began to change for the better. As he continued blessing his employees, they were soon producing double work. After constant blessing of his business affairs, his employees increased their work tempo to such an extent that they saved him thousands of dollars in one transaction alone.

COLLECT MONEY THROUGH BLESSING

A credit manager heard of the dynamic power of blessing and began using it for collection of accounts. In one instance, a customer owed his company $2,500. The customer kept evading payment. The credit manager extended the time of payment as long as he could. Finally, he realized he could not extend it further and would be forced to take legal action for collection, if the money was not paid very soon.

One night when he could not sleep because of concern about this account, he began to intensify his blessing of the man, the account, the entire situation. Over and over he decreed: "I BLESS YOU AND BLESS YOU FOR THE GOODNESS OF GOD THAT IS WORKING IN YOU AND THROUGH YOU." After a time, he felt peaceful and went to sleep.

Early the next morning, the customer telephoned him at the office and said, "I will be in to see you at noon with the money." As promised, he arrived and paid the delinquent account with twenty-five 100-dollar bills!

BLESS WHEN YOU'RE TEMPTED TO CURSE

A businessman once read these words of Emmet Fox, which describe the dynamic power of blessing:

Bless a thing and it will bless you. Curse it and it will curse you. If you put your condemnation upon anything in life, it will hit back at you and hurt you. If you bless a situation, it has no power to hurt you, and even if it is troublesome for a time, it will gradually fade out, if you sincerely bless it.[1]

This man decided to start using the power of blessing, instead of cursing, on a troublesome co-worker. For a time, he was able to silently bless the one in question. One day, in a state of agitation, however, he was tempted to curse instead of bless. Trying hard to think and say the right thing, with clenched teeth he blurted out, "God *bless* you and you know what I mean!"

Sometimes we begin using the power of blessing in a similar way. A mind that has long been trained to criticize may not always wish to bless and behold the good. But as we persist in training our thoughts to bless, it becomes easier; and each happy result obtained from the habit of blessing makes our efforts well worthwhile.

BLESSING MAKES BAD CHECK GOOD

Another businessman recently proved that it pays to bless and not curse a troublesome situation. He was asked by a superior to take two "bad checks" to the bank and try to cash them. When his superior had previously attempted to cash them on various occa-

---

1. From the book *Power through Constructive Thinking,* published by Harper & Row.

sions, he had been informed that there were insufficient funds in the account. The superior spoke strong, critical words about the checks and about the customers who had written them, as he handed them to this employee.

The employee began immediately blessing them, thinking of them as "good checks." At the bank he was informed that this time there *was* a sufficient balance in the customers' accounts to make these checks "good."

When he returned to the office, with cash in hand, his superior was amazed. He said to his boss, "Let me share a little success secret with you. Curse a thing and it will curse you. Bless a thing and it will bless you." The boss replied, "I like that approach. It sounds reasonable, especially since you just proved it!"

BLESSING FOR HEALTH

The power of blessing knows no limit. It can be successfully applied to every phase of life.

A businessman recently spoke of how the power of blessing had worked to help him and his wife experience renewed health, youth, and vitality after many years of health problems. They learned of the power of blessing and began to daily bless their bodies with the thought of renewed health. Gradually, a number of healings took place, and for the first time in years they were free from pain.

A little later, friends visited them whom they had not seen for many years. The friends knew of the various health problems that had plagued them, and expected their appearance to bear witness to ill health.

Their friends were amazed at how youthful and healthy this man and his wife were.

Of course, they immediately wanted to know how this couple had managed to regain their health and to look so young. The reply was that the habit of blessing the body as a temple of the living God was their secret. They had literally followed the advice of the apostle Paul: "Know ye not that your body is a temple of the living God, which is in you. . . . Glorify God therefore in your body" (I Corinthians 6:19-20). The statement of blessing they had daily used to help restore their health had been: "I GIVE THANKS THAT MY BODY IS A TEMPLE OF THE LIVING GOD. I NOW PRAISE, BLESS, AND GLORIFY DIVINE HEALTH IN MY BODY."

BLESSING REDUCES WEIGHT

A mother used the power of blessing to help her teenage son lose 17 pounds of excess weight in three months. This boy had been overweight since birth. Doctors had said repeatedly that it was a "gland condition," and that nothing could be done about it.

In his early teens, this child became very conscious of his weight problem and felt he could bear it no longer. The usual methods for losing weight had not worked for him over the years, and so it seemed a hopeless problem.

Finally, his mother heard of the dynamic power of blessing. She and her son agreed that instead of criticizing or condemning his weight problem further, they would begin to praise and bless his body with the thought of "perfect weight." It was agreed that whenever the boy thought of the subject, he would say to himself, "I am not fat. My body is blessed with perfection now."

Meanwhile, his mother began to take a little time daily to bless him with the thought of perfect weight. The statement she used was this: "I BLESS YOU AS A RADIANT CHILD OF GOD. I BLESS YOUR MIND, BODY AND AFFAIRS AS THEY NOW EXPRESS RADIANT PERFECTION."

This young man shed 17 pounds in three months. He and his mother plan to continue this blessing technique until his weight is completely normal.

BLESSING IMPROVES EUROPEAN TRIP

A retired businessman used the power of blessing to produce happy results in still another area of life — on a trip to Europe. His wife had recently passed on, and her death had naturally been a shock to him. Finally, he decided to take a trip abroad in an effort to gain a new lease on life.

At first, it looked as though the trip was a mistake. Everything was going wrong. There was one couple in his tour group who were particularly unpleasant. They loudly voiced their criticism of the travel and hotel accommodations and of the European way of life generally.

This businessman silently blessed this couple for a number of days, and finally felt the time had come to speak to them directly. He said, "Why don't you try holding some good thoughts about this trip, instead of criticizing it? You are making everyone's trip unbearable by your own unpleasantness. You are being very selfish. Why don't you stop criticizing and start blessing this fine trip and these wonderful European people?"

At the time of this conversation, the tour group was in Spain. This couple meekly asked what his religion was and how they could use the power of blessing. He explained that he was a student of Practical Christianity. He then took from his pocket the well-known *Daily Word* magazine, published by the nondenominational Unity School, which is read daily by people around the world. He explained that its daily messages helped him to successfully practice the ancient art of blessing by holding good thoughts.

Upon hearing the conversation, a woman in the group exclaimed that she was also a *Daily Word* reader and she took an identical copy of the little magazine from her purse!

It was then agreed that each morning, in order to help the entire tour group hold good thoughts, to bless and enjoy the day's trip, this businessman would read the *Daily Word* message for that day to the entire group. Then the group would declare aloud together the day's affirmative prayer statement found in the *Daily Word* lesson.

It proved an enjoyable experience for the entire group, and it changed the atmosphere of their trip.

MORE POWERFUL THAN MONEY OR POLITICS

In these times, many people have come to believe that money and politics are all-powerful. There is nothing wrong with money and politics, when rightly used. But the power of blessing is more powerful than either of these, when they are being wrongly used. I once had the privilege of observing the power of blessing as it delivered a group of 40 businessmen out of the clutches of the wrong use of money and political power.

These men were being prosecuted in court by a group of several hundred professional people. The larger group claimed that these 40 men were operating illegally in their business affairs, and they meant to put them out of business. Knowing several of the 40 men, it seemed highly improbable to me that they were handling their business affairs illegally. The larger group had $300,000 with which to obtain the best legal counsel and to prosecute these 40 men.

As I read the news accounts of this situation, the reports seemed biased in casting the men being sued in an unfavorable light. Indeed, it seemed from all reports that the powerful money and politics involved might be sufficient to accomplish the purpose of the larger group.

Not only did the men being sued have little money, but they had absolutely no political "pull." However, they did believe in the power of prayer and success attitudes. They began saying, "We will not accept the idea that we are going to be put out of business by money and politics." They asked me as a non-denominational minister to meet and pray with them about the matter.

I shall never forget the experience. These men and their wives of various faiths and denominations gathered in family fashion at one of their homes. They joined me in meditating upon the divine promises of protection found in the 27th Psalm: "Jehovah is my life: of whom shall I be afraid? Though a host should encamp against me, my heart shall not fear. Though war should rise against me, even then will I be confident . . . I had fainted, unless I had believed to see the goodness of Jehovah in the land of the living. Wait for Jehovah, be strong and let thy heart take courage, yea, wait thou for Jehovah."

It was then explained how we could "see the goodness of Jehovah in the land of the living" by blessing all concerned rather than criticizing or condemning them. We then blessed the entire group of men who were suing them: "I BLESS YOU AND BLESS YOU FOR THE GOODNESS OF GOD THAT IS NOW WORKING IN AND THROUGH YOU." We then named the specific leaders of that group and verbally blessed those men with the same statement. The names of the judges, the attorneys for both sides, the newspapers reporting the news, and the leaders of the group of 40 men being sued were all blessed individually. Words of blessing were spoken by the group in unison for everything and everybody involved.

Almost from the instant the power of blessing was decreed, the troublesome situation began to improve. The attitude of the larger group of men began to soften and seem less harsh. The judge and attorneys for the other group became more cooperative. Less adverse publicity appeared in the papers. The trials of these 40 men continued, though every case ended in a mistrial.

Finally, the prosecution of these men was rescheduled for another court term several months later. During this interval, the men being sued continued to bless the entire situation and to decree the goodness of God concerning it. During this period of several months all the previous excitement, commotion, and bad feeling seemed to completely vanish.

When the rescheduled cases began trial again, everything was very quiet. There was almost no publicity given to the situation. The first man's case ended in a verdict of mistrial. On the morning that the case of the second man was scheduled to begin trial, all 40 men were called into a private room by one of the court authorities, who informed them that the judge had a statement to make. The court official stated that newsmen would be present when the statement was made, and this official asked these men not to display any emotion or reaction to it. Obviously, something startling was to be announced.

When the judge appeared, he briefly stated that the court had decided it would not be necessary to continue hearing these cases, and that all charges against these 40 men were being dismissed! No visible emotion was displayed by these men, only silent gratitude and thanks that the goodness of God *had* prevailed. The power of blessing had done for these men what $300,000 and supposedly vast political influence had not been able to do against them. I soon received a letter of thanks from the 40 men who had been exonerated, and several of them began attending my church services.

I have witnessed the power of blessing work the miraculous and impossible in legal conflicts. Usually, when the power of blessing has been invoked early in the conflict, the problem never reaches a court, but is quietly and harmoniously settled out of court.

BLESS THE TRAFFIC

I recall how the power of blessing helped me in heavy traffic. One afternoon I found myself at a busy intersection, where there was no light that would allow me to get into the stream of homebound traffic.

There seemed no possibility of my entering it from a side street at this busy hour, until I remembered the power of blessing. It was then that I began to declare for each car that passed by, "I BLESS YOU AND BLESS YOU FOR THE GOODNESS OF GOD THAT IS AT WORK IN YOU!" Suddenly, a man looked at me from the busy stream of traffic, immediately stopped his car, and waved me into the homebound stream of cars. I silently gave thanks for the power of blessing working through that man as I waved at him.

A few days later, not realizing how late it was, I again found myself at that same intersection, futilely hoping to again get into the five o'clock rush. My first reaction was to condemn myself for having not remembered to take another route home at this busy hour. Realizing, however, that this line of thought did not solve the problem, I again began to bless the stream of traffic passing before me.

This time, suddenly, it was a woman driver who noticed my plight. She slowed down and waved me into the stream of cars. When the power of blessing causes one woman driver to respond to the need of another, it is truly a success power!

BLESS EVERY SITUATION

Begin now to bless every experience that comes into your life. When you bless a problem, injury, lack, or an enemy, you are calling forth the good within them, and you will be pleasantly surprised at the good that comes through them.

Bless your money, bless your debts, bless your problems. Bless your food, bless your body and your health. Bless your mail, your work, your tools. Bless your family, business associates, and friends. Above all, bless your enemies or those troublesome, trying people in your life. Wherever there is a lack, slip in a blessing. You can bless an empty purse into a full, happy one. Say to yourself often, "I IMPROVE EVERY CONDITION IN MY LIFE BY BLESSING IT."

EVEN BLESS YOUR INCOME TAXES

A businessman learned a lesson in blessing the last thing that most people ever want to bless—the payment of their income taxes! For some time this man had been criticizing the payment of his taxes. One year he had been particularly critical, but he had the money on hand to pay the taxes by the deadline. Only after grudgingly waiting until the last minute did he pay them, along with speaking words of strong condemnation about his taxes.

The next year, even though he had had a good year financially, he found as the tax deadline approached that he did not have any money in reserve with which to pay his taxes. Finally, in desperation he borrowed the money from the bank at the last minute. He then spent the rest of the year struggling to repay the loan.

By the time he finally repaid all of it, it was time to pay the next year's taxes! For several years this man struggled along, in this manner, complaining every step of the way about paying his taxes.

Finally, he heard that if he blessed a thing, it would bless him; whereas, if he cursed a thing, it would hit back at him and curse him. He realized that perhaps he had been his own worst enemy where his income tax payments were concerned. He thought back to previous years before he had become so critical of his tax payments, and realized that he had always had the money to pay them. It was only after he began to condemn the tax situation that he had to borrow the money each year and then struggle to repay it, just in time to start the process all over again.

Though it meant adopting a whole new line of thought, this man decided to bless the payment of his taxes, deliberately, hoping that the act would bless him with enough money to pay them, without struggle.

As he began blessing the payment of his taxes, he *was* able to pay them with cash on hand, though he had to wait until the last moment to do so. He continued to bless them, and never again had to borrow money or struggle to get them paid, for the money has always been available to meet this obligation.

As this man continued to bless the payment of his taxes, he was able to begin filing a tax estimate at the beginning of the year, and to pay his taxes in advance. This has given him real peace of mind and a feeling of prosperous security. Now he feels that he is "ahead of the game," instead of lagging and struggling behind it. He has proved to his own satisfaction that if you bless a thing, it will bless you; and if you curse a thing, it will curse you.

Interestingly enough, as he continued blessing the tax situation, he felt guided to tithe, thereby greatly reducing his taxes.

USE THIS ANCIENT SUCCESS SECRET OFTEN

As Paul advised, "Bless, and curse not" (Romans 12:14). Never underestimate this ancient secret for happy living. It is a simple but powerful way to release great good into your life, and it will work to improve every phase of your world, if you will invoke it.

Use often the dynamic power of blessing by declaring, "I BEGIN NOW TO BLESS EVERYTHING IN MY LIFE AS GOOD, GOOD, GOOD!" It can then prove to be so.

PART II

THE SUCCESS ALLEGORIES
Their Hidden Meanings for You

SEVEN SECRET ATTITUDES
FOR SUCCESS
FROM THE CREATION STORY

— Chapter 3 —

The success symbology given in the seven days of creation is terrific! The seven stages of creation are symbolic of seven mental attitudes you can use for creating your own success!

It is not necessary that you know or remember all seven of these attitudes. Holding mentally to any one of them can start you toward a successful new beginning. Holding to any one of them can prove to be the turning point in past or present difficulties.

However, you should be familiar with all seven, so that you can refer to the particular attitude that seems appropriate as you travel the path to more successful living. The more often you use these success attitudes, the more they will work for you.

YOU CAN CHANGE YOUR WORLD

Along with the symbolic meaning of the creation story, there are several literal success principles available to you, too. You will notice in the first chapter of Genesis that God created a rich, lavish universe for all men to enjoy. He then created man in His own image and likeness, and gave man dominion over the entire universe. He even instructed spiritual man to subdue his world, if necessary. In other words, man was instructed to conquer, vanquish, bring into subjection or change his world for the better, if such a need arose.

How often you need to remind yourself of this great success secret, when you are tempted to settle for failure and limitation in your life experiences.

You are clearly shown how to subdue, conquer, vanquish and change your world: God created this rich universe through definite words and decrees. "Let there be" is the phrase constantly used, followed by a detailed description of the next phase of creation which was spoken forth into the ethers.

You can begin changing your world in the same simple way. Further evidence that you should do so is shown in the fact that a loving Father later brought the birds of the heavens and the beasts of the fields to Adam to see what he would "call" them, declaring that whatever Adam named them, that they would become (Genesis 2:19). *Whatever you call or name your experiences, that they become, according to your decree.* Your thoughts and words are filled with that same creative power for success or failure.

Your basic success secret, therefore, lies in studying the seven decrees of the creation story, learning their secret meaning for you, and then boldly applying them.

YOUR *FIRST* SUCCESS ATTITUDE

1. *"God said, Let there be light and there was light."* (Genesis 1:3)

Always when you are trying to either bring forth new good in your life, or solve a troublesome problem from the past, you can start getting results by decreeing, "LET THERE BE LIGHT." Do nothing until you get that light in the form of new ideas, an intuitive leading, or until you observe something happen that indicates light has come into the situation.

Decree: "LET THERE BE LIGHT," rather than rushing about trying to force things, people, and events to your way of thinking. This is your first success secret from the creation story.

A PHOTOGRAPHER PROVED THIS

A photographer had long sought to collect thousands of dollars due him on a judgment. At the time of the court decision, this man's creditor had been unable to pay. Later, he had prospered, but still he refused to pay. Legal action had been taken, lawyers had conferred, but nothing happened. This photographer needed the money and pressed the matter, yet to no avail.

One day he heard a lecture in which it was explained that along with their literal meaning, the seven steps in creation as given in Genesis 1 also denote the seven secret attitudes for success. As he heard this first success attitude explained, he realized that for several years he had tried to humanly push this legal matter through to the conclusion *he* desired; and that he had not asked for divine guidance in the matter. He decided to change his thinking and to constantly declare for this unpleasant situation: "LET THERE BE LIGHT. LET THERE BE ENLIGHTENED IDEAS AND ENLIGHTENED RESULTS IN THIS SITUATION!"

One day, as he was thinking in this way, it suddenly flashed into his mind to write a relative whom he had lost contact with some ten years previously, and to ask his advice about this legal matter. In his reply, this relative explained that during the ten-year interval, he had enjoyed great success and was now in a position of influence and authority to help quickly clear up the legal matter amicably.

Thereafter, the case that had been pending for years quietly moved toward settlement, to the satisfaction of all involved. Since that time, this photographer has found this success prayer to be his prime help in handling his business affairs victoriously. Constantly he decrees, "LET THERE BE LIGHT."

THIS SUCCESS ATTITUDE HEALS

A housewife spoke of her concern for a friend who was very ill. Both medical and spiritual help had not seemed effective. One day as this housewife was praying again for her friend's healing, she remembered this decree from Genesis and began affirming over and over, "LET THERE BE LIGHT." She remembered what scientists have said—that at the center of each atom of man's being, there is light. When there is a healing need, it is as though the light in the diseased area (which appears dark) needs to be contacted and released. When it is, healing results.

Remembering this scientific explanation, she began affirming for her sick friend, "LET THERE BE LIGHT, LET THERE BE LIGHT." Suddenly, it was as though someone had turned on an extremely bright light in the room where she was. The whole area seemed flooded with light. She also had a feeling of peaceful assurance that her friend would be all right. All previous anxiety and fear left her.

She learned later that the turning point in her friend's health came that day. Thereafter, she steadily improved until she was completely well again.

Thus, begin now to decree for any situation that troubles you, "LET THERE BE LIGHT." You will experience success from this point on in meeting that situation victoriously!

YOUR *SECOND* SUCCESS ATTITUDE

2. *"God said, Let there be a firmament in the midst of the waters."* (Genesis 1:6)

The word "waters" here symbolizes any situation you are trying to master. In order to master that situation, you want a firmament in the midst of it; that is, you want a "firm feeling" about it and some firm results. The word "firmament" denotes faith. Faith is an assurance, a conviction, an inner knowing about any situation you are trying to master.

After you affirm light for a situation, often the first thing you notice is that you begin to get a firm feeling of assurance, a conviction, an inner knowing that, at last, things *are* going to work out. At this point, you may get nothing more than that assured feeling. Fine! That is your second success secret, from the creation story. Recognize that assured feeling as an indication that things *are* working out; the very sense of assurance and peace is proof enough.

A WEST BERLINER PROVED THIS

A minister from West Berlin spoke of how this success secret worked for one of his parishioners, whose father had died in the Russian sector of East Berlin. This parishioner's great desire was to have the body delivered into West Berlin for a Christian memorial service. In talking with his minister, he expressed fear that the Communists would not grant his request to transfer the body to West Berlin.

The minister said, "Let us have faith and just know that if it is for the highest good of all involved in this situation, the Communists will grant your request." They then quietly prayed and affirmed a divine solution for the situation. During their prayer time, they both got a calm, peaceful, "firm feeling." An inner knowing, a conviction, a sense of peace came upon them.

The next day, the Communists notified this parishioner that they were sending the body to West Berlin for burial!

When you seem to be floundering in the "waters" of a negative condition, you want a firmament or a firm feeling, that things are going to work out. As you get that feeling, you can be assured that everything else will follow in divine order.

YOUR *THIRD* SUCCESS ATTITUDE

3. *"And God said, Let the waters under the heavens be gathered together unto one place and let the dry land appear."* (Genesis 1:9)

After you have decreed light as step number one, after you have gotten an inner conviction, a firm feeling that things are going to work out in step number two, you then want to see something quite definite happen. You want the ideas that have already come to you to be "gathered together in one place" in your thinking and you want the "dry land," the results, to appear.

You can help the ideas that have already come to you to be gathered together and you can help the visible results begin to appear, by picturing it as already so in your mind. Mentally image the highest and best result you can, at this point. This helps your mind to begin working to produce definite, visible results.

To help your imagination form a clear picture of definite, constructive results, you should decree: "LET THE LIGHT AND THE INNER CONVICTIONS THAT HAVE ALREADY COME IN THIS SITUATION NOW BE GATHERED TOGETHER IN ONE PLACE. LET THE DIVINE RESULTS BEGIN TO APPEAR!"

IMAGING SAVED A GRAIN CROP

A doctor bought a cattle ranch. He was especially anxious to succeed in this new financial venture. After the grain, which would be used to feed his cattle, had been planted, unseasonable freezing weather set in. Other ranches in that area were lamenting, "Our crops have frozen, and we have lost our grain crops for this year."

After the first freeze, this doctor inspected his ranch, heard these woeful statements, and repeated them that night to his mother, a schoolteacher. She had learned of the tremendous success power to be found in the right use of the imagination.

She said to her son, "Do not believe what the other ranchers are saying. It is not necessary for you to lose your crop. Use your imagination constructively to picture an abundant crop of grain. Mentally see it the way you wish it to be, green and growing, with your cattle grazing upon it."

For several weeks, freezing weather persisted. The doctor continued to hear discouraging remarks from neighboring ranchers about their doomed crops. As best he could, he tried to picture a rich harvest of grain for his own cattle, and he tried to eradicate any fear or doubt about it, but it was not easy.

One day, to help him hold to the picture of a green crop, his mother brought home from her classroom a sheet of green drawing paper. It was a shade of light green similar to the color of grain on which cattle would graze. She asked her son to sketch on that green paper an outline of his ranch property. She suggested that he place the sketch in his office, where he could view it every day. Whenever he was tempted to worry about the grain crop for his cattle, he was to look at that green sheet and picture his entire ranch as covered with healthy, green, growing grain!

In spite of several severe freezes, this success technique worked. His grain was saved, even though crops on adjoining ranches were lost.

You should picture definitely and in detail the highest and best results you can image for a given situation. Decree: "THIS OR SOMETHING BETTER; LET THE DIVINE RESULTS APPEAR!" You can harvest real blessings of health, prosperity, and happiness in this simple way.

YOUR *FOURTH* SUCCESS ATTITUDE

4. *"And God said, Let there be lights in the firmament of heaven to divide the day from the night."* (Genesis 1:14)

The lights mentioned here are symbolic of your will and understanding. When rightly used, the will and understanding can separate the darkness from the light in the heavenly realm of right thinking and right action.[1]

After you become enlightened about a situation, after you have a firm feeling that it is going to work out harmoniously, and after you have pictured the highest and best result that you can conceive, these two lights or mind powers can come alive—your will and understanding—and they usually do so in that order.

Of these two "lights" or mental faculties, the will wants its way first. Your human will usually strives to tell your understanding what to do. In fact, your human will, at this point, often tries to force you to take hasty action to produce an immediate result.

---

1. See Chapters 8 and 9 on the will and understanding in the author's book *The Healing Secrets of the Ages,* published by DeVorss & Company. Rev. ed., 1985.

It is impatient for results and can trip you up, if you aren't careful.

When your human will tries to push you around and impatiently forces you to take action, remind yourself that the will and understanding should work together. But the understanding must lead the will, not vice versa.

To help your understanding gain control of the will and of the situation generally, declare: "LET THERE BE DIVINE UNDERSTANDING IN THIS MATTER." Bring your will into line with your understanding by decreeing: "I WILL TO DO THE WILL OF GOD THE GOOD IN THIS SITUATION. I AM WILLING TO ACHIEVE SUCCESS THROUGH DOING GOD'S GOOD WILL." In effect, Jesus was using this success attitude in the Lord's Prayer when he decreed, "Thy kingdom come, Thy will be done."

LAWSUIT RESOLVED THROUGH THIS SUCCESS SECRET

A woman owned a farm which she wished to sell. She had not been able to do so because it was involved in court action. She was being sued by a nearby mink rancher, who claimed that the noise from the airplanes, which her employees had used for crop-dusting, had frightened his mink and had caused them to destroy their young. Thus, he had no crop and no income — or so he claimed.

However, this woman felt his charges were unwarranted for a number of reasons. This man had often made the statement to neighbors that this woman was "rich," and had implied that he intended "cashing in" on her presumed wealth.

Her human will told her to fight this man in court,

but she did not desire such an unpleasant experience. Furthermore, to pursue court action was costly and would only delay her main desire, which was to sell her farm and retire to a quiet life, after years of hard work.

Every time her human will tried to force her to take action, she would decree: "LET THERE BE DIVINE UNDERSTANDING IN THIS MATTER. I AM WILLING TO ACHIEVE SUCCESS THROUGH DOING GOD'S GOOD WILL." Instead of retaliating through court action or through attempting to force a settlement outside of court, she became very quiet and sought a peaceful, harmonious feeling about the situation.

As she began to bless the man who was suing her, gradually all feeling of willfulness, strife, and hostility faded out of her thinking. After months of quietness, a buyer appeared who wanted to purchase her farm. She happily wrote, "The matter had been settled out of court, and has not cost me a cent." How different it might have been had human will, rather than divine understanding, been allowed to rule in her emotions and affairs.

Subdue your will! Insist that it follow your understanding, not force it. When the will cooperates with and is led by the understanding, it becomes a dynamic, constructive power within you and within your world. Most human-relations problems could be easily solved, if those concerned would let their understanding rule their will.

YOUR *FIFTH* SUCCESS ATTITUDE

5. *"And God said, Let the waters swarm with swarms of living creatures, and let the birds fly above*

the earth in the open firmament of heaven." (Genesis 1:20)

The swarms of living creatures and the birds mentioned here symbolize ideas that become active in our thinking, which is our heavenly firmament. After having decreed light, obtained a firm feeling, mentally pictured the best result you can conceive, and having restrained your human will from forcing a result by decreeing that divine understanding is showing you what to do—you then reach this fifth success attitude in creating your good.

All kinds of ideas come alive and seem to swarm through or even fly about in your mind. You may become confused by these teeming ideas, unless you know the meaning of this fifth step in creation.

When these ideas swarm into your thinking, you can know that your good is mightily at work. Things are getting ready to happen! So that you will know which ideas are worthwhile and which are not, decree judgment and discrimination. Solomon knew the success power of ideas, and he acquired great wealth by using them with judgment and discrimination.

Paraphrase his advice from the Book of Proverbs, and you will be on the royal road to success, too: "LET DISCRETION WATCH OVER ME AND LET UNDERSTANDING KEEP ME" (Proverbs 2:11).

Declare to the swarming ideas that surge up in your thinking: "LET THERE BE DIVINE JUDGMENT AND DISCRIMINATION. LET THE RIGHT DIVINE IDEAS AND THE RIGHT RESULTS APPEAR. LET DIVINE ORDER, HARMONY AND BALANCE NOW REIGN IN THIS SITUATION." To help make it so quickly, declare: "I KNOW WHAT TO DO AND I DO IT!"

You will be surprised and delighted how fast your mind will quickly respond, and the various ideas will quietly find their right place.

SHOPPING QUICKLY ACCOMPLISHED

A woman in the real estate business was asked by a relative who lived in a rural area to shop for a certain item of clothing that was not available in the rural shopping area. This item of clothing was needed immediately for a special event that had suddenly arisen.

After being informed of the need, the businesswoman had only her lunch hour in which to shop for this item of clothing. She felt confused and uncertain about making the right selection so quickly, until she remembered to decree: "DIVINE JUDGMENT AND DISCRIMINATION QUICKLY LEAD ME TO MAKE THE PERFECT PURCHASE AT THE PERFECT PRICE. DIVINE ORDER GOES BEFORE ME AND MAKES EASY MY WAY."

In the first few stores in which she shopped, the items shown her were not in the desired price range. Other stores did not seem to offer the right size, color or style. Toward the close of her lunch hour, when she was tempted to give up, she again decreed: "DIVINE ORDER, JUDGMENT AND DISCRIMINATION."

She then decided to try one more store. The clerk there quickly brought forth the desired garment, beautifully styled, in the right color, size, and priced unusually low! The clerk also graciously agreed to airmail the garment that afternoon to the relative.

When your mind is teeming with ideas, or your world is bustling with activity, and you are trying to produce quickly a right result, remember to decree: "DIVINE ORDER, JUDGMENT AND DISCRIMINATION." You will then know what to do and you will do it!

YOUR *SIXTH* SUCCESS ATTITUDE

6. *"And God said, Let the earth bring forth living creatures after their kind . . . and God saw that it was good. . . .*

"And God said, Let us make man in our image, after our likeness . . . and let them have dominion . . . over the earth . . . and subdue it. And God saw everything he had made and behold it was very good." (Genesis 1:24, 25, 26, 28, 31)

After you have acted in an orderly way, with discrimination and good judgment, as evidenced by the fifth success attitude, then more ideas "after the same kind" may come to you upon which to also take action. You will recognize them as they come; and since they are "after the same kind" as those previously acted upon, they will produce further good in the situation.

After you have taken what seems to be the best action in the matter, it is good to remember God's words, after He had decreed the sixth step of creation: "AND GOD SAW IT WAS GOOD."

Often we have tortured ourselves, after following through in an orderly way upon the ideas that our judgment gave us about a given situation. We then look back, undecided as to whether we had done the right thing. When such fear, indecision, or questionings come upon you, after you've already done the best you knew in a situation, firmly decree: "AND IT WAS GOOD!"

This helps all elements of the situation to accept and respond to the idea of good, whereas fear and negative questionings at this point can tend to dissolve the good that is at work in the matter.

HOW TO OVERCOME DOUBT AND FEAR

It is also helpful to remember the success secret contained in the next passage: "And God said, let us make man in our image, after our likeness, and let them have dominion . . . over the earth and subdue it." In other words, you should take dominion in your thinking and actions, over all that has been thought and done.

You do not have to doubt, fear or question whether you have done the right thing or whether the right results are working. Remind yourself that your discrimination and good judgment have done their perfect work, regardless of what seems to be happening. Such an attitude helps you to "subdue" various events that are taking place, and to remain in control of the situation in your own thinking. When dominion and control are maintained in your mind, the right results will surely come forth in the "earth" as visible results.

If you remember nothing more from the creation story but this one phrase, you will have gained a valuable success secret. Declare often for past, present and future events that come to your attention: "BE-HOLD, IT IS VERY GOOD!" Your very words "subdue" an old condition and can still produce good from it; your words can help create good in a new situation, too.

NO MISTAKES HAVE BEEN MADE

A dental technician found her job becoming quite dissatisfying. The doctor for whom she worked was negative and disagreeable. She realized that, as a child of a loving father, she did not have to tolerate the circumstances. After having blessed the situation for some time, with no apparent improvement, she realized that perhaps the highest good of all concerned would be for her to seek employment elsewhere.

She had long desired to live and work in a distant state. She decided to quietly make plans to resign her present job, and to arrive in the distant state in time to take the required licensing examination. Without this license, she could not obtain work in her chosen profession.

She decreed, "LET THERE BE LIGHT," following through step by step on the ideas that came to her. Every detail worked smoothly for her to make this change. She was easily able to rent her home and to arrange other business matters.

However, upon arrival in the distant state, in spite of much affirmative prayer, she did not pass the state examination required for licensing. She applied for several other types of work, but no appropriate job was offered her. As she awaited further guidance in the matter, she rested, relaxed, and became acquainted with her new surroundings.

She found the new area to be quite crowded with many people seeking work. Somehow she could not get the settled, stable feeling which she had hoped this new area would give her. She became increasingly disappointed with this new situation. Instead of condemning herself for having apparently done the wrong thing, she constantly decreed, "AND BEHOLD IT IS VERY GOOD!"

After several weeks, she still had not been able to obtain suitable work. Since it would be months before another examination for licensing would be offered, she decided to return to her home state. At first, to return home seemed an admission of failure. But she continued to decree, "AND BEHOLD IT IS VERY GOOD!"

Upon arrival at home, she immediately found a fine new job in her chosen profession. She discovered that she was easily able to relocate in familiar surroundings.

Before long, she realized that the trip to the distant state had proved most worthwhile. It had helped her to see that perhaps the time was not right for her to live there. She had learned that working conditions were better and salaries were higher in her home state. By going to the distant state and by taking the examination, her earlier desire to live in that new area had been resolved.

During her stay there, she had been able to enjoy several weeks of change, rest and relaxation, which she had long needed. She had also found freedom from her former unpleasant job. She now feels that, as the decree from Genesis declares, "BEHOLD IT WAS VERY GOOD!"

Hold to this decree when it seems you have failed; or when things have not worked out as you had expected. Declare the good anyway; and you will be guided into it, despite changes or rearrangements in your plans and results.

YOUR *FINAL* SUCCESS ATTITUDE

7. *"And on the seventh day, God finished His work and rested . . . from all His work, which He had made. And God blessed the seventh day and hallowed it."* (Genesis 2:2, 3)

The term "let go and let God," which is symbolized in this final success attitude, has confused a lot of people. Often, they ask, "How can I know when the time has come to let go and let God?"

The creation story clearly shows that you do not "let go and let God," until the last step. You do all that you can mentally and visibly to make a situation right, as evidenced in the first six success attitudes; and *then* you let go and let it work out completely, in God's own way.

Please note carefully that this is your last success attitude, not your first. A businesswoman was frantic because her beauty shop business was in a decline. Instead of using some of the foregoing success attitudes first, she had attempted to just "let go and let God." Well, nothing happened, at least nothing prosperous.

When she contacted me, she reported that she was padlocked out of her beauty shop because of non-payment of rent. She shouted on the telephone, "Why doesn't God do something about this? After all, I have let go and tried to let God work this out!"

It was necessary to explain to this beautician that God can only do *for* us what He can do *through* us; that our minds are divine instruments for God's blessings. It was suggested that she first begin to "think straight" about this situation, affirming, "LET THERE

BE LIGHT." It was suggested that she next follow through on whatever ideas for straightening out this situation came to her.

It was quite a shock to her that she still had to do something; and that God would work *through* her for her success. Indeed, it came as a further shock to her that she was to literally take action in the matter. She said, "You mean it's all right with God if I borrow money from the bank to pay the rent, and if I advertise to bring in new business?"

When assured that all these methods are God-given, she asked, "Well, when do I let go and let God?" The answer was, "Not until you've done all you can in your thinking and in your actions to make this situation right!"

NOTHING MORE TO DO

You can tell when you have reached this last step, because *there will be nothing more you can do in the situation.* When there is nothing more you can do to make a situation right, then there is nothing else you are supposed to do! That is the time when having done all, you let go and let God's infinite intelligence work out the details and bring forth the perfect results.

Sometimes, you will have done all you can and still there will be no immediate visible evidence that your good is working or about to manifest. But you will simply feel there is nothing else to do. In fact, you will probably have lost interest in even thinking about the subject any more, and will find rest in just shifting your attention to something else. As the first verse of the second chapter of Genesis declares, you will intuitively know that, "The heavens and the earth were finished, and all the host of them."

At this point, instead of fretting or trying to force your good into visibility, decree: "IT IS DONE! THIS IS A TIME OF DIVINE COMPLETION. THE PERFECT FINISHED RESULTS NOW APPEAR. THEY NOW MANIFEST IN GOD'S OWN WONDERFUL WAY. I REST, RELAX AND LET THEM!"

The Bible often speaks of things coming to pass "in due season" or "in the fullness of time." As wise old Solomon wrote, "For everything there is a season, and a time for every matter under Heaven" (Ecclesiastes 3:1). What a terrific success secret this is! Often there are many invisible elements to a situation that have to be worked out and rearranged before the visible results can successfully appear. Only Divine Intelligence is aware of the host of details that must be handled, so remind yourself, when you reach this final step and are resting in that quietness and stillness: "DIVINE INTELLIGENCE IS NEVER TOO LATE. DIVINE INTELLIGENCE IS ALWAYS ON TIME WITH MY GOOD!"

Then gather your forces together, rest, relax and enjoy this quiet time. This opens the way for your desired good to burst forth full-blown!

YOUR GATEWAY TO SUCCESSFUL LIVING

FROM THE GARDEN OF EDEN

— Chapter 4 —

The Garden of Eden allegory in Genesis 2 and 3 contains a simple formula for attaining health, happiness and satisfying results. The word "Eden" means "pleasantness," and the Garden of Eden symbolizes a harmonious, pleasant, blissful state of mind. *It is the harmonious, pleasant state of mind that contains all possibilities for achieving favorable results in your life.*

The success symbology of the Garden of Eden story shows you *how* to develop that harmonious, pleasant, blissful state of mind which can produce satisfying results for you:

Adam symbolizes your intellectual faculty of wisdom, Eve symbolizes your emotional nature of love. These two powers of the mind, when expressed in a harmonious, balanced way, can lead you into greater good than you have ever known! All mankind longs to know about and give balanced expression to wisdom and love. "LET LOVE AND WISDOM BE UNITED IN ME" is an ancient prayer.[1]

ONE PERSON CAN CHANGE A SITUATION

When you constantly use your faculties of love and wisdom to dwell on the thought of good in yourself, in others, and in the world, you find yourself in an Eden state of mind. In this pleasant and productive state of mind, you have access to all the possibilities of God's good and to His lavish abundance for you. Health, happiness, and prosperous accomplishment can come easily to such a state of mind.

A delightful success secret is that *only one person who dares to get into an Eden state of mind is all that is needed to change an entire situation.*

A housewife related this story:

> At the time I learned of success attitudes through your writings, I felt I had reached the end, that I could not go on. My husband was on the brink of a nervous breakdown and in deep depression. Our oldest son, age 19, was struggling to stay in college, doing it all on his own, without a dime of help from us. Our middle son, age 12, had been under treatment for several years as an 'emotionally disturbed' child. He had periods of becoming quite angry, on the edge of violence. Our daughter, age 11, was

---

1. See Chapters 8 and 9 on love and wisdom in the author's book *Open Your Mind to Prosperity,* published by DeVorss & Co., Marina del Rey, CA 90294.

beginning to react to all this discord with temper tantrums and sulking spells. She seemed unable to get along harmoniously with her friends or teachers. I kept getting one kidney infection after another. Since I have only one kidney left, you can imagine the concern I felt when my doctor warned me to be especially careful.

After learning of the power of a pleasant, harmonious state of mind to improve personalities, situations, events and even one's health, I bought a notebook and a pen, and every time I started to worry, feel sick, or afraid, I sat down, wrote the name of the family member or the situation that was bothering me, and then I wrote down a pleasant, positive statement about it. For my husband, our children and for myself, I often wrote: "I BEHOLD YOU WITH THE EYES OF LOVE AND I GLORY IN YOUR PERFECTION."

My husband was at a standstill when I began using this success attitude six weeks ago. Recently, *he took a bath, the first in weeks!* He got his hair cut and turned out some work on his own, without a word of prodding from me. Our son in college received a $100 refund on income tax. He also got a job managing the baseball team, so his tuition will be provided. Our middle son has gone for several weeks now without displaying violent behavior. His disposition has greatly improved. Our daughter is getting along better with her friends and teachers. As for my kidney infection, it has cleared up completely, and I am now launching on a health program to build up my resistance. I shall always be grateful for learning of the power for good that one person has in a situation when that person holds to pleasant, harmonious thoughts.

PARADISE: YOUR CHOICE

The serpent, who led Adam and Eve astray, symbolizes your five senses of sight, hearing, touch, taste, smell. These senses often try to call the attention of your wisdom and love (Adam and Eve) mind powers to appearances of failure, limitation or evil in your world.

Adam and Eve were placed in a garden of lavish abundance, and given access to all its blessings. A loving Father expected them to use their mind powers of wisdom and love to "dwell" upon the abundant good He had lavished upon them.

All the birds and beasts were brought to Adam, who was given authority to name them. Whatever he named them, that they became to him. As long as Adam and Eve remained in a harmonious state of mind, and dwelled upon the goodness of God in their midst, they remained in Eden. *They were driven from Eden and were subjected to pain and hard work only after they misused their power of choice.* In choosing to dwell on the "knowledge of good and evil," rather than continuing to dwell upon the good only, they lost their paradise.

You, too, have been divinely endowed with the power of choice. Like Adam, you have been given authority to name your experiences either good or evil. Whatever you name them, that they become to you.

How often have you made the same sad mistake as Adam and Eve and misused your power of choice to dwell on appearances of evil in or around you? If so, you drove yourself from Eden, but you can return!

BLIND TO THE GOOD

The success attitude you learn from Adam and

Eve's downfall is that *attention to evil doubles evil;* also, the description of evil doubles evil. The thrilling thing is that the reverse is true, too: *Attention to good doubles good;* also, description of good doubles good!

Whatever of evil you see in others will happen to you in some negative form. When you "run down" someone else with your criticism and condemnation, you are opening the way for some phase of your mind, body and affairs to become "run down" in the form of ill health, unhappiness, confusion or lack.

A woman once wrote asking for prayers about her eyes. She said, "I am still a young woman, yet I have gone almost blind, and it has happened so fast." She then spent the rest of her three-page letter "running down" her family, friends, neighbors, church and city officials. According to her, there was something wrong with everything and everybody in her world. The miracle of it was that there was *not* more wrong with her than just sudden blindness. Because she had become blinded to the good in life and was partaking of the tree of "knowledge of good and evil," she was reaping in her own body what she had sown in her thoughts about other people.

But there is good news! Along with the tree of knowledge of good and evil, there was another tree in the Garden of Eden: *the tree of life.* When you partake of the fruit of the first tree, dwelling upon appearances of evil, you are prevented from eating the fruit of the tree of life. But when you by-pass the first tree, beholding only the good in every experience, then the tree of life with its abundant "fruits" of health, abundance, and happiness can be yours.

I CAN HARDLY WAIT!

An employee of a large organization once proved that a harmonious state of mind can be the gateway to successful results. This worker had one statement he constantly used when evil tried to appear in his world. He would boldly declare for the challenging experience: "I CAN HARDLY WAIT TO SEE WHAT GOOD IS COMING FROM THIS!"

One day, this worker was driving home from work on icy streets. He was involved in an automobile accident. Instead of becoming upset and fearful, he jumped out of his car and declared: "I CAN HARDLY WAIT TO SEE WHAT GOOD IS COMING FROM THIS!" Good *did* result. A medical examination revealed he had suffered no physical harm, and his insurance paid the damages on his car. This man had been divinely protected in an experience that might have caused him serious physical injury and financial loss.

Another businessman heard this story and decided to try this idea on a troublesome situation that had arisen. He had been informed that his job would soon be terminated because of his age. He did not wish to retire, but job prospects seemed dim. Nevertheless, whenever he thought of the termination of his job, he would declare: "I CAN HARDLY WAIT TO SEE WHAT GOOD IS COMING FROM THIS!"

As he persisted in knowing there was good in this experience, it came in the form of another job offer. Because of many factors involved, the new work proved to be much better in every way than his previous job.

When you are tempted to say of a situation, "Here is a hopeless problem for which there seems no answer," say instead: "THERE IS GOOD IN THIS EXPERIENCE AND THE GOOD IS REVEALED TO ME NOW. IN FACT, I CAN HARDLY WAIT TO SEE WHAT GOOD IS COMING FROM THIS!"

A FORMULA FOR HARMONY

Remind yourself often that there are two ways of living open to you. One is that through all types of negative experiences, you gain by contrast an appreciation of good. This is the hard, dreary, and unnecessary way.

The other way is God's way: Through developing a harmonious, pleasant state of mind that dwells on the good in yourself, in other people and in outer events, you see that evil is needless in your life. Every person in the world is following one or the other of these two paths.

To be sure, good and evil seem to be pitted against each other in the world. But it is not necessary for you to eat of the tree of good and evil. You need not have a knowledge of evil in order to realize the power of good in your life. If you follow God's way — which is to know the good first, last and always — your mind will become so charged with good that evil will become to you totally unreal and lacking in power. Evil appearances will then fade out of your life.

EVIL IS NOTHING

It is easier to remain poised in the face of evil appearances when you realize that the Hebrew word for evil, "aven," means "nothing." *The ancient Hebrews knew that evil is nothing!*

All around us there are people who are quietly living in an Eden state of mind. They are harmonious; they are serene and secure; their lives are productive of good, because they are "knowing the good, affirming the good, and experiencing it." They know that evil is nothing — nothing at all. Therefore it can have no power. They are using their God-given dominion to name their experiences good. The Eden state of mind is their gateway to successful living.

A BUSINESSMAN'S SUCCESS FORMULA

A businessman related how he overcame ill health, financial failure and family difficulties by daily dwelling on the good, in the face of apparent evil.

At the time he began to daily affirm, "THERE IS ONLY ONE PRESENCE AND ONE POWER IN MY LIFE: GOD THE GOOD," both he and his wife were in ill health. They had spent much money on various health treatments, but they were still suffering. This man had also gone from one job to another, and had never found his right work. Their only child had proved to be a problem to them in many ways.

As this man began to affirm only the good in his life, things gradually improved. Nothing spectacular happened, but he could see that good was becoming more evident in all phases of his life. It encouraged him and gave him hope to persevere in claiming God's blessings.

First, his wife's health improved. Soon they were both able to give up the expensive drugs and health

treatments so long prescribed. As he continued affirming the good, he was offered the kind of job he had
long desired. Later the way opened for him to buy
this business. This had long been his dream. His
business then prospered in ways he could not have
foreseen. Their child matured and found work that
challenged and satisfied him; he married and settled
down to a harmonious, successful way of life.

This businessman still keeps this statement where
he can see it and use it daily: "THERE IS ONLY ONE
PRESENCE AND ONE POWER IN MY LIFE, GOD THE GOOD."
He continues to prove that by knowing the good,
affirming the good and living it, you can develop a
harmonious, pleasant, productive state of mind that
will lead to successful results.

EVIL IS UNDEVELOPED GOOD

The "fall of man," which caused Adam and Eve
to leave Eden, symbolizes the fall of man's thinking
from the constant thought of good. If they had held
to the thought of good only, they could have remained
in Eden. We still experience the "fall of man" when
we "stumble" on the mixed idea of good and evil.

When you are tempted to misuse your power of
choice and become upset by appearances of evil in
your world, remember that *what appears to be evil
is only undeveloped good!*

If you will begin to dwell on the thought of good
right in the midst of evil appearances, you will develop
the good and bring it forth. The troublesome situation will fade away. Declare: "MY GOOD IS AT HAND
AND QUICKLY APPEARS NOW." Decree for others: "YOUR

GOOD IS AT HAND, AND QUICKLY APPEARS NOW." For yourself and others involved, decree: "OUR GOOD IS AT HAND AND QUICKLY APPEARS NOW."

A schoolteacher brought forth good where there had seemed to be none. She was working with a practice teacher who was very uncooperative, inharmonious, and who had not adjusted to her teaching job. Her attitude and conduct were affecting her training as a teacher; they were upsetting the teacher who sought to help her; and they were disturbing the children in her classes.

Her supervisor finally realized that perhaps the highest good in this situation would probably be for this practice teacher to work with someone else, so he began to decree: "YOUR GOOD IS ELSEWHERE AND YOU GO TO IT NOW!"

In a few days, the practice teacher announced that she was changing her college major, because she realized through her practice teaching experiences that she would not be happy as a schoolteacher. Thus, her practice teaching came to a conclusion, and she departed.

HARMONY HEALS HEART CONDITION

There are countless ways you can get into and remain in the Garden of Eden as a pleasant, productive state of mind. It is worth the effort that is required to discipline your mind to think consistently of good, because of the wonderful results that will follow.

We can all look back on some of our life experiences and see where, like Adam and Eve, we misused our power of choice, dwelled on the appearance of evil, became negative and brought on hard experiences. But we need not continue doing so!

An industrial worker proved this after he had developed a serious heart condition. While hospitalized, he remembered having heard a lecturer speak on the power of one's thoughts and feelings to affect one's health. From his hospital bed, he began to analyze his life experiences and realized that perhaps the bitter feelings that had long existed between him and his wife were related to his heart condition. He resolved to become more considerate in his marriage relationship and to deliberately think, speak and affirm only good to his wife. He resolved to praise her more and to criticize her less.

Right from his hospital bed, he began to do this, and he immediately felt more peaceful. During his weeks of recuperation at home, he continued this plan of thinking about the good, and speaking good words. His marriage relationship improved and soon he was back at work.

Some months later, he and his wife decided to take an automobile trip to the northwestern part of the United States and then drive down the coast to California. On leaving Seattle, an old point of grievance was mentioned, and he and his wife began arguing again, as they had often done before his heart attack. By the time they had reached San Francisco, he had to be hospitalized again for another heart attack.

From this experience, they both learned the power that one's thoughts, words and feelings have to kill or cure. They resolved to think, know, see and state only the good about each other. They had learned, as Solomon wrote, that "The tongue of the wise is health" (Proverbs 12:18). This man is again enjoying good health, which came quickly after he and his wife established pleasant, harmonious states of mind.

YOU ARE RADIANT SUBSTANCE

You can get into a harmonious state of mind, which helps produce good health, by speaking of your body only in good terms. Indeed, you should praise your body as good, for according to the Garden of Eden allegory, we are told that man was formed from the "dust of the earth" (Genesis 2:7).

In man's ignorance, he has often felt he was a "worm of the dust," a miserable sinner, because he was formed from the dust of the earth. But quite the opposite is true. The "dust" from which the body was made is *radiant substance,* of which the whole universe is formed. Man, God's highest creation, is a splendid example of radiant substance and radiant energy in expression.

Thus, you should regard your body as the temple of the living God, as radiant substance. Just thinking and speaking of it in this way can help you to maintain good health or to reestablish it.

A schoolteacher had long declared that she had "bad teeth." Frequent visits to the dentist always verified her words. In spite of fine dental care, her teeth continued to give her trouble and caused much financial expense. One day she learned that the "dust of the earth" of which the body is composed was actually radiant substance. She began to speak good and healing words about her teeth.

Whereas she had previously decreed that she had "bad teeth," she now began stating often, "I have good teeth. They are radiant substance." On her next visit to the dentist, examination revealed that the health of her teeth had greatly improved. Within two years, as she continued speaking good words about her teeth, they gave no more trouble. On her last visit to the dentist, he found no irregularities and simply cleaned her teeth. He also remarked that it was amazing how much her dental health had improved.

YOUR WORDS CAN HEAL

A nurse who has realized, through her spiritual study and through her nursing experience, the power of thoughts and words upon one's health, had occasion to prove it when her teenage son became very ill with a dread disease. Upon being hospitalized, he was placed in a room with two other patients, neither of whom was expected to live. In this depressed atmosphere, he continued to grow weaker, in spite of receiving the finest medical treatment.

His mother daily spoke words of life and health to him, but he did not respond. Finally, she realized that if those administering treatment spoke encouragingly to him, it would help her own good words to have more effect. She confidentially talked with the nurse in charge of his floor, asking that she and all who had contact with him speak encouragingly to him of his recovery. The nurse replied, "I will be glad to see that this is done, though I cannot see how it can help your son. He is getting weaker every day." The mother replied, "I am also a nurse and I have seen many patients recover who were supposed to be dying, after someone began firmly encouraging them to live."

Soon a nurse's aide, following instructions, said to this woman's son, "You are looking much better than you were yesterday. You are now on the road to recovery!" Later, when an intern made his nightly check, he said the same thing. Immediately, this woman's son began to respond to these ideas of life and health. The very atmosphere in his hospital room changed from depression and death to hope and life. As this mother continued talking health to her son, he responded. Quietly she said over and over to him, "You are on the road to recovery. You are getting better. You are getting stronger. You are getting well." She realized the wisdom of the Proverb: "Pleasant words are as a honeycomb, sweet to the soul and health to the bones" (Proverbs 16:24).

As she continued to speak simple, pleasant words to her son, the other two people in the room began to recover, too! One man later told her that when she first began to speak words of life and health to her son, he immediately began to silently repeat over those words for himself. Gradually, new hope for his own recovery came to him, although he knew he was expected to die. After he had completely recovered, he later told this woman's son, "Your mother not only talked you back to life, but her words gave me new life, too. Had it not been for your mother's daily encouraging words, I believe we would both be dead today." Again, the words of Proverbs had proved themselves: "A cheerful heart causeth good health. But a broken spirit drieth up the bones" (Proverbs 17:22).

Whatever you name an experience, that it becomes. It is much more pleasant to speak good words and obtain good results, than to settle for lack, limitation, and ill health.

LAVISH ABUNDANCE

Along with the harmonious state of mind, which Eden symbolizes, we find several other prominent success attitudes indicated in this famous allegory. As described in both Genesis 1 and 2, a loving Father created a world of lavish abundance, in which He then placed man to reside, giving him complete dominion over it.

But to call our attention to the prosperous world that has been created for us, in Genesis 2, we are told that water flowed forth from four rivers to water the Garden of Eden. In describing one of these rivers, the passage states: "The gold of that land is good" (Genesis 2:12). Had you ever realized that the second chapter of the Bible speaks of our universe in terms of gold? In fact, there are 409 references to gold in the Bible!

Say often to yourself for every aspect of your world: "THE GOLD OF MY LAND IS GOOD." This helps to release prosperity and success in every phase of your world.

Also, think of your world in terms of "lavish abundance." A housewife, upon reading Genesis 1 and 2, realized that these chapters gave a detailed description of the lavish abundance that has been prepared for mankind. She began to decree to herself often: "THE GOLD OF MY LAND IS GOOD. I LIVE IN A WORLD OF

LAVISH ABUNDANCE!" Soon her husband received a check for $1000 unexpectedly with which they paid off a number of worrisome bills.

As she continued to think of a golden world of lavish abundance, she was offered not one but two jobs, neither of which she had solicited in any way. Her husband seemed happy for her to return to work, now that their children were grown. She accepted the job for which she best qualified. In a short time, she became the leading representative for her entire area in this type of work. Lavish abundance truly did its perfect work for her, after she "named" her world in rich terms!

MARRIAGE ADVICE

There is some fine advice for a happy marriage given in Genesis 2, also, though few people have recognized it. After the Lord created Eve for Adam, the passage reads, "Therefore shall a man leave his father and his mother, and shall cleave unto his wife: and they shall be one flesh" (Genesis 2:24).

A private nurse talked with me at various times over a long period about her financial affairs. She could not keep a job though she needed to work. Every patient assigned to her either died immediately or recovered almost as fast. She and her husband were heavily in debt. Most of her husband's income went for monthly payments on these debts. Her own income was needed for current expenses of rent, food, and clothing for the family.

In spite of her use of various prosperous attitudes and actions, nothing seemed to bring this couple out of a financial slump. I sensed that there was something deeper that was causing this—something hidden which she did not wish to reveal. I also realized that until it was revealed and cleared up, success would not come.

Finally, in consultation with her one day, my intuition told me to try to talk with her about her husband —a subject she had always evaded. She hedged, but I insisted. Their deep-seated problem was then revealed—the one that was keeping their success from them. Though they were living under the same roof, that was the extent of their marriage. This woman had been an only child. She had insisted, after marriage, upon moving back to her small home town near her parents, although it meant sacrificing her husband's career. She had also demanded that her husband change his religious faith and join her church.

Over the years, he had consistently followed her wishes and had consistently failed in the business world. Furthermore, when he did not succeed in this small town in a career for which he was not fitted, his wife began to turn to her parents for extra money for herself and the children. Her husband rightfully began to resent not being the man of the house, and their marriage had become a thing of appearances "for the sake of the children" only.

It is little wonder this woman was having financial problems, health problems, and trouble with her children. Even her parents finally realized their lack of wisdom in assisting her financially over the years. They now wanted to be free from her many demands upon them. Amid all her frustration, this woman had also become dangerously overweight, which led to various other health problems as well.

When this passage from Genesis 2 was pointed out to her, "Therefore shall a man leave his father and his mother and shall cleave [be faithful] unto his wife," she indignantly said, "Don't ask me to clear up my marriage. *After* the children are grown and gone; and *after* my parents have passed on and left me their wealth, then maybe I can straighten out my marriage, but not before." It was pointed out to this woman that she was not only violating the holy vows of marriage, but that her own health, happiness and success had been endangered by her attitudes and actions.

It was only some months later that this woman was willing to speak words of release, declaring, "I FULLY AND FREELY RELEASE MY PARENTS TO THEIR OWN GOOD. I LOOSE AND LET GO. I LET GO AND LET GOD HELP ME WITH MY MARRIAGE." That was the turning point. As she began to show her husband the respect and appreciation to which he had long been entitled, it gave him the confidence and incentive needed to realize greater prosperity in his work—so that, at last, this woman did not have to continue working.

One of the greatest success attitudes of all is that of being willing to try a new approach, a new method, rather than continuing to lament your present difficulties. So that you will not close your mind to the very good you desire and the good that is seeking you, say to yourself often: "I AM NOW OPEN AND RECEPTIVE TO MY HIGHEST GOOD IN MIND, BODY AND AFFAIRS!" Then get ready to receive new ideas, new methods, new approaches, as well as tangible new blessings!

Never underestimate that one little passage in Genesis 2: *A right relationship in marriage can be the key to success in matters of health, finances, and social relationships.*

YOUR STORY AND MINE

I trust that by now you are viewing the Garden of Eden allegory in an entirely new light. It is not just a story of a man and woman who made mistakes eons ago and who suffered as a result. It is also your story and mine.

As you return to a state of thought in which you dwell on the good, you return to the harmony of Eden. As you think in terms of lavish abundance, you return to the bounty of Eden. As you think in terms of right relationships, getting them into their true perspective, you return to the happiness of Eden that Adam and Eve enjoyed in the beginning.

The Eden state of mind is your gateway to successful living. Use it often.

THE SECRET OF
OVERCOMING HARD CONDITIONS
FROM CAIN, ABEL AND SETH

— Chapter 5 —

You can do one of two things when hard conditions arise in your life—you can fight them or you can overcome them.

The word "overcome" means to "come up over." The success symbology found in the story of Cain, Abel, and Seth, children of Adam and Eve, shows you how to come up over hard conditions, rather than continuing to fight them.

Cain was a tiller of the soil. The name "Cain" means "possession." He symbolizes the earthly, human phase of man's being that is self-centered, possessive, fearful of its rights, always trying to "grab" or force its will on others. It is the Cain phase of man's being that usually produces the hard conditions in life which he must face and either fight or overcome.

Abel was Cain's brother. The word "Abel" means "breath," symbolizing man's invisible or spiritual nature, which constantly tries to harmonize, balance, adjust, refine, and bring forth the good in man's mind, body, and affairs.

Just as these two brothers were in conflict, often the human and spiritual phases of your being are in conflict. The Cain phase, man's human nature, wants to possess, control, dominate; the Abel phase, man's spiritual nature, wants to harmonize and produce good results in a quiet, unassuming way.

In this famous old allegory, Cain killed Abel, and Cain then went into the Land of Nod (Genesis 4). At times, we all try to force our good—the human (Cain) tries to destroy the higher ideas of good within us (Abel) that desire expression. When this happens, we find ourselves also in the Land of Nod—in a state of confusion, uncertainty, fear, and bewilderment, which the Land of Nod symbolizes.

FORCE CAUSES MENTAL ILLNESS

All kinds of problems—mental, emotional, financial, family, social—result when man "raises Cain" by trying to force his will and his way upon other people.

Our mental hospitals and our divorce courts are filled with people who are in the confused Land of Nod, because they tried to force their good to them, through willfulness and domination; or because they were the victims of someone else's strong will, which sought to force them into certain patterns of thought and action, against their better judgment.

Often parents are guilty of trying to force their children into the parents' own patterns of thought and action, and then they find themselves and their children in the confused Land of Nod.

A couple strongly insisted that their daughter should become a doctor. The daughter obediently attended medical school. Toward the conclusion of her medical training, however, she became mentally confused and emotionally upset. She was confined to a mental institution, and was given psychiatric treatment.

Close examination of her situation revealed that her parents had insisted that she specialize in a certain field of medicine, which they felt would make her a "rich society doctor." But she was interested in specializing in a quite different field, in which there would be less financial income, but from which she would derive great satisfaction through the service that she could offer suffering mankind.

Thus, a conflict of wills had ensued. This young woman had tried hard not to show her resentment of her parents' interference, and she had repressed her feelings. In due time, her accumulated hostility resulted in mental imbalance.

Only after this young woman had been confined for months in a mental institution and thousands of dollars had been spent in treating her, did her parents finally seek spiritual help in the matter. They were immediately advised to stop trying to force their child into a field of medicine she cared nothing about; to consider her an adult, allowing her to follow the course of study in which she was interested. They were also advised to give her emotional freedom in other phases of her life as well. For instance, they had objected to her marrying while in medical school, though all concerned could well afford it.

When the Cain power of human will, domination, and possessiveness was cleared up in this situation, and the Abel or spiritual method of emotional freedom, balance and adjustment was used, this young woman returned from the confused Land of Nod! She was soon released from the mental hospital, happily married, and returned to her studies. She has since become a competent, successful doctor.

However, her parents' human force, possessiveness, and domination cost them thousands of dollars, much heartache and worry, and their daughter untold suffering, before they emotionally released her to follow her will and her way. Only then did her good—and theirs—come forth.

THE SECRET OF FREEDOM

Parents sometimes think they are doing the right thing when they try to force their will on children, saying, "We have lived longer than you, and we know what is best for you."

How often parents try to protect their children from all of life's "hard knocks," not realizing that their children need a few "hard knocks" along the way for their growth and mature understanding.

How wise are the birds of the air who push their young out of the nest at a certain point in their growth and insist that they learn to fly, rather than trying to do everything for them. Birds seem to know that if they shelter their young too long, their little ones will soon turn on them, because they know they should be free to rise or fall on their own.

When you are tempted to dominate, possess, and force others to your way, remind yourself that only more problems and difficulties will result. Setting others free emotionally means setting yourself free from problems as well. Recently, a distraught businesswoman, whose financial affairs and health had hit rock bottom, wrote me. She asked for prayers for guidance about her apparently hopeless financial and health problems. In the last line of her letter, she added what I suspect may have been the whole secret of her problems: "Please pray with me, also, for my 30-year-old problem child." Obviously there was more than a problem *child* involved in this situation! This mother has since realized that the only way to be free from financial and health problems is by freeing her "child" emotionally, allowing him to rise or fall on his own.

Your dear ones must have liberty to live their own lives, and you must grant it to them, or else you will create problems for them and for yourself. Here is a great secret: *If you really want to free yourself from all types of problems in mind, body and affairs, then emotionally you must release other people to their good in their own way. Nothing is ever lost through release.* Instead, the way is then opened for great good to come to all involved. Your own freedom and well-being depends upon such release, as does the freedom and well-being of your loved ones!

As Job's friends reminded him, "There is a spirit in man" (Job 32:8). Bless that spirit of good in your loved ones. Cast all burdens and problems on the spirit of God within them. Bless their divinity, and loose them to find it and develop it in their own individual way. The results will be infinitely better than anything you could foresee or create for them in the final outworking, though this good may not appear immediately. Like the prodigal son,[1] your loved ones have to have time to find themselves, to come to their spiritual senses. Let them!

DIVORCED WIFE DISCOVERS RELEASE

The Cain phase of man's being as human will, human force, possessiveness, and domination can cause great havoc in the realm of marriage and family relationships.

A divorced woman could not understand why her husband had left her after 30 years of marriage. Nor could she understand why he then married his secretary and moved to another state, where they were living happily.

This woman's lawyer informed her that, since the divorce had been obtained out of state, it was not legal if she wished to contest it. Her friends advised her to accept the fact that her marriage of 30 years was over, and that her husband was now happily remarried. But she said, "I am waiting, as long as it takes, for my husband to come to his senses and return home."

This woman seemed to think that she could use human will to force her former husband to return to her. She was advised to make a new life for herself; to realize that a cycle had ended; to emotionally release her former husband; to know and decree that a new cycle of good was trying to appear for her, just as it already had for her former husband. Otherwise, she would remain in the confused and lonely Land of Nod.

---

1. See Chapter 8 of the author's book *The Millionaire from Nazareth.*

Some distraught, troubled husbands or wives try to force their spouses back to them, not realizing that the use of such human force caused them to leave in the first place! Every soul is born with freedom of choice. When that freedom of choice is restrained by another—whether by husband, wife, parent or child—a rebellious desire to run away usually develops. The one being forced or dominated inevitably does get away, either through physical absence; by turning elsewhere and becoming emotionally involved; through losing themselves in their work or other activity; or perhaps by turning within themselves too much, so that mental illness or physical illness results. *Illness is their way of fighting back!*

HOW TO RESTORE YOUR GOOD

As previously stated, the Cain phase of man's being as human will, human force, possessiveness and domination can cause great havoc in the realm of marriage and family relationships.

When you, like Cain, try to force your good, you seem to "kill it." That is, it disappears for a time and serious problems result. Then you find yourself confused, bewildered and fearful in the Land of Nod, but you do not have to remain there.

Always the Abel or spiritual phase of your being is at work trying to harmonize, balance, refine, readjust and bring forth good, even in the midst of inharmony and confusion.

This is shown in the fact that even though Abel was killed, a third child was later born to Adam and Eve. This son's name was Seth, a word which means "compensation, substitution, restoration." Today the fields of philosophy, psychology, psychiatry, and holistic medicine, as well as religion, all advocate the use of the spiritual law of substitution and compensation. You are using the law of substitution and compensation every time you accentuate the positive in the face of negative experiences.

For instance, when it seems that your good has been lost, it is time to let your Seth power of substitution be born into the situation. It is time to substitute a new approach to the situation.

Instead of condemning yourself or the others involved in your apparent problem or loss, substitute this thought: "MY GOOD IS NOT LOST IN THIS EXPERIENCE. MY GOOD CANNOT BE TAKEN FROM ME; IT CANNOT BE WITHHELD FROM ME. IT CANNOT BE DIMINISHED, DISSIPATED, OR EXHAUSTED. MY GOOD AND THE GOOD OF ALL CONCERNED IS NOW REBORN, RESTORED, IN GOD'S OWN WONDERFUL WAY."

A DIVORCEE PROVES
THE SUCCESS LAW OF SUBSTITUTION

Does this success attitude of substitution work?

A woman was deserted by her husband and left with several children. Her family and friends spoke of her "sorry husband" in no uncertain terms, but this woman refused to criticize or condemn him. She knew he had never found his right place in life, and that he was still confused and uncertain about many things. When he asked for a divorce, she granted his wish. She refused to be bitter or to attempt to legally enforce the financial settlement and monthly payments due her and the children. She knew that what she fought to get from her former husband, she would have to fight to keep. She was not interested in that arrangement.

Instead, every time she thought of her former husband and his actions, she blessed him and said to herself: "MY GOOD CANNOT BE WITHHELD FROM ME. THE BLESSINGS THAT BELONG TO ME AND MY CHILDREN BY DIVINE RIGHT CANNOT BE WITHHELD FROM US. THEY NOW COME TO US IN HARMONY AND DIVINE ORDER, AND WE WELCOME THEM."

She then returned to the profession in which she had served prior to marriage. In due time, she heard from her former husband. He had joined the armed forces. He advised that he made an allotment to her and their children; and they would begin receiving monthly support payments immediately. For many years his financial support continued until he retired from the armed forces. He helped to educate all their children, and even made his former wife beneficiary to his estate.

All concerned prospered and led satisfying lives. How different it might have been if this woman had tried to force her former husband to provide for her.

WHEN ALL SEEMS LOST

When it seems that you have made grave mistakes in some situation, so that all seems lost, remind yourself of this great success law of substitution and restoration:

There is in all the universe, including man, a balancing power for good ever at work. This balancing power of good causes readjustment and healing to overcome every transgression or every wandering away from that which is wholesome and best in life. This great law of restoration is clearly set forth in Biblical history and symbology.

Each time that man has wandered away from his good or gone to some extreme, he has experienced a negative reaction. He has entered the confused Land of Nod. But such reaction has led man back to a saner point of view. It is through this process that man has evolved and continues to grow into a greater understanding of his divine potential, and of the countless blessings that are his by divine right.

CALL ON THE SUCCESS LAW OF RESTORATION

When you find you have made mistakes, instead of condemning and blaming yourself, other people, or the unpleasant results, use your Seth power of substitution and try a new approach. Know that you can overcome or come up over the hard experience (which will then dissolve), by calling on the great success law of restoration.

So many people miss their present blessings because they are still lamenting unhappy experiences of the past and blaming themselves or other people for them. Often they say, "If that had not happened, then I would be happy today, but that experience or those people ruined my life."

Never fool yourself into believing that anyone or any experience can "keep you down," unless you let it! Don't give people or experiences that much power over you. Unfortunate, unhappy experiences of the past or present have only the power you grant them in your thinking. Instead of blaming difficulties, unhappiness, or failure on others, call on the success law of restoration to restore your good to you.[2]

A COSMIC SECRET

Let me share with you one of the great cosmic secrets of the universe. This one secret has had an electrifying effect for good on the lives of countless people as they have learned and applied it. It can also make the difference between success and failure in life for you.

God, as a loving Father, has prepared unlimited, boundless good for each of His children, including you. When your good seems to have been withheld or taken, it is because your own attitudes and actions have withheld it. Not the attitudes or actions of others, but your own attitudes have caused the lack.

However, since this unlimited good is your divine heritage, it forever awaits your recognition and claim. When you do claim it and call it forth, that good will appear. Furthermore, all the good that you have not recognized or claimed in the past has not been lost. It has become dammed up in the invisible, awaiting your recognition of it. In other words, *the good that seems lost from the past is still yours!* It has accumulated and still wants to materialize as new blessings. *Your good wants you as much as you want it.*

When there seems to be great pressure in your life —when difficulties, problems, challenges seem to press upon you—in reality that pressure is your good

---

2. See Chapter 10 of the author's book *Open Your Mind to Prosperity.*

of the past and present, dammed up in the invisible, trying to come forth. Often, it takes form as the pressure of challenges so as to get your attention strongly focused on the desire for good. When the idea of good gets your attention strongly enough, it then has a channel through which to be born as great blessings in your life.

I shall never forget the first time I stated this great cosmic secret in a lecture. A housewife got so excited that she squealed with delight and I had to stop the lecture until she calmed down. During the following months, she proved that her good from the past was not lost. So many new blessings came to her and to her family that people said, "What is her secret? What great power for good has she turned on in her life? Where is her Aladdin's lamp?"

Just as this housewife demonstrated, your good can still be born into your present circumstances, even though it has been seemingly lost, withheld, or dammed up in the invisible. Push your faith button! Declare often these words used by this housewife:

"I CALL ON THE GREAT LAW OF RESTORATION. MY GOOD OF PAST AND PRESENT IS NOW DIVINELY RESTORED. ALL THE BLESSINGS THAT SHOULD HAVE BEEN MINE ARE STILL AVAILABLE TO ME, IN WHATEVER PRESENT FORM IS BEST. THEY HAVE NOT BEEN LOST. THEY STILL COME FORTH IN GOD'S OWN WONDERFUL WAY. I CLAIM MY PRESENT BLESSINGS, TOO. THE GOOD THAT IS FOR ME NOW PRESSES UPON ME, AND I ACCEPT IT. I AM RECEIVING MY HIGHEST GOOD OF MIND, BODY AND AFFAIRS NOW! MY ACCUMULATED GOOD OF PAST AND PRESENT NOW POURS FORTH INTO MY LIFE AS RICH BLESSINGS, AND I WELCOME THEM."

It will be as though the windows of Heaven have opened to you as you *persevere* daily in affirming these success attitudes.

BUSINESSMAN RISES TO GREATER SUCCESS

A businessman had been refused a number of pay raises and promotions, though employees around him, with less seniority with the company, were being promoted and given general raises — a most unfair situation. This man had appealed to his superiors, to no avail.

His good seemed lost completely in this situation. Of course, he was resentful and felt that great injustice had been done him. Then he learned of the success law of restoration. He learned that his good, which seemed to have been withheld or even lost in the past and present, could still be restored to him.

It was at this point that he realized he had gone as far as he really cared to go in his present position. For several years he had been interested in another field of work, but lacked the courage to make the change toward it, since it would mean starting at the bottom of the pay scale again. Nevertheless, as he called on the success law of restoration to bring forth his good of past and present, an offer was made him to go into the desired field of work. This time, he found the courage to accept it, though it meant a reduction in immediate salary.

As he continued to affirm that all the good of past and present that belonged to him by divine right was now appearing, it did. Within a year, this man was making several times the income he had enjoyed in his previous job. Furthermore, he had greater freedom, responsibility, and self-expression than the previous job could have ever offered. His accumulated good poured in and piled up, after he decreed and accepted it.

HELP OTHERS RESTORE THEIR GOOD

The wonderful thing about the success law of sub-stitution and restoration is that you can help others restore the good that seems lost from them. For in-stance, an accountant was working in an office with a group of businessmen, most of whom felt dissatisfied with their jobs. It was discouraging to listen to all the criticism, dissatisfaction, and negative talk that was daily voiced by these men. This accountant knew his fellow workers were killing or dissolving their good by their negative talk.

He began arriving at the office half an hour early each morning. He would then write down the names of all the men in the office, and write out this state-ment for them: "THERE IS GOOD FOR YOU, YOU OUGHT TO HAVE IT, AND YOU CLAIM IT NOW. YOUR GOOD IS AT HAND AND YOU EXPERIENCE IT NOW!" During the day when these men spoke in terms of job dissatisfaction, this man would silently declare for them: "YOUR GOOD IS AT HAND AND YOU EXPERIENCE IT NOW!"

Within a few short weeks, nice things began to happen to these men. One man decided to retire from his job, to move permanently to his ranch, and to do the work he loved most. Today he is a much happier man for having done so.

Another man in the group, a lawyer, received an offer of a promotion if he would transfer to another city with a leading law firm. He is now happily relo-cated there. Several men passed tests for better jobs with their present company. One employee finally passed the required tests and was certified as a public accountant, after having sought it for ten years. This entire group was blessed, after only one of them began

to declare: "YOUR GOOD IS AT HAND AND YOU EXPERI-
ENCE IT NOW."

A CONTRACTOR USED THIS SUCCESS ATTITUDE

A wealthy contractor and his wife found it necessary
to use the law of substitution for their son, who
dropped out of college. They could well afford to
give their children every advantage, and it was quite
a blow to them when their son left school. Their first
reaction was to force him back into school. But they
realized that force was not the highest or best way of
handling the situation. After discussing the matter
fully, this man and his wife agreed to emotionally
loose their son, let go and let God help all concerned
in this experience.

Often they affirmed together for their son: "YOU
ARE GOD'S CHILD. GOD REIGNS SUPREME IN YOU AND IN
THIS SITUATION. THE GOOD SHALL BE VICTORIOUS!"

For almost two years, their son loafed, and worked
at odd jobs. He refused to join his father's construc-
tion firm. For a period he went on emergency calls
with the city policemen, many of whom became his
friends.

At country club parties, on the golf course, and at
the bridge table, his parents refused to discuss this
son negatively. Instead, they would say, "All is well
with our child. Everything is working out fine." For
some time, it seemed more a statement of faith than
of fact. But it paid off.

Substituting the thought of good brought forth the
good. This son finally made the decision to go back
to college, where he later graduated with honors. He
is now an Air Force officer, happily married and

serving overseas in work that he enjoys. The good has been victorious.

HEALING OF CANCER

A salesman's wife became quite ill. Hospital tests indicated that she had cancer. This man consulted with his minister and asked, "Shall I tell our children how sick their mother is? Shall I tell them she may even have cancer?" The minister advised, "No, if you want her to get well use the law of substitution in this situation. Refuse to speak in terms of the diagnosis. Speak in terms of her getting better and getting well, if you want to help her recover. Under no circumstances mention cancer, unless you want it to become a reality."

He followed this advice. He told his children that their mother had been quite ill, but was on the road to recovery. Thus, no fear about her condition was generated, only hope and expectancy of recovery.

After several weeks of treatment, further tests were made, and all evidence of cancer had faded from this woman's system. Soon, she was released from the hospital, returned home, and fully recovered.

The good was victorious as the good thought was persistently held.

FEELING OF LOSS MAY CAUSE CANCER

Cancer has recently been described as an "anxiety disease." The emotional history of many cancer patients shows that in some period of their lives they felt anxious, insecure, unloved. They subconsciously retained that feeling, which often turned into bitter-ness, a critical state of mind, and may have even generated strong feelings of hostility and hate.

One psychologist has stated that 62% of his cancer patients related stories of loss, intense grief, depres-sion, and despair that led to the diagnosis of cancer. As far back as 1925, an analyst declared that after studying hundreds of cancer patients, she found most of them had lost an important emotional relationship prior to the development of the disease, and they had been unable to find any effective outlet for their deep emotional reactions.

In many cases of serious illness, there is a feeling of loss of good in some form. If that feeling of lost good can be divinely restored, if the patient can real-ize his good can still appear, that attitude can help him recover from his illness rather than succumb to it.

Many people who are not under the dread diag-nosis of cancer, but who fear it, can neutralize and dissolve any possibility of cancer, if they can neutralize and dissolve the feelings of bitterness, disappointment, and hurt caused by unhappy experiences and rela-tionships of the past or present.

Just to declare: "MY GOOD IS NOT LOST. MY GOOD IS AT HAND AND APPEARS NOW. THE GOOD IS NOW VICTOR-IOUS IN MY PAST, PRESENT AND FUTURE," may actually add many pain-free years to your life!

WHAT TO THINK ABOUT DEATH

A businessman became quite upset when his only daughter was killed suddenly in an accident. He felt that a cruel fate had cut her down in the prime of life. He felt cheated, defenseless, bitter, and rebellious. Instead of realizing that his daughter had apparently completed her life cycle, in spite of her youth, and had gone on to another phase of eternal life, he grieved, bitterly dwelling on his tragic loss. Within a year he developed cancer. Within two years he had passed on, too.

His wife was then left alone, having lost both her daughter and husband within a few short years. To all appearances, it seemed a heartless situation. But this woman had learned of success attitudes and knew how to face death, so that it could not defeat her. Though she loved and missed both daughter and husband very much, she realized that the soul of man, created in the image and likeness of God, has power of choice to come into this world and to leave it, when the unfoldment of the soul warrants such changes. Thus, what seemed a sudden, premature death on the part of her daughter, was in reality *soul choice.* It was definitely not the cruel action of blind fate or a supposedly "vengeful God."

She also realized that her husband had not emotionally released their daughter. By nourishing a feeling of loss, through soul choice he had followed their daughter into the next plane of eternal life. With this realization, the wife has been able to release them both and begin building a new life for herself. It has not been an easy adjustment, but this woman realizes that her first responsibility is to her own spiritual, mental, emotional and physical unfoldment on this earth plane just now.

Of all the hard conditions man has to overcome in the business of living, rising above the loss of a loved one through death is among the greatest challenges of all. But it can be met victoriously, when you realize there is no death, only new experiences in eternal life, which come when the soul of man is ready for them.

As in all situations involving human relationships, it is necessary to loosen up emotionally, let go and let God work for good in His own way. Someone has said that when you take the "u" out of "mourning," it becomes "morning"—a new morning for your loved one in another phase of life, and a new morning for you in your present life experiences. Grief must give way to the new dawn.

WELCOME CHANGE AND CALL IT GOOD

A phrase I heard years ago has helped me through many changes in my life experiences: "Welcome change and call it good." It applies to all phases of life. Your good is often reborn through unexpected changes that come into your life, almost in spite of yourself. What you may at first be tempted to look upon in scorn may be the good being reborn into your life and affairs. Welcome change and call it good.

I trust that this chapter has covered some of the hard conditions in life you have been concerned about. If you have been in the confused Land of Nod, you now know how to reclaim your good. It is not lost; it never has been. Your restored good now awaits you!

A FLOOD CAN BE A HEALING

FROM NOAH'S ARK

— Chapter 6 —

Your flood experiences are for good! A flood can be a healing.

We find this success symbology in the famous story of Noah and the flood. This flood allegory has been an important part of the sacred teachings of many cultures, including Babylonia, Greece, Persia, India, China, Australia, Polynesia, Hawaii, Europe, the Scandinavian countries, Wales, East Africa, North, Central and South America — as well as being a part of Hebrew lore. Ancient though it is, this allegory also contains important success teachings for us today.

Noah was a descendant of Adam and Eve. He lived at a time of great wickedness upon the earth. According to the Bible, the Lord sent a flood to cleanse the world of evil (Genesis 6 and 7).

Noah, however, was saved from this flood as he followed the Lord's instructions, which were to build a huge ship, one almost the size of a modern ocean liner. When this huge ship or ark was finished, Noah and his household gathered many animals that were to be saved from the flood and placed them on the ship. Finally, Noah and his family also went on board. After they had followed complete instructions in faith, the rain began and continued for 40 days and nights. At the end of this time, the whole earth was covered with water. Later, the water subsided so that Noah and his family were able to go ashore and again became farmers and shepherds. The Lord made a covenant with Noah that He would send no more floods, displaying a rainbow in the sky as a guarantee.

This famous flood story is symbolic of those periods of healing and readjustment that come to all of us, to balance and perfect the negative experiences through which we have passed.

As stated in the last chapter, there is in all the universe, including in man, a balancing power for good ever at work. This balancing power for good causes readjustment and healing to take place, after man has wandered away from that which is best for him.

In history and in Bible symbology, we are shown that every time man wandered away from the path of his good, he experienced a reaction that led him back to a saner point of view. It is through this process that man ever evolves into his divine heritage of greater good.

In Bible symbology the word "Lord" not only means the Supreme Being, but it can also mean the law of mind action, whereby man reaps as a result what he has previously sown through his thoughts and actions.[1]

In this flood story, it was not so much the Supreme Being who brought about the flood that cost many lives as it was the law of mind action whereby the people brought it on themselves, through their previous wickedness, which was now catching up with them. Those wicked people symbolize our negative thoughts that have to be flooded out of our minds and bodies, so that new health and well-being can flow in.

GREATER BLESSINGS ON THE WAY

Don't panic and give up when you find yourself flooded with negative experiences. Like Noah, you can know a cleansing is taking place. That which is no longer for your highest good is being cleansed, released, dissolved from your life—whether you want it to be or not. Greater good, greater blessings, are on the way!

For instance, the experience of ill health, in which you seem flooded with pain, weakness, and inharmony in the body is a time when your body is attempting to throw off, release and dissolve much that is no longer of any use in mind or body.

A flood experience is good! It is a purifying, balancing process that is helping you get ready for greater good. Often after severe illness, a person feels and

---

1. See Chapter 2 of the author's book *The Millionaire Moses*.

looks better than ever. Often after dire financial strain, a person is more prosperous than ever. Often after prolonged emotional stress in one's human relationships, the whole picture changes and greater happiness comes than one has previously known. *Your flood experiences are for good!* That is the success attitude you need to know and hold to when it seems much of the past or present is being swept away from you on a floodtide of negative experiences which may seem beyond your control.

Flood experiences come to you in the guise of confusion, loss, disappointment, ill health, hard financial conditions, inharmony, even betrayal in human relationships. However, a flood of such circumstances is not an unfortunate experience at all. It is a time when your whole being is being purified, cleansed, and readjusted. It is a time when balance and equilibrium are taking place. It is a time to release, loose, let go and let your new good come forth in ways you may not have even dreamed possible.

When you recognize these flood experiences for what they are—for good—then you will no longer be overwhelmed or frightened by them. You can rejoice, knowing you are being freed, cleansed, healed and that divine adjustment is taking place. *Greater good always comes to you after these severe periods, if you dare to expect it!*

AFTER THE FLOOD, A HAPPY MARRIAGE

A housewife in San Francisco was contemplating divorce when an old friend paid her a visit. The friend, a reader of my books, suggested that instead of thinking of divorce, this unhappy woman get busy planning how she would like her life to be. The friend insisted if this housewife would set her thinking straight, her life would become straight, too.

Having nothing to lose, this unhappy woman began spending time daily in prayer and studying inspirational books. She began to make lists of the kind of life she wished to lead: one of peace, harmony, contentment, and soul-satisfaction, as well as one of service to others, travel, and general life expansion. She then made a prayer map or "wheel of fortune" picturing these blessings as hers.

She decided to bless her husband and release him to act any way he wished. She began to affirm daily, "I WALK IN PATHS OF PLEASANTNESS, PROSPERITY AND PEACE." In due time, a peaceful relationship was established between them. Then, quite suddenly, her husband passed on to the next plane of life.

Feeling that their mission together had doubtless been completed, she emotionally released her deceased husband and continued with her inspirational studies. Later, she attracted to her a very fine minister, whom she soon married, and she wrote her former houseguest, "My life is happier now than I had ever dreamed it could be!"

Out of her flood of severe negative experiences had come a healing.

NERVOUS BREAKDOWN CAN BE GOOD

What has been commonly called a "nervous breakdown" is often a flood experience—for good!

Doctors now tell us that when the mind or body

reaches a strained or tense state, the law of balance and equilibrium forces a "showdown." That showdown takes place in the emotions, and may "show up" as complete nervous collapse.

A nervous breakdown is a polite term for a not-so-mild emotional illness. The body often responds through certain physical symptoms, but it is actually the subconscious mind (man's emotional nature, where all old, forgotten memories and hurts are stored up) that plays havoc in a nervous breakdown.

A nervous breakdown occurs when there has been some severe strain, either physical or mental, or both. Suddenly, this strain triggers and stirs up old emotional conflicts that the person presumed were dead and buried, or perhaps he never realized that they existed consciously. There is nothing disgraceful or even unusual about a nervous breakdown. It releases inner tensions and conflicts that have risen to the surface of one's mind and emotions. They are trying to pass away, to be dissolved, to be healed, as they rise up to the surface. They are like the flare-up of an old fire, just before it flickers out and is gone completely. These old conflicts can be upsetting emotionally because they stir up a person, but if a person realized that those old conflicts are now being resolved and dissolved forever, he is not unduly upset, because he knows that healing is taking place.

As one woman who had gone through a nervous breakdown said, "I remembered everything I wanted to forget and I forgot everything I wanted to remember." It is an uncomfortable experience, but it does not last, and while it is in process, healing is taking place. Afterwards, the person usually feels unburdened and free. When a nervous breakdown seems to linger, it is because the persons involved are usually holding to the hurts of the past, thereby delaying the healing.

A nervous breakdown can be for good—and that's all you need to remember or hold to concerning it.

FREEDOM COMES AFTER NERVOUS BREAKDOWN

Once I was called to the hospital to visit a young lady who had had a nervous breakdown. She was having severe headaches and prolonged crying spells. Drugs and medication had brought no relief.

Her mother was frantic with fear for her daughter, saying, "I can't understand what has happened. This girl has always been such an obedient child. She has never disagreed with me, nor crossed me in any way. But now she is saying terrible things to me. She is telling me I've ruined her life, that I have kept her from getting a job and working, that I've kept her from marrying and having a normal life. To be sure, I never encouraged her to work, because she has always been a timid, shy, sickly child. There was no financial reason for her to have to work, and so I insisted that she remain at home and help out there, thinking it would provide her with a more pleasant way of life. Now she is criticizing and condemning me for it. She suddenly seems to hate me."

Her daughter, who was at last reacting in an emotionally healthy way by rebelling against her mother's domination and "smother love," was hardly a "child." She was past 30, though she still wore long hair and teenage clothes. She also seemed to think and talk like a teenager. She was a pathetic sight to behold.

The daughter felt quite guilty in having "turned on" her mother, but she said she could not help it. When assured that she was only reacting in a normal

way, she began to relax. As she did, the severe headaches left her completely; and the periods of uncon-
trolled crying ceased, too. She was then able to retain
food and liquid again, and her strength returned.
Much of the hostility toward her mother soon faded
away.

Further talks with this mother and daughter helped
them both to realize that this experience had been for
good. Had this daughter not been able to finally
release her accumulated hostilities toward her mother,
had she not been able to begin claiming her emotional independence, she would doubtless have been
confined to a mental hospital in due time.

As it worked out, her emotional experience was
sufficient to convince her mother to release her emotionally to a normal way of life. After leaving the
hospital, she went to business school and took up
several artistic hobbies that enabled her to further
release deep hostilities and resentments. She obtained
secretarial work, and went on to build a happy life.
Her health was then better than it had ever been in
her life.

How different it might have turned out had she
never undergone a severe flood experience. Instead,
her extreme experiences led to greater good in her
mind, body and affairs.

INSURANCE EXECUTIVE MAKES COMEBACK

A housewife was quite concerned about her husband. He was drinking heavily, had become involved
with another woman, and was on the verge of being
fired from his job as an insurance executive. His wife
stated, "This is the second time in 20 years of mar-

riage that this has happened. If he gets fired again, his future is ruined. He is getting too old to find another good job."

She then related how during all the years of their marriage she had "covered up" for her husband, in an effort to push him up to the top. She felt that she had renounced the development of all her own talents and abilities in an effort to make him a success.

Though this woman had doubtless tried in her own way to help her husband, it appeared that in reality she had only attempted to control and dominate, rather than inspire him.

Perhaps he resented her possessiveness and domination, and was subconsciously trying to claim his freedom by retaliating in his drinking and immoral behavior. In his effort to be free from his wife's domination, all involved were being hurt.

When these possibilities were pointed out to her, the wife agreed that trying to control her husband had become a mental and emotional burden, and that she had given up any life of her own in the process. Her husband no longer respected her for failing to be creative in her own sphere.

She agreed to mentally free him to find his own way, and to know that there was a power within him that could lead him aright. She was assured that *we never lose anything that is for our highest good through emotional release and freedom,* but we only draw greater good into our lives, and into the lives of those about whom we are concerned. *Freedom and release are magnetic!* They cause our dreams to come true and our ships to come in.

She was further assured that when severe experiences come, it is for good, because that good is forcing a showdown and demanding expression.

Accepting these ideas, it was easier for this woman to face the difficult experiences that came upon them. Everything that she had feared might happen did happen, but she realized that this was part of the balancing, freeing, cleansing process. Her husband was fired from his job; his secret prolonged drinking was exposed; the "other woman" made herself known to everyone, including this man's employers.

When secretaries in her husband's office telephoned to offer their "sympathy," the wife refused in declaring, "This has happened for the best. A better way of life is trying to reveal itself to us. This experience is for the good and only good shall come from it!" Soon the telephone calls ceased.

As she became more relaxed and harmonious about the situation, so did her husband. He seemed relieved that she was not calling him or their predicament hopeless. As she continued to say, "Somehow this experience is for the good," he began to think in those terms, too.

He soon received a long-distance call from an insurance executive in another state, who said that he had heard the man was available. This executive stated that he knew why this man had been fired from his job, and that he would tolerate no such activities from one of his assistants. But he also knew of his talents and abilities, and was interested in interviewing him for a job.

This jobless executive was interviewed and offered the best job of his life. He was subjected to none of the tension of his previous work, he was granted wide freedom, and the new job provided him with a fine future.

This man asked his wife to join him and to give their marriage another chance. The "other woman" faded quickly from their lives. Soon they were settled in the new area, surrounded by happy circumstances and new friends, who knew nothing of their previous difficulties. Suddenly, all their dreams of many years began coming true.

But those dreams came true only after a flood of challenging experiences had been faced and decreed as good.

MIRACLE FORMULA FOR SUCCESS

The wonderful thing about the story of Noah and the flood is that it gives us a miracle-working formula for meeting extreme experiences successfully.

The Lord told Noah to build an ark, to take his family and two of each animal, go into the ark and remain there while the wickedness was being washed from the earth (Genesis 6 and 7).

The word Noah means "rest, calm, peace." When extreme experiences seem to flood your life, meet them calmly in a non-resistant state of mind, and you will be victorious.

Prayer is powerful because it gives you the sense of peace needed at such a time. In the midst of a hectic, trying experience you can achieve a peaceful, calm, non-resistant, state of mind if you will prayerfully affirm to the experience that is trying to upset you: "PEACE. BE STILL." Then say to your own thoughts and feelings: "BE STILL. BE STILL AND KNOW THAT GOD'S GOOD IS AT WORK IN THIS EXPERIENCE."

We are all seeking "peace, sweet peace," of which the old hymn speaks. There is something within us that intuitively knows that the peaceful state of mind has access to every good thing. *Health, happiness, prosperity, and spiritual enlightenment all come easily to a peaceful state of mind.*

The people who are the most peaceful are the most powerful. The really great people in this world are invariably the quietest and most peaceful. In their peace lies their power.

In his book *As A Man Thinketh,*[2] James Allen writes of the strength of serenity:

> Calmness of mind is one of the beautiful jewels of wisdom. . . . The more tranquil a man becomes, the greater is his success, his influence, his power for good. . . . The strong, calm man is always well-loved and revered. . . . How few people we meet in life who are well-balanced, who have that exquisite poise which is characteristic of the finished character. Self-control is strength; right thought is mastery; calmness is power.

You need to get into a calm, peaceful, poised, serene state of mind, particularly in times of stress and strain. And you can! Deliberately do so by saying to yourself over and over: "I KNOW THAT GOD'S GOOD IS AT WORK IN THIS EXPERIENCE." Dwell often upon the words, "peace, sweet peace." In this way you become master of a situation, no matter how fearsome or distressing it seems.

In such mastery is your strength and power for good. The strength and mastery of your peaceful state of mind is like a healing balm for the situation, helping to bring order and right results into the experience. You are the master of the situation, no

---

2. Published by DeVorss & Co., Marina del Rey, CA 90294.

matter how negative it seems, when you are in a peaceful state of mind.

When you have built your ark and entered it, nothing can harm you or keep your good from you. Your sweet peace will indeed bring sweet results.

If you do not have a peaceful state of mind, but fight and resist the rising flood of negative experiences that surge around you, you only prolong and multiply the very problems you are trying to solve and be free from. If you resist an experience, you only bring about further problems, and you delay the good that is trying to come to you. Furthermore, you will be hurt in the process. Remember the age-old axiom: *A weak man fights, but a strong man governs himself to higher purposes.*

Noah was a strong man who governed himself to higher purposes. He did not fight or resist the flood. Instead, he got into a peaceful state of mind, built an ark of protection, went into it and remained there until the flood passed.

HOW TO BUILD YOUR ARK OF PROTECTION

Now for the success attitude to be found in the word "ark:" An ark is a place of refuge or protection. The ark symbolizes an affirmative, saving state of mind. Your ark of protection in the midst of stormy experiences is constructed and entered into by your declaring over and over success attitudes that are uplifting and satisfying to you.

When you are flooded with negative experiences, first get peaceful, as did Noah. Then build an ark of protection and go into it by affirming positive statements and prayers. This is your sure protection. This method will bring you through the most searing experiences unharmed, leaving you stronger and wiser for having had the experience.

A businessman who had protected himself from a business experience in which it seemed he had lost his job of a lifetime, recently stated, "If people only knew the power for health, wealth and happiness there is *within* them! If they only knew to release that power through making daily, affirmative statements, their lives would be transformed almost effortlessly." He then related how daily use of success attitudes had caused his dreams of a lifetime to begin coming true, after all had seemed lost due to a job change.

A CHIROPRACTOR'S SUCCESS SECRET

A successful chiropractor has stated that his daily prayer for getting into a calm, peaceful state of mind and staying there amid a busy day is this: "I AM CENTERED AND POISED IN THE CHRIST MIND, AND NOTHING CAN DISTURB THE CALM PEACE OF MY SOUL."

This man spends an hour early each morning in meditation and affirmative prayer. He decrees success, prosperity, and healing results for his patients; he uses specific healing affirmations for troublesome cases of healing.

He decrees for his own prosperity and success: "THE SPIRIT OF SUCCESS IS WORKING WITH ME, AND I AM IN ALL WAYS GUIDED, PROSPERED, AND BLESSED." For his patients, he decrees: "DIVINE ORDER AND HARMONY ARE QUICKENED IN YOU, AND YOU ARE HEALED THROUGH AND THROUGH." In those quiet morning meditations, he

often visualizes the patients who are to be treated that
day; and he deliberately pictures them as whole and
perfect.

Before he begins his day officially, he calls in his
staff and asks that they become quiet and prepare
themselves for a perfect day. For about 15 minutes,
he quietly meditates with them, often declaring whatever affirmations come to him, such as: "WE FEEL THE
PRESENCE OF GOD'S HEALING POWER, GUIDANCE, DIREC-
TION. WE GIVE THANKS THAT WE CAN HELP ALL PATIENTS
WHO COME TO US THIS DAY. WE GIVE THANKS THAT
TENSION IS RELEASED, HARMONY IS EXPRESSED, WHOLE-
NESS IS RESTORED. THIS IS THE DAY WHICH THE LORD
HAS MADE. WE WILL REJOICE AND BE GLAD IN IT!" Such
prayers set the pace for a perfect day of healing and
prosperity.

This chiropractor also ends his professional day
prayerfully: at the close of each work day, he mentally goes over the names of the patients of that day
and blesses each one with health. He thanks God for
healing each one. As he thinks of the following day,
he blesses the appointment book, and affirms that
the right patients will come whom he and his staff
can help. He also blesses the money that came in that
day, thanks God for it, and asks for divine guidance
and wisdom in its use. It is little wonder this doctor
has been able to help so many people, who, in turn,
have greatly prospered him!

However, the most interesting aspect is how this
doctor meets the flood experience of many patients
and various demands *during* the day. When things
become hectic, so that there are more patients waiting than it seems he can treat, when the telephone
rings incessantly requesting home calls, etc., instead

of getting tense in trying to meet these demands, this man stops everything, lets the people and telephone wait.

He then goes privately into a little "meditation room" he has created in his suite of offices. There he becomes still, quiet, composed, relaxed. He gains new strength and new wisdom through quiet meditation. When he goes into his meditation room, his nurse knows that he is not to be disturbed. Always after such a peaceful meditation period, he is able to return to his patients renewed, and to treat them more effectively, often in half the time it would have required had he not become renewed and poised through meditation. That is how one busy professional man meets his daily flood experiences successfully!

A SALESWOMAN'S SUCCESS SECRETS

A woman in sales work proved that we can all go into the ark of protective affirmations and find deliverance from the negative experiences of life.

This woman had worked long, hard hours most of her adult life. Her husband had passed on, leaving her with an invalid child to rear and support. It was no easy task.

This woman knew she could never take care of herself and her child, unless she could maintain a positive, uplifted state of mind. As she daily affirmed God as her supply and health, she met every challenge in business and at home successfully.

One day she became very ill and then was unable to work for several months. Because of her continuing

financial obligations during this period, it was necessary to use all her savings and later to borrow money
on which to live.

At first, she thought, "Why is this happening to
me?" But she realized that instead of analyzing the
situation, it was best to know that this experience
was for good, and that only good would come from
it. As she began to daily affirm that there was good
in this experience, she realized that there literally
was!

For instance, it was such a blessing to have a quiet,
peaceful time of rest, relaxation and recuperation.
For many years, she had been so busy that she had
not taken time for adequate spiritual study, prayer,
and meditation. She now had time to relax and study
all the books she had long been accumulating. She
began to enjoy all the little things in life, which she
usually did not have time to notice. During this recu-
perative period she realized how thoughtful, kind,
and generous people really are. She realized how
much she had needed this quiet period for contemplating and enjoying the simple blessings of life.

In due time, she returned to work, enjoying better
health than ever before. People commented on how
beautiful she was; she radiated a new look of health,
youth, beauty and well-being not previously apparent.

Soon her sales had increased sufficiently to compensate for the period when she had no income.
Later, she received a transfer and became assistant
manager of a new store opened by her company.

This woman now looks back on her flood experience as good. Through those long weeks of illness,
her mind and body were freed of all kinds of negative
thoughts and emotions. The time of change, rest and

relaxation prepared her for the even greater blessings that were trying to come to her.

We learn from Noah's experiences that regardless of how destructive conditions about us may be, we can go into the ark of God's goodness, and find protection from those flood experiences that might otherwise drown us.

INSURANCE AGENTS BEGIN TO SELL AGAIN

A group of insurance salesmen were not selling as they should. The vice-president of their company realized that they needed someone constantly giving them the "will to win," and he hit upon the idea of having someone else to express success attitudes to them directly.

He arranged for these agents to meet weekly with a doctor who was a psychologist and who knew the power of suggestion. These salesmen met in a group with this doctor once a week. He would first have them become still, quiet, relaxed. Then he would affirm for them: "YOU ARE RELAXING, YOU ARE RELAXING NOW. YOU ARE RELAXED IN MIND AND BODY. YOU ARE OPEN AND RECEPTIVE TO SUCCESS. YOU ARE RECEIVING SUCCESSFUL IDEAS NOW. YOU ARE EXPERIENCING SUCCESSFUL RESULTS NOW." Each week he would declare their success to them directly. The group would then take up the name of each man present, and affirm for him directly, "JOHN BROWN, YOU ARE RELAXED, OPEN AND RECEPTIVE TO SUCCESS. YOU ARE RECEIVING SUCCESSFUL IDEAS AND YOU ARE EXPERIENCING SUCCESSFUL RESULTS NOW!"

These weekly get-togethers gave these men a terrific boost. It was as though they received a "shot of success." Within a week, one man's sales had risen considerably. Within a few sessions, all of these men were selling again. Before long, several of these men were at the top of the list as the company's most successful salesmen.

This insurance company has found this method a terrific success technique for encouraging salesmen who "slow down" to make a successful comeback.

HAVE OTHERS AFFIRM SUCCESS FOR YOU

In your own life and affairs, if you grow stale in using success attitudes convincingly for yourself, ask someone who is success-minded to speak success attitudes for you directly at regular intervals. At times the mind more easily accepts impersonal suggestions than those uttered by the individual himself.

Speaking words of health, happiness, and success is also a marvelous prayer method that you can use for others. In a prayer group I once asked the ladies to think of someone they were interested in helping while we affirmed success attitudes out loud. Our statement for those being blessed was: "THE SPIRIT OF SUCCESS IS NOW WORKING WITH YOU, AND YOU ARE IN ALL WAYS GUIDED, PROSPERED AND BLESSED." The next week, one lady reported that she had directed that success attitude during our prayertime to her mother who lived in a distant state. Her mother had written excitedly that very day saying she had just returned from a party where she won $50 playing bingo!

Your success attitudes and prayers for others do reach them and help them, often more powerfully than you ever know.

DO NOT BE DISCOURAGED

Do not be concerned if you do not immediately get results for yourself or others from success attitudes. Further success symbology given us in the flood story points this out. After Noah had followed instructions on how to meet his flood experiences constructively, it rained for 40 days and for 40 nights. Forty is a mystical number that always symbolizes a period of balance and completion. Sometimes a trial period or challenge continues for a period after we begin invoking success attitudes, but as we quietly persist, we are always safe and secure from the challenge.

This is indicated by the fact that the ark came to rest on Mount Ararat. The word "Ararat" means sacred or holy. We are to rest in or remain in a holy, whole, balanced state of mind as long as the problem continues, knowing it will pass and be dissolved. A success attitude that has helped many people do this in the midst of challenging experiences, "I GIVE THANKS FOR THE PERFECT, DIVINE RESULTS NOW."

Another success clue given us is the fact that Noah was instructed to take one of both male and female of each animal into the ark. In Bible symbology, the male always symbolizes the mind power of wisdom, while the female symbolizes the mind power of love. It is good to take the thought of divine love and wisdom with you into your ark experiences. Affirm often: "LET DIVINE LOVE AND WISDOM DO THEIR PERFECT WORK IN THIS EXPERIENCE HERE AND NOW." When divine love and wisdom are truly released, the problem will be solved! Often, it is because divine love and wisdom are not being properly expressed that the flood experience arises in the first place.

AFTER THE PROBLEM IS SOLVED

After the flood was over, Noah went forth, built an altar to Jehovah, and offered sacrifices. This was his way of giving thanks for having been divinely protected. People so often affirm guidance and deliverance in the midst of problems. But how seldom they remember to give thanks that their prayers were answered once the challenge passes. Usually they are already too busy making decrees about some new problem or desire.

In the Old Testament, the great men constantly built altars to Jehovah and offered sacrifices. They knew that the thankful, grateful state of mind is a magnet for rich blessings. They knew that *it's great to be grateful*. The "attitude of gratitude" is one of the most powerful of all success states of mind. Thanksgiving is truly the royal road to successful living.[3]

---

3. See Chapter 8 in the author's book *The Millionaire Moses;* and Chapters 6 and 13 in her book *The Dynamic Laws of Healing.*

SHOWERS OF BLESSINGS FOR YOU

The main success secret you learn from the flood story is that a flood of negative experiences in mind, body or affairs can result in blessings in disguise when you follow Noah's example in meeting your challenging experiences. When you meet your flood experiences nonresistantly, declaring that they are for good, you then open the way to receive showers of blessings from them. Declare often: "THERE ARE SHOWERS OF BLESSINGS FOR ME IN THIS EXPERIENCE, AND I CLAIM THEM NOW." Remember, too, that a flood experience is a period of balance, adjustment, a time of letting go the lesser to make room for the greater good, a time of release and healing.

Declare often for the flood experiences of life: "I AM SHOWERED WITH GOD'S GOODNESS IN MIND, BODY AND AFFAIRS NOW." It is thus that you enter the ark of divine protection, and that your flood experiences bring you good and only good.

SPECIAL NOTE: Also see Chapter 12, "Chemicalization, A Healing Process," in *The Dynamic Laws of Healing*.

TURNING FAILURE INTO SUCCESS

FROM THE TOWER OF BABEL

— Chapter 7 —

The story of the Tower of Babel shows you how to turn failure into success and how to banish failure from your life. The descendants of Noah also show you what most people do to bring about failure in the first place.

Throughout this book, I seek to bring to your attention something that is a shock to many people: what you think about *everything* in life affects your health, wealth, and happiness.

What you think about God and man; what you think about life and death; what you think about marriage and divorce; what you think about your husband, wife, children, in-laws, business associates, neighbors and friends; what you think about world affairs in general and your own life in particular— all these attitudes and many more affect your success.

131

The symbology in the Babel story especially emphasizes this important and little-known success secret.

Noah's descendants became very ambitious and
built a city (Genesis 11). Later, they built the Tower
of Babel, which they hoped would reach Heaven.
The word "Babel" means "confusion," and it is confusion that brings failure in life.

Confused thinking, confused standards of living,
confused emotions that are a mixture of good and
evil — all cause failure. Often man is like the descendants of Noah as he builds confusion into his thoughts,
feelings and actions. It is then that failure seems to
tower over him, just as the Tower of Babel overwhelmed the descendants of Noah. Noah's descendants were scattered abroad by their confusion. So
does man often lead a scattered, dissatisfying, unsuccessful way of life when confusion towers over him.

SECRET THOUGHTS PRODUCE FAILURE

The story of the Tower of Babel begins by saying
that the descendants of Noah journeyed east, where
they found a plain in the land of Shinar in which they
settled. The secret formula for failure is found in
this one statement!

As stated in the last chapter, the word "Noah"
means a peaceful, calm state of mind. The "descendants of Noah" would also symbolize your peaceful,
calm, even secret states of mind, which journey east.
The word "east" always means "within" in Bible
symbology.

Your journey east in your thinking occurs when you
turn within and *secretly* think deeply or *secretly* feel

deeply in certain ways. Your secret thoughts are always your thoughts which go deep, deep within and affect your mind, body and affairs in powerful ways. The science of holistic medicine has known and taught this great truth since ancient Egyptian times.

It was those powerful secret attitudes and emotions that Solomon was warning man about when he said, "As he thinketh in his heart so is he" (Proverbs 23:7). Solomon was saying, "What you think, feel, and do secretly is sooner or later shouted from the housetops, either as failure or success in your life!"

People who think they can "get by" with leading a double life are often surprised when they find their secret thoughts and actions have led to anything but secret results. People who think they can "get by" with things in life have not yet learned the age-old truth: as you sow, so you will inevitably reap. It cannot be avoided. We have to learn through experience that we "get by" with nothing in life; that a man cheats only himself out of health, wealth and happiness when he tries to cheat on life. The Epistle of James describes this kind of person as the "double-minded man, unstable in all his ways" (James 1:8).

DIVIDED THINKING PRODUCES FAILURE

Let us now pursue our success symbology a little further to discover the other reasons for failure.

After the descendants of Noah journeyed east, they found a plain in the land of Shinar and they dwelled there. A "plain" in the Bible symbolizes a low state of mind, while mountains symbolize uplifted states of mind. Not only did Noah's descendants find a plain or get into a low, depressed, fearful, negative state of mind, but they *dwelled* there.

It is no sin to get into a discouraged state of mind. In fact, psychologists say there are times when man's emotions demand a housecleaning. At such "low" times, many negative emotions rise to the surface of our thinking, and we feel depressed, perhaps for no particular reason.

When this happens to you, you can know that a healthy adjustment is taking place. Your emotions are mercifully throwing out and dissolving many old negative thought patterns that have been buried deep in your subconscious mind. Do not resist these low periods, but just give thanks that a deep emotional cleansing is taking place. After such low periods pass (and they will pass soon, if you do not resist them or condemn yourself for them), you always feel relieved, unburdened, and are better able to "take hold" and meet the challenges of daily living victoriously.

It is no sin to get into a low state of mind, but it is dangerous if you deliberately dwell there. A continuing state of depression, anxiety, fear, and pessimism leads to confusion, ill health, financial problems, and general failure in life.

Some authorities have even said that if you can keep your thoughts and feelings uplifted only 51% of the time, you can avoid confusion and you can experience success in life. Of course, the more uplifted your thoughts are above the 51%, the more able you are to avoid confusion and achieve success consistently.

Not only does a "plain" symbolize a low state of mind, but the word "Shinar" means a "divided state of mind"—a mind that emphasizes evil instead of good; a mind that believes it has to fight for its good, scheme for it, outwit others for it. A Shinar state of mind is a confused, upset, inharmonious, fighting state of mind that is filled with violent emotions and that tries to have its own way, regardless of the rights and feelings of others. Getting into and remaining in a Shinar state of mind always leads to divided thinking which results in confusion and failure.

SECRET ADULTERY CAUSES ILLNESS

A businesswoman who had been divorced by her husband became bitter toward the world and decided to "get even" by leading a double life. In her bitterness, she began going with a married man, and soon she was secretly living with him. But in due time, the results of such a confused, divided, bitter state of mind were no secret to the world, because her health reacted in such a way that certain areas of her body became pained and swollen. She was in a type of business where beauty and good looks were required. To lose her health meant ultimately that she would lose her job. Of course, in the meantime, as her health declined, so did her sales and financial income.

Finally she became very frightened when her health problem did not respond to the finest medical treatment available. In desperation she sought spiritual help. She was informed that the swelling and pain were the result of wrong thoughts, feelings and actions. She obviously had been dwelling in a low state of mind in the divided land of Shinar. She was informed she would have to make right whatever was *secretly* wrong in her world, as the only hope for solving her health and financial problems.

This was not an easy prescription to follow, but this attractive woman realized that it was foolish to lose her health and job for a married man who planned to stay that way. Soon she gave up her married lover, moved out of his apartment, went to another town and began her business career anew. As she found the courage to make these changes, she found that the pain and swelling gradually left her body, responding to the medical treatment previously prescribed. As she continued to make right what had been secretly wrong in her life, every phase of her world improved. She is a much happier woman today for having risen out of a confused, divided, low state of mind and circumstances.

GIVING UP MARRIED MAN BRINGS MARRIAGE

Many an unmarried woman has kept a happy marriage from coming to her because she has closed that channel by "playing around" with a married man. In our modern society there are those people who consider such an activity both sophisticated and clever, for they reason that half a loaf is better than none. Little do they realize that instead of getting by with anything, they are only causing their good to slip by them. When they make right their secret life, their life in general will be worth living again. They must eventually learn that life is governed by divine laws which cannot be "played" with, or serious consequences will follow.

A career woman met and fell in love with a married man who seemed everything she had ever dreamed of in a husband. But he *was* married. At first that made little difference, because he seemed so right for her in every other way. As time passed, and he remained married, this career woman realized that perhaps meeting such a man had been good for her, since it had helped her to realize that the type of "man of her dreams" *did* exist in this hectic world. But she knew that someone else's husband could hardly be the man of *her* dreams, no matter how ideal he seemed. With this realization, she began to lose interest in him.

They went their separate ways, and it was then that she did meet the man of her dreams. They were soon happily married. This woman realized that by comparison, the first man did not in any way measure up to her husband, who came into her life only after she freed herself of a man already married.

SECRET RELATIONSHIP CAUSES HEART TROUBLE

A businessman was in love with one woman but did not trust her, so he married another woman whom he knew he did not love but could trust. At this point, he was already in a confused state of mind which was bound to lead to failure, unless he changed his thinking.

Soon the woman he had been in love with also married, but not happily. She then sought emotional satisfaction by secretly contacting this businessman at regular intervals. Since he thought he was still in love with her, this secret association led him to emotional turmoil, dissatisfaction and confusion. His wife and the children recently born to them bore the brunt of his frustration and that of the other woman, because of the excessive inharmony which their confused relationship caused.

Over a period of several decades, this confused relationship continued to cause great unhappiness for all concerned. During this period, the "other woman" married and divorced several times. Between each divorce and marriage, she tried to lure this man back to her. He thought he still loved her, but he lacked the courage to make a break from his now established way of life. He held a prestige job, was an officer in his church, and was a respected citizen in his community. No one outside his immediate family knew of his secret love life which had caused so much anguish to his wife and children.

As the years passed, this man's children grew up and no longer had to endure the inharmony caused by this secret love affair. Without their father's knowledge, they visited this woman. They were surprised to find a haggard, dowdy, frustrated, overweight woman. They warned her that no further contact with their father would be tolerated. Having received expert advice on the matter, they pointed out the legal steps that could be taken against her. She who had gleefully and scornfully caused so much trouble in the past, now actually seemed frightened. She made no further contact with their father.

Meanwhile, he had developed heart trouble which forced him to retire from his job several years early, on a reduced retirement income. The result of trying to lead a double life had caused great unhappiness over several decades. It had brought on an early look of old age, attended by overweight, for the "other woman." It has caused heart trouble and had cost this man the love and respect of his family.

A heart condition often indicates that some deep, secret emotion or affair of the heart needs to be set right. The heart is especially sensitive to man's emotions. When his deep feelings are confused, upset, or secretly involved in a life of contradiction, a physical reaction in the heart area usually results.

Of course, there is much that could be analyzed about the foregoing story. Perhaps this immature, unstable, confused man would have been equally as dissatisfied had he married the other woman in the beginning, since he would have soon discovered that marriage is not an immediately perfect relationship, but one that has to be perfected, step by step. Had his wife known some of the success attitudes given in this book, she could have doubtless *blessed* the other woman right out of her marriage! She should have also blessed and praised her husband, rather than making a habit of criticizing and condemning him. This had only led him to turn again and again to the other woman.

SECRET HATES CAUSE OVERWEIGHT

Often people who are suffering from overweight are those who are either secretly or not so secretly holding strong thoughts of ill will, hate or antagonism. It is as though these confused, negative emotions have become blown up in their thinking and in their bodies, causing an excess of weight which diets and exercise rarely can help, until their attitudes change.

A witty, cultured woman finally admitted that her overweight problem began after her husband divorced her. She felt the separation poignantly, and felt frustrated, unwanted, unloved. Her frustration soon developed into intense hate for her former husband

ily. As her antagonism increased, so did
At times, her body would painfully swell
..... an extent that she had to be hospitalized for
special reducing therapy. For more than a decade,
she was forced to undergo these very expensive treatments for her health.

One night she heard a lecture on the power of one's
secret thoughts and actions to cause ill health and
financial failure. She sensed that her hate for her
former husband and his family was not hurting them
in the least — but it was killing her!

At this point, this woman realized she could no
longer afford to hate anything or anybody — that her
every secret thought of hostility, resentment, criticism,
antagonism, and hate was hurting only herself.

From a financial standpoint, she further realized
that one reason a book which she had written may
have been delayed in publication was due to her strong
antagonism toward her literary agent and publisher.
They were apparently reacting subconsciously to her
secret, critical thoughts about them.

Upon advice of a spiritual counselor, she began
to daily declare forgiveness toward everything in her
past and present: "I FORGIVE EVERYTHING AND EVERY-
ONE WHO CAN POSSIBLY NEED FORGIVENESS IN MY PAST
AND PRESENT. I FORGIVE POSITIVELY EVERYONE. I AM FREE
AND THEY ARE FREE TOO. ALL THINGS ARE CLEARED UP
BETWEEN US NOW AND FOREVER." Shortly after she
started to speak these words of forgiveness daily, she
began to see various people whom she had hated in
the past. Each time, she made it a point to be kind
and gracious to them. Each time, they seemed amazed
and relieved, and invariably responded to her with
equal kindness.

This woman soon felt unburdened mentally and emotionally. As she did, she began to lose weight for the first time in years. The book which she had previously pulled every string to get into print, was now quietly and easily published. Several professional honors came to her in her work. This woman felt that for the first time in years, she was coming alive. Often she declared for a happy future: "NEW DOORS OF GOOD NOW OPEN TO ME, AND WITH A CONFIDENT SPIRIT, I GO FORTH INTO A LIFE OF HEALTH, HAPPINESS, SECURITY AND ABUNDANT LIVING, IN GOD'S OWN WONDERFUL WAY." Recently she confided that she is now considering a proposal of marriage! In any event, she is relieved to have risen out of that low, divided state of mind, which the Tower of Babel allegory describes as a "plain in the land of Shinar."

FORCING YOUR GOOD PRODUCES FAILURE

Another cause of failure is found in the fact that the descendants of Noah tried to build their tower from brick and slime. Brick is made of the earth and instead of real mortar, these people used some kind of slime. In other words, this tower was made of earthy or unstable materials that could not be expected to hold the tower together.

When man labors to build his tower of good from earthy, human, or slimy materials, his good soon comes tumbling down around him. So many people experience all kinds of troubles in mind, body and affairs because they are laboring hard under the human belief that they personally have to force their good into being. They are straining physically, mentally, and emotionally to compel their good into expression, yet they are experiencing exhaustion, frustration, and failure on every hand.

Such people do not realize that there is a loving, powerful Presence and Power for good in their midst that wishes to work for them and through them. This God-Presence will help them accomplish easily what they are trying so hard to accomplish alone.

After the descendants of Noah built their tower of brick and slime, the passage says that the Lord was angry and that He did just what the people had feared might happen — he scattered the people abroad and confounded their language, so that they could not understand one another's speech.

In this instance, the word "Lord" means the law of mind action. The law of mind action is that what you sow you reap; what you think you produce as an outer result. What you really believe, expect, and think about activates the law of mind action in that direction. These people had dwelled in the plain in the land of Shinar — in a low, pessimistic state of mind. Furthermore, they had built a tower of confusion with inferior materials by using brick and slime. Thus, they had sown confusion and were bound to reap confusion and failure, because of the unwise manner in which they had invoked the unfailing law of mind action. It is little wonder they were scattered abroad, and that further confusion became their lot. They had not asked God's help in their endeavor. They had tried to go it alone, and they got the usual human result of failure.

You may have heard the once amusing television ad which had the punchline, "Please, I'd rather do it

myself!" When you are tempted to feel so self-suffi-
cient, remember the sad story of Noah's descendants
who said the same thing and who experienced only
scattered results of confusion and failure.

Instead, be big enough to become peaceful, quiet,
and then affirm that there is one Presence and one
Power in your midst — the Presence and Power of God
the Good. Know and declare that He is helping you,
guiding you every step of the way. Then the right
ideas and right results will come, so that the good
you build will not come tumbling down. This is one
of the great success secrets which the descendants
of Noah had not yet learned.

OTHERS HEALED OF DRINKING HABIT

Once upon a time there was a bartender who wondered how he could claim the presence and power
of God's goodness in his job. He heard of affirmative
prayer as a scientific and simple method, and hit
upon the idea of silently affirming this thought for
his customers: "YOU DRINK TO THE SPIRIT, YOUR THIRST
IS FOR GOD." His customers began to dwindle and soon
there were not enough left to keep the tavern open!
This bartender and the proprietor then went into a
different type of business together, which proved to
be much more successful than their first.

Many people in modern times drink socially. People of the Bible times drank socially, too. In many
instances, they drank wine because water was either
scarce, impure, or unavailable.

However, excessive drinking usually indicates that
the person really thirsts for more good in life, and

that liquor does not quench that thirst. Yet they seek to compensate by excessive drinking. The greatest help you can give such a person is not by preaching to him about the sins of drink, but by affirming for him: "YOU DRINK TO THE SPIRIT, YOUR THIRST IS FOR GOD."

A very devout woman once told me that her entire family considered her a mental case for years because she refused to condemn a member of her family who drank excessively. Instead she prayed and affirmed a perfect healing. Eventually, he was completely healed of the desire for strong drink — the desire waned and left him completely, without one word being uttered to him.

People who drink excessively are usually very sensitive and quite talented people who are trying to find their right place in life. As they do, their drinking problems are often resolved. The greatest thing you can do for them is to refrain from criticism and preaching to them. Silently affirm that there is a divine place for them in life, and that they are being led into that divine place where they fully express their talents and abilities in rich and satisfying ways.

MAKE NON-VIOLENT DECREES

Along with affirming the presence and power of God's goodness, so that we do not build our towers of good with brick and slime, our affirmations should be made in a certain way to insure success in a non-violent "Noah" state of mind. People who complain that their affirmative prayers have not been answered often have made their affirmations in an excited, emotional, violent frame of mind.

I once knew a woman whose prayers were always answered, but usually in some violent or dramatic way. She was a very excitable woman and lived in a state of intense emotional turmoil all the time. Once she affirmed that she would receive $5,000 which she needed to clear up certain financial obligations. She got the $5,000, but it came as an insurance settlement following an automobile accident. Through a lot of pain and suffering, her prayer was indeed answered!

She had had three or four children by her three or four husbands, and she loved to dramatically relate all the troubles she had endured with both husbands and children. She constantly went from one predicament to another, and would then affirmatively pray her way out of each one in some dramatic way.

When it seems that you have one thing after another to meet, check your emotions to see if you have not been exaggerating, playing up and showing off your troubles. If you are dramatic about your troubles, you will always have troubles to be dramatic about. As you give up the drama, you give up the troubles. Get still and quiet about your troubles, if you want your troubles to become still, quiet, and then fade away.

BE FIRM BUT HARMONIOUS

You should make firm decrees, but be sure to make them in a harmonious, poised, non-violent state of mind. A secretary had tried every mental method she knew to demonstrate a car of her own, which she urgently needed. One night, feeling she could stand the privation no longer, she calmly walked the floor of her living room (there was no one else in the house at the time), and in a calm but loud, firm voice she decreed: "I GIVE THANKS THAT THE PERFECT CAR NOW COMES TO ME FOR MY PERSONAL USE, IN GOD'S OWN WONDERFUL WAY."

For perhaps half an hour she decreed this over and over. Finally, a sense of relief came and she "felt" that the car was very near. Thereafter, whenever she thought of this desire, she simply said to herself, "I GIVE THANKS THAT GOD HAS MET THIS DEMAND! I HAVE THE PERFECT CAR NOW!" She then got busy studying the required tests for a driver's license.

Within a week, a friend came to her, talked about her need for a car, and insisted upon arranging a personal loan, so that she could obtain the car at once. Before she had time to obtain a driver's license, the lovely new car of her choice was sitting in her driveway! God did meet her demand, after she had decreed it in a firm but non-violent way.

IDEAS ARE THE SECRET OF SUCCESS

The main lesson we learn from the Tower of Babel story is to not attempt to force our good in a given situation, for force only brings confusion and failure. Emerson said, "All advancement and progress come through ideas, not through physical force or mechanical force."

Perhaps it surprises you that several of the allegories in Genesis point this out in various ways. Had the descendants of Noah been open and receptive to the inflow of other ideas, rather than trying to force their own, their story might have had a happier ending.

You will see as you analyze your failure experiences

in life that you made the same mistakes as Noah's descendants. You tried to force your own limited ideas in a situation, rather than being receptive to the highest and best methods of accomplishment.

When it seems you have failed, it is good to know you can still become open and receptive to the highest and best for that situation by meditating upon this statement: "DIVINE INTELLIGENCE, WHAT IS THE DIVINE IDEA THAT CAN HEAL AND ADJUST THIS SITUATION? LET THE DIVINE IDEA NOW APPEAR!" The right idea or the next step of accomplishment will then reveal itself to you personally; or someone else will take the right action; or some unforeseen opportunity or event will point the way.

72-YEAR-OLD EMPLOYEE REINSTATED

A 72-year-old businessman had been released from his job, presumably because of his age. His first reaction was to try to force his way back into the job by filing a protest, demanding a hearing, etc. But he knew, as did Emerson, that all progress comes through ideas, and not through physical or mechanical force.

He began to hold to these ideas for his continued progress and success: "MY GOD-GIVEN SUCCESS CANNOT BE WITHHELD FROM ME. MY GOD-GIVEN SUCCESS CANNOT BE TAKEN FROM ME. ALL OBSTACLES AND BARRIERS TO MY SUCCESS ARE DIVINELY DISSOLVED NOW, SO I MOVE INTO THE MOST AMAZING, MIRACULOUS CONDITIONS OF HEALTH, WEALTH AND HAPPINESS."

Within a few days, he received a long-distance telephone call from the home office of his company, asking him to please return to his former job!

A FITTING CONCLUSION

From the Tower of Babel story, you have learned what *not* to do so as to avoid failure or overcome it. This is a fitting conclusion to the success allegories of Genesis.

Now proceed quickly to the upcoming chapters. There you will learn from the Bible's early millionaires their specific success secrets for you!

PART III

THE PROSPEROUS PEOPLE
OF GENESIS
Their Success Secrets for You

YOUR OCCULT POWER FOR SUCCESS

PICTURING FROM ABRAHAM

— Chapter 8 —

In the 12th chapter of Genesis, you meet the man who became the Bible's first millionaire, Abram, later called Abraham. From him you can learn certain ancient secrets that can lead to your own greater wealth.

Abraham's life began in the Babylonian city of Ur. Historians tell us that the Babylonians were very advanced in many ways. By their ingenious techniques in agriculture, commerce, and finance, Babylon's citizens became the richest of their era. They understood financial principles through which they developed ideas for insurance, savings, home ownership, and investments that are considered sound and worthwhile by financiers today.

Into this advanced and prosperous civilization, Abraham was born and grew to adulthood. Even later in Canaan, Abraham was still under the influence of the Babylonian government.

The story of Abraham begins when the Lord told him to get out of his old country and go to a new land which the Lord would show him — a land in which the Lord promised to bless him and make him great (Genesis 12:1, 2). When you want to experience success in life, you need to get out of the old country, or an old state of mind. You leave the old country as you release negative thought patterns, old, limited ideas and attitudes, doubts, fears, resentments, prejudices, criticisms. Sometimes it is even necessary to release old relationships and old ways of living, too, if they stand in the way of a higher viewpoint that is necessary for a better way of life.

You rise out of an old set of circumstances into greater good when you dare to boldly try a new, uplifting viewpoint.

A LITTLE-KNOWN POWER FOR SUCCESS

In Canaan both Abraham and Lot became very rich in cattle, silver, and gold (Genesis 13:2, 5). In fact, their substance became so great that the land was not able to sustain them. When strife arose among their herdsmen, to keep peace in the family, Abraham offered Lot any land that he desired.

Considering himself a shrewd businessman, Lot chose the fertile Plain of Jordan, leaving Abraham with the hilly country near Hebron. At the time, it seemed that Abraham lost much by his generous nature.

It was then that the Lord pointed out to Abraham an occult power for success. The word "occult" simply means "secret, hidden, esoteric, mysterious, or that pertaining to the mystic arts." The secret power for success, which was pointed out to Abraham, has been used since ancient times — the picturing power of the mind:

> Lift up now thine eyes, and look from the place where thou art, northward and southward, eastward and westward; for all the land which thou *seest*, to thee will I give it. (Genesis 13:14, 15)

When it seems that someone has grabbed your good or cheated you; when it seems that someone else has gotten the best in a situation, and you have gotten the worst; or when it seems that success constantly evades you; that is the time for you to "look up" from the rough circumstances where you are and picture your good in a big way; for all that you "see" will be given you.

Psychologists tell us that the picturing power of the mind is one of man's strongest powers for success. They say that any picture firmly held in mind is bound to come forth as a result. How often have you pictured failure and gotten it, when you might just as easily have pictured success and produced it? Your picturing power is one of your greatest success powers. You should boldly use it to create whatever you want in life. Image what you want instead of what you do not want, because *what you constantly image, you will get!*

IMAGING MONEY BRINGS MONEY TO YOU

A businessman first brought to my attention the success power of the imagination. This man had gone through a period of severe financial privation and felt he could endure it no longer. Learning of the imaging power of the mind, he purchased some "play money" and placed the bills of large denomination in his wallet. Every time he opened his wallet, his eyes would first see those large sums of money, and subconsciously the thought would register, "I have money!" It was a nice, new thought for his subconscious, which had so often been fed the idea, "I have no money." From this point on, he began to make more money as a salesman, and gradually he became quite prosperous. He feels that the turning point from financial lack to financial abundance came the day he placed "play money" in his wallet. This helped him to begin to "see" plenty instead of lack.

It may sound like a kindergarten idea to you, but who cares, if it works? And it does! Actually, this is an old occult secret for prosperity that was known and used by the ancients. When they desired more money, they would sit in meditation, picture definite sums of money, and then demand of universal substance, "Give me this!" They would picture definite sums of money, over and over, day in and day out, until the money came to satisfy their needs in some way.

I cannot recommend this method for producing more financial supply too strongly to you. It is a simple, easy, delightful way of expanding your imaging power to picture definite prosperity instead of lack.

A housewife heard me lecture on this method for realizing greater supply. Afterwards she said, "I know that that method works, because many years ago my husband was not selling as he should, and he began to carry play money in his wallet. Every night, as he was relaxing after dinner, he would take certain denominations of play money from his wallet — usually sums of $50 and $100 — and hold it in his hands, looking at it for some time. He would concentrate on one bill which represented the amount of sales he wanted to make the next day. Gradually, he was able to increase his daily sales, as he nightly looked at larger and larger sums of play money in denominations of $500, $1,000 and $5,000. He still carries play money in his wallet, but now only in larger amounts of $10,000, $20,000, $50,000 and $100,000, since he has over the years moved into a much bigger sales bracket."

I confess that my husband and I both carry play money in our wallets all the time, along with genuine cash. We find that when our cash is getting low, if we will take the play money from our wallets, look at the definite amounts and decree, "I AM RECEIVING, I AM RECEIVING NOW!"—more money appears, sometimes in surprising ways. My husband's favorite denomination of play money is a $5,000 bill, which he places next to his genuine cash in his wallet. He has often said, "When I get down to that $5,000, more real money always comes in." That alone is a nice prosperity decree: "When I get down to $5,000, more money comes in!"

A domestic worker once informed her employer that she needed more money for daily living. Her employer told her to get some play money to help her think definitely about prosperity. This maid needed two new uniforms which cost $7 each. She had managed to save $2 for one uniform but needed $5 more. An extra $5 at this point would have seemed a tremendous prosperity boost to this woman.

Daily she began to look at the $5 in play money given her and to mentally accept it by declaring, "I AM RECEIVING, I AM RECEIVING THIS $5 NOW IN GOD'S OWN WONDERFUL WAY." Shortly after this, she was walking down an unpopulated street and as she looked down, she saw a $5 bill lying on the pavement in front of her. Since there was no one in the vicinity to claim it, she did! She immediately bought one uniform for $7. Within a week, two more new uniforms were given to her by her daughter for her birthday. Recently this woman said, "Since I began this practice of keeping play money in my purse, I have not been without cash. More money and other types of prosperity have come to me than ever before, in both expected and unexpected ways."

MAKE A WHEEL OF FORTUNE FOR MONEY

One young couple, recently married, incurred many financial expenses while setting up housekeeping, and soon found themselves about $2,000 in debt. Upon learning that they could picture money and attract it to them, they decided to make a "wheel of fortune" as described in my book *The Dynamic Laws of Prosperity* (Chapter 5). On their wheel of fortune, they placed only play money in various denominations of $20, $50, $100, $500, and $1,000. In bold letters, amid all this money, they placed these words, "ALL OUR NEEDS ARE MET NOW!" They placed their money wheel of fortune where they could view it often daily.

Within a short time, the husband received a check for $1,000 for some work he had done before his marriage, for which he had never been paid. Later he decided to cash in some financial assets he owned because they were of no immediate value. From this transaction, he received another $1,000.

This couple continues to make "money wheels" in order to expand their thinking, and they continue to attract more and more money to them in usual and unusual ways.

WIDOW MARRIES THROUGH IMAGING

A lonely widow decided to make a wheel of fortune for a husband and happy marriage. She was a housemother in a college dormitory. Her regular social activities centered around other housemothers in nearby dormitories, who constantly spoke of how lonely they were, how they yearned to marry, and how they were never able to meet eligible men.

This widow became bored with their negative line of thought. Quietly she went through magazines, cutting out pictures of a beautiful home, travel by boat, new clothes, and large sums of money. She also found and clipped a picture of the type of man she thought she would like to marry. After making her wheel of fortune, she put it in a private place where she could view it daily, but where it was not available for others to see.

As she daily viewed this marriage wheel of fortune, she began to feel that somehow the blessings depicted on it were possible for her. In due time, friends wrote that they were coming to town to attend a cattlemen's convention, inviting her to be their guest at several events during the convention. Her first reaction was to decline since she would be unescorted. But then she remembered her wheel of fortune, and courageously she accepted their invitation.

The main social event of this convention was a dinner dance, which she attended with her friends. There she was introduced by her hosts to a wealthy cattleman, a long-time friend of theirs whose wife had recently passed on. As she shook hands with him, she was aware that he resembled the attractive man pictured on her wheel of fortune. Later when she looked closely at that picture, she was startled to see for the first time that her "dream man" wore some sort of badge on his coat lapel, similar to the nameplate worn by her new friend at the convention banquet!

Their friendship grew and deepened into love, and within a year they were happily married. As a wedding gift, her husband gave her a substantial sum of money. They then left on a honeymoon cruise aboard an ocean liner similar to the one pictured on her wheel of fortune. She settled down to a joyous new life, in a lovely home, stating she would have to make a new wheel of fortune since every item on her first one had come forth in wonderful detail! Her former housemother friends left behind in that college town have not recovered from the shock of seeing one of their group actually prove the picturing power of the mind in such a marvelous way.

NO IMAGE, NO MARRIAGE

A doctor's wife recently complained about her 40-year-old daughter who had never married, who she feared might never marry. She said, "My daughter is a member of a prominent church and is active in various clubs. She does everything she knows to circulate so as to meet the right man. She has been doing this for years, but still nothing happens."

What this mother had to be told was that both she and her daughter needed to circulate the picture of marriage in their minds more, and do less worrying about outer circulation. Until the mental image of marriage has been set up and accepted in their thinking, this daughter will not marry, no matter how desperately she circulates socially. When she does accept the mental image of marriage, it will come with no great effort on her part. I referred both mother and daughter to the chapters on radiation and attraction (Chapters 2 and 11) in my book *The Dynamic Laws of Prosperity* as well as to the chapter on imaging (Chapter 5). As stated therein, you must first radiate in order to attract. The mental image makes the condition; without the mental image, there can be no condition!

THE DANGER OF IMAGING WHAT BELONGS TO ANOTHER

Many single women have complained that they only meet married men who measure up to their standards for a husband. When they meet such men, they should realize that their image is working! They have met the "type" of man they would like to marry. This should help them to mentally accept the idea that the "type" of man they wish to marry is, at least, on this planet. But they should not continue association with that particular man, for if they do, they will stop their image from manifesting the next step, which would be the man of their dreams, unattached and available.

I know of a woman who met a married man whom she considered the man of her dreams, rather than realizing he was only the "type" she wished to marry. She imaged him as her own husband and finally got him. But he was not what she had anticipated. Meanwhile she met and fell in love with someone else who was the man of her dreams, and who was free to marry her. But sadly she had taken another woman's husband and was then not free to marry. Through imaging something that belonged to someone else, she came to grief and disappointment.

ADOPTION OF CHILDREN THROUGH IMAGING

A schoolteacher was heartbroken because after many years of marriage, she and her husband still had no children. Several times they had attempted to adopt children, but always something had happened so that their plans had never worked out. This couple had become so thoroughly disillusioned that the husband had said, "Never mention the word 'adoption' to me again. There's just too much red tape connected with that procedure, and I am not willing to go through it."

This unhappy schoolteacher attended a lecture I gave on the picturing power of the mind, and decided to quietly make a wheel of fortune for a baby. On it she placed pictures of beautiful babies, bottles, cribs, toys and baby clothes. Daily she looked at these pictures, giving thanks that the perfect child was being given to her in God's own wonderful way.

While housecleaning, she later came across an adoption form which she had earlier obtained from an out-of-town adoption agency. She felt led to fill it out and mail it. The authorities from this agency soon visited her and her husband, explaining the simplicity of their adoption method. Her husband then completely changed his mind and seemed more anxious for a baby than she did! The first child shown them was a little girl, and it was her husband who said, "You need not show us any more babies; we want this one."

It proved to be a happy choice, and the presence of this baby in their home has added much to the happiness of their marriage. This woman is now picturing another child, a little boy, to complete their family group. She also recently made a wheel of fortune for a larger home to provide more room for their growing family.

Be sure when you picture definite tangible things, such as a car, home, clothes, trips to far-off places, that you also picture the money to pay for these things. Otherwise, these items will come, but you may find yourself heavily in debt for them because you did not also picture the money to pay for them!

PREPARING NURSERY BRINGS CHILD

Another childless couple had also attempted to adopt a child, but to no avail. Upon learning of the picturing power of the mind for producing results, the wife decided to go ahead in faith and prepare a bedroom in their home as a nursery, rather than to wait until an adoption was definite.

As she began to furnish this nursery for a little girl, both she and her husband were better able to mentally accept the idea that there would soon be a child in their home.

After this wife had completely decorated the nursery in every detail, their minister learned of a baby—a little girl—who was available by private adoption. Investigation revealed that this was the child they had long dreamed of having. All adoption details moved swiftly and smoothly, and this couple was soon proudly putting their waiting nursery to use!

SALE OF PROPERTY THROUGH IMAGING

The picturing power of the mind works to produce good results in all phases of life. Many people seem to have trouble selling their homes when they have decided to move elsewhere. Difficulty in selling a home is often due to the fact that the persons who have lived in it still feel strong emotional ties for their home. They find it hard to release such sentimental attachments. But until that emotional release comes, the house will not sell. Many families must actually move out of a house and leave it in the hands of realtors, before it will sell. Often such an act of release seems necessary.

When you are trying to sell property and have not been able to do so, deliberately declare: "I FULLY AND FREELY RELEASE YOU. I LOOSE YOU AND LET YOU GO. I PICTURE YOU AS SOLD NOW!" Then picture a "sold" sign in front of the house, instead of a "for sale" sign. For a time, think of the house as completely empty of your own furnishings and then think of it as re-occupied by new owners. As you completely change the mental picture you are holding of the house, it will then sell at the right time, to the right people, for the right price.

IMAGING CLOTHES BRINGS THEM

It is amazing the numerous ways in which one's pictures can produce happy results. A doctor shopped all over town trying to find a type of sport jacket which he wished to wear, but did not find it in any of the stores.

Upon returning home he thought, "Why should I be concerned about how this sport jacket comes to me? Why don't I just mentally image it and let it appear in whatever way seems best?" In his meditation times daily, he imaged this jacket in detail, dwelling on the fine texture, the weave, the color, the design he admired in this jacket. He then pictured himself wearing it.

Then he dismissed the matter from his mind, giving thanks it would come at the right time in the right way. A few days later, an out-of-town patient came to his office for treatments, carrying a large package. He presented it to the doctor saying, "We just received a new shipment of sport jackets at my store, and when I saw this one, I thought of you. If you like it, I hope you will accept it as a gift from me." It fitted him perfectly, and was almost exactly the jacket he had imaged!

PUBLIC-RELATIONS MAN IMAGES FOREIGN TRAVEL

A friend in the public-relations business proved the result-getting power of mental images, when he decided he would like to take a trip to some faraway place in connection with his work. We agreed that it might be fun to see what happened if he would mentally accept that desire for a pleasant, expense-paid trip and then began entertaining the image of its perfect outworking.

He did this in three ways: *First,* he mentally pictured himself taking a trip. Since he enjoys flying, he pictured himself boarding a plane for a distant place and enjoying a wonderful flight. Having no particular place in mind, he did not think of any specific destination, but simply entertained the idea of flying to some faraway spot.

Second, he made this decree many times both verbally and silently, so that this conscious and subconscious phases of mind would accept the idea: "I GIVE THANKS FOR THE PERFECT ALL-EXPENSE-PAID TRIP TO THE PERFECT PLACE WHERE I ENJOY PLEASANT ACTIVITIES WITH CONGENIAL FRIENDS. I GIVE THANKS THAT THIS TRIP NOW MANIFESTS QUICKLY, EASILY, AND IN DIVINE ORDER."

Third, to clarify his thoughts on the matter, he then made a list of desires in connection with the all-expense-paid trip, and he also wrote out words of thanks for the happy manifestation of these things.

In less than two weeks, the results came!

At the conclusion of an evening lecture, this public-relations executive excitedly showed me a telegram he had received from the president of a Central American country. It was an invitation for him to spend a long weekend in Central America as the president's personal guest. Their friendship dated back ten years earlier to the time when this man, as a newspaper reporter, had interviewed this Central American president while in exile. They had become friends and had communicated occasionally, but there had been no contact in recent years.

Of course, this invitation was quickly accepted and my friend flew to a Central American city. Upon arrival, he was provided with an aide, an interpreter, even secret service agents. He was given a royal tour of the country, and wined and dined by the president and his family. He also met with the president's cabinet members. They discussed various prospects for better public relations between the United States and Central America. They exchanged views on progressive ideas concerning the economic and political structure of both areas.

When his American friend departed several days later, the Central American president presented him with more gifts for his wife and daughter. After returning home, this public-relations man sold several news stories about his visit to Central America. He later did some public-relations work at the request of the Central American president. Thus, his deliberate images of a pleasant airplane trip had brought fulfilling results for all concerned.

HOUSEWIFE IMAGES SUCCESS FOR ENTIRE FAMILY

Twelve years ago a housewife learned of the astonishing power of mental imaging. At that time, she and her husband were living meagerly in a garage apartment. They owned a worn-out car which her husband used in his work. She did the housework, since they could not afford a maid.

Across the street lived a neighbor who was obviously prosperous. Her husband was an important executive; her children seemed happy, well-nourished, and beautifully clothed; and she had her own new car, a maid, and time and money to entertain graciously.

Instead of envying or jealously criticizing her neighbor's prosperity, this woman would view her activities with delightful interest and appreciation. Every time she noticed her neighbor's maid coming to work, she would mentally picture her own beautiful home with a maid at work. Whenever she saw her neighbor's husband coming and going to his office, she would think of her own husband and of how he would look when he, too, had a responsible, well-paying position.

She steadily built the mental picture of a better way of life, and lived with it daily. She said nothing about this dream to anyone, since to all appearances, it seemed impossible of ever coming true.

Although it was a gradual process, it did come true! Things just got better and better, until today that housewife's husband is president of his company. They have a beautiful home and a full-time maid. This wife has her own car, which she uses to take their children to and from private school. All that this woman has mentally pictured has come to pass and much more.

OUR GO-KART CHRISTMAS

I shall never forget how my son once proved the power of imaging many years ago. Christmas was fast approaching and I was apprehensive because I did not have much money for his Christmas gifts. Undaunted by this fact, he had great expectations, as do most children at that time of the year. For months he had been eyeing a little gasoline-powered "go-kart" on display at a nearby hardware store. He had been telling his playmates that this little go-kart would be his for Christmas. He had even invited the neighborhood children to drop by on Christmas morning for a ride in this go-kart.

I had prayed and affirmed that God's goodness would manifest in the matter, but at the beginning of Christmas week, no money had appeared with which to buy the go-kart. My son was unimpressed by this, however. He was busy clearing an area in the garage in which to keep the go-kart.

Rather weakly, I inquired how he could be so sure he would receive the kart as a Christmas gift. He replied, "Mother, I am practicing what *you* teach. I have prayed and asked God for that go-kart. I have affirmed that it is coming to me in God's own wonderful way. Months ago, I placed a go-kart picture on my wheel of fortune, and I have been picturing it parked in the carport. I have even imaged myself riding it all over the neighborhood." He then gave me some of my own medicine by concluding, "Don't worry, Mother, everything will work out! The imaging power of the mind is taking care of this."

It was after that conversation, early in Christmas week, that I finally released the matter into Higher Hands. Several days later we received a nice gift of money which was a Christmas bonus from my employer. At first, I thought that we could then buy the go-kart, but when I counted the money, my heart sank. It was $80 less than the amount needed to pay cash for the go-kart. My financial affairs that season would not allow for a long-term credit arrangement for this luxury toy. It was either pay cash or no go — and no go-kart.

I was grateful for the money, however, thinking it would cover other financial needs nicely. My son seemed to think that we had enough money to buy his go-kart, even after I explained that we still needed $80. He merely replied, "Our prayers have been answered. Let's go down and see about the go-kart."

Late that afternoon, when I could stall no longer, I finally consented and we drove through the heavy holiday traffic. We entered the crowded store, and I allowed myself to be led over to the much discussed go-kart on display.

As I stood there, trying to fully appreciate this little machine before me, I suddenly became aware that a man was talking quietly to me. At first, I assumed that he was a sales clerk. But as his conversation progressed, I realized that that was hardly possible. He was saying, "Lady, that's a fine little go-kart. If you are interested in getting one for your son, I know where you can get one at wholesale price. It is available for $80 less than this one, but it is basically the same kart."

In stunned silence, I listened as he explained that a business friend had ordered one for this man's own son, but that his son had changed his mind, preferring a bicycle instead. This man, who introduced himself as a local insurance executive, said that he had just returned to this hardware store to purchase the bicycle. He felt that he was still financially responsible for the go-kart which his friend had ordered at a discount price as a special favor to him.

On the reverse of one of his business cards, he then wrote the name of his friend and the address where he and the go-kart could be found.

My son and I quickly made our way to the other shop. There we found the little kart still packed. The owner seemed quite happy to sell it to us at the same wholesale price for which he had purchased it for his insurance friend. When we had paid him for the little kart, somehow there was enough money left over for my son to purchase some extra accessories he wanted for it.

As we drove home in the late afternoon with the go-kart packed in the car trunk, I marveled at the way the imaging power of the mind had worked through people, situations, and even the element of time to give my son his special Christmas gift. Never was any toy so thoroughly enjoyed as was that go-kart, for it was a long-imaged desire come true.

IMAGING PRODUCES DOMESTIC HELP

A friend of mine in the Midwest related how she used the imaging power of the mind to locate an unusual type of domestic help that she wanted. She had been without domestic help for some time. Busy with her television career, she could hardly keep up with the increasing demands of her home life with her husband and children.

One night as she watched a television drama, she was fascinated by one of the characters, an Oriental houseboy, who played an important role. She thought how nice it would be to have a similar domestic arrangement in her home. But finding an Oriental houseboy in the Midwest seemed an impossibility. She was about to give up on the idea when she chanced to mention it to her father. He replied, "Just for fun, why don't you telephone the employment agencies and let them know of your desire?" She did. As the days passed she continued to mentally picture an Oriental cook and butler working in her home.

One month later an employment agency called to say they had located her Oriental houseboy! An Army couple, who brought him with them from Guam, were now being transferred to Europe. The boy wished to remain in America, and he proved to be the perfect answer to her domestic problem.

IMAGING FOR YOURSELF AND OTHERS MAKES DREAMS COME TRUE

Along with picturing greater good for yourself and your own life situations, be sure to image good for others. Often a person who is beset by unhappiness, ill health, or financial difficulties finds it hard to mentally accept the idea that a better way of life is possible for him. If someone can impersonally picture it for him, it helps to bring it to pass.

Where there is inharmony, picture love, understanding, good will. Where there is lack, picture abundance. Where there is ill health, picture wholeness. Where there is confusion, picture peace.

This occult power for success is so important that we find it emphasized not only in the life of Abraham, but also later in Genesis in the lives of Jacob and Joseph, who became millionaires, too.

Your picturing power of the mind is your occult power for success. Use it constantly to image greater good for yourself and other people. It is a simple, delightful way of making your dreams come true.[1]

---

1. The power of picturing is also described in the author's books: *The Dynamic Laws of Prosperity*, Chapter 5; *The Dynamic Laws of Healing*, Chapter 10; *The Healing Secrets of the Ages*, Chapter 7; *Open Your Mind to Prosperity*, Chapter 4; *The Prospering Power of Prayer*, Chapter 5; and her series of books on "The Millionaires of the Bible."

THE PROSPERITY SECRET
OF THE AGES

GIVING FROM ABRAHAM

— Chapter 9 —

This book shares many prosperity secrets with you. But the supreme prosperity secret of the ages is that *your giving can make you rich!* This is a prosperity secret that was known long before Biblical times. The ancient Egyptians, Babylonians, Persians, Arabians, Greeks, Romans, and Chinese knew and practiced this universal prosperity law.

Abraham learned this prosperity secret from the Babylonians. His grandson, Jacob, used it when he left home to seek his fortune in a new land. That Jacob did follow this success principle is obvious since he became very rich. Moses later emphasized this same success principle, and it was practiced by the Hebrews, who became one of the wealthiest groups the world has ever known. They credit their wealth over the centuries to their use of this prosperity idea: you will be made rich by giving.

Many of our modern millionaires have used this prosperity secret and have often pointed it out as the formula that brought them riches. The list includes the Colgate, Heinz, Kraft, and Rockefeller families.

Giving can make you rich, for when you systematically give, you open the way to systematically receive. But when you do not give, you stagnate, dam up, and close many channels to your prosperity.

Perhaps you are thinking, "But I *do* give every cent I can find to pay the bills and to keep going financially." Yet there is another kind of giving you must know about and practice in order to prosper. When you practice this other type of giving, putting it first in your financial affairs, then divine order will come. You will find yourself prospered in both expected and unexpected ways; your money will begin to go further, and other financial surprises will come forth so that it becomes easier and easier for you to pay the bills and "get ahead financially."

The ancients, who knew the wisdom of the ages, understood the nature of universal substance out of which all wealth is created. They knew that by consistently giving, you move on universal substance, forming a vacuum which substance then rushes to fill with new supply. That is the nature of substance: it abhors a vacuum and always rushes to fill it. *Giving in order to make room to receive is a scientific method that always works to prosper those who use it consistently.* It can work for you, too!

CAUSE OF CONSTANT PROBLEMS

This is a giving universe. You have to constantly give in order to constantly receive, because the universe is constantly giving to you. If you do not balance the act of receiving by giving voluntarily in some good and happy way, the universe will force you to give in some unhappy way. But give you must!

The universal law, "Give and it shall be given unto you" (Luke 6:38), works whether you want it to or not. *Where there is no voluntary giving, something is taken from you.* People who think they cannot afford to give constructively and freely have to give anyway, destructively and involuntarily—to doctors and hospitals for their ill health; to lawyers for their accidents, legal and business problems; to accountants and to the Internal Revenue Service for their income tax problems; and in other reluctant ways. If you do not give voluntarily of your financial resources, you can expect that body ailments, financial entanglements, human-relations problems, and general confusion in your affairs will follow.

When you see a person who has constant problems of ill health, financial difficulties, family inharmony, general confusion and dissatisfaction in his life, not only is he not thinking right, but neither is he giving right. *Where there is no voluntary giving, something is taken!*

You cannot cheat the basic law of the universe, which is giving and receiving. It works regardless of your misworking it. You can only cheat yourself out of much health, wealth and happiness by trying to foolishly bypass it.

THE MAGIC NUMBER OF INCREASE

How can you practice this other kind of giving constructively, so as to avoid giving destructively? The ancients believed that the number "ten" was the magic number of increase, and they invoked this magic number by regularly giving one-tenth of all channels of income to their religious leaders. Later, the Hebrews were commanded by Jehovah to give a tithe (or one-tenth) of all channels of income to their priests and temples. This included giving a tenth of their gold, silver, jewels, land, cattle, sheep, goats, camels, and other flocks; a tenth of all fruit, wine, grain, oil and other crops; a tenth of all financial income and all financial assets.

The first instance of tithing recorded in the Bible occurred when Abraham gave his tithe to the High Priest of Salem (Genesis 14:20). After Abraham had tithed, Jehovah plainly promised him riches and protection from the negative experiences of life: "Fear not, I am thy shield, and thy exceeding great reward" (Genesis 15:1).

That same divine promise of protection and prosperity also applies to you and me, when we invoke the prosperity secret of the ages through tithing.

Ten is still the magic number of increase! Regular, consistent tithing of a tenth of all channels of your *gross income* (before taxes and other deductions) to the priest, minister, church or spiritual organization which inspires and uplifts you, is still one of the surest ways to permanent, satisfying prosperity.

One of the wealthiest men who has ever lived, Solomon, promised that tithing invokes the magic law of increase for you. He advised: "Honor Jehovah with thy substance, and with the first fruits [tithe] of all thine increase. So shall thy barns be filled with plenty, and thy vats shall overflow with new wine" (Proverbs 3:9, 10).

THE AUTHOR'S EXPERIENCE WITH THIS PROSPERITY LAW

Although I had heard tithing mentioned in church for many years, I had not realized it was a prosperity law for my personal benefit. I assumed it was the minister's way of trying to raise money to support the church.

As a $25-a-week secretary, desperately struggling to find *any* prosperity law that would work, I read L. E. Meyer's fascinating booklet, *As You Tithe So You Prosper*.[1] This booklet contained many thrilling stories of people in every walk of life who have prospered through consistent tithing, and I began to think seriously about the subject. I also remembered that my own parents had been much more prosperous when they tithed.

One of the stories in Dr. Meyer's booklet that especially interested me was this one:

> He who said that he found it necessary to tithe in order to get out of debt voiced a truth that has become evident to thousands. A man who was $10,000 in debt, with his credit gone and a wife and four children for whom to provide, took a job as a day laborer in a mill and with his family was compelled to live in a tent. He met two Divinity students who convinced him that if he wanted to again prosper, he should tithe. The same week that he began tithing the company offered him one of its houses in which to live. Within a year, he was promoted to foreman. Ten years later, he was free from debt, the owner of a large lumber company, owner of his own home,

---

1. Published for free distribution by Unity School of Christianity, Unity Village, MO 64065.

which was large and beautifully furnished, and owner of a large car, an airplane and other things on a similar scale. He attributes his success to first recognizing his debt to God and faithfully tithing of his income.

At the time I was considering the tithing law of prosperity, I was also debating whether I should start a savings account. From a business standpoint I felt that it was more important to begin saving than to begin tithing. "Tithing can come anytime," I thought. Instead, the savings account was opened. Everything went along fine for a time as I proudly watched my savings account grow, week by week.

Then one day my son became violently ill. Only after he had had the finest doctors and medical care in a local hospital did the turning point come and he recovered. His hospital bill was more than the amount I had painstakingly managed to place in my savings account!

A valuable lesson came from that experience. I learned that if I did not put God first financially and give to His work voluntarily, I would have to give anyway—involuntarily to pay for the unhappy experiences in life which I did not want.

I immediately began to tithe from my gross weekly income of $25, giving $2.50 to the spiritual organization that had taught me this ancient prosperity secret. Upon receiving my pay check and depositing it, the first check I always wrote was the tithe check. This act gave me a feeling of protection and security. By putting God first financially, I assumed my own needs would be met; and always they have been, sometimes in the most amazing ways.

The week I began to tithe was truly the turning point for me financially! Soon I began receiving pay raises, so that my income doubled and later tripled its original amount. It has continued to steadily rise over the years as I have continued to tithe faithfully. My husband and I now tithe three-tenths or 30% of our gross incomes, and we look forward to bigger giving as our prosperity consciousness continues to expand.

The wonderful thing about my son's health has been that, although many years have passed since he was so ill, he has had few major health problems since, and he did not have any of the usual childhood diseases.

I, too, have been much healthier since I began tithing. Having been underweight, nervous, and anemic as a child, it was a great blessing to finally be free of ill health. I have found that I am now able to produce much more work in a much shorter length of time. Whenever I hear of loss, theft, accident, illness and the high emotional and financial costs that usually accompany these experiences, I cannot help thinking: "It's too bad those persons do not tithe. They would be protected from such negative and unhappy experiences if they did!"

By giving voluntarily at least a tenth of my gross income to spiritual work, I have been saved from giving *many times that amount* to the negative experiences of life such as illness, accidents, thefts, etc. I am grateful that I learned this lesson early. It is one of the most valuable success secrets that I can point out to you.

To be sure, there is nothing wrong with the prosperity practice of consistent saving, which I had in mind during that experience many years ago. The Babylonians' great success secret for their riches was that they tithed one-tenth and saved one-tenth of their income. It is still a fine prosperity practice. The Rockefeller family has mentioned their use of this idea. However, if you have a choice between tithing or saving, be sure to put first things first, by beginning to tithe first. That act will insure your growing prosperity, so that consistent savings will then naturally follow. *Both the ancient and modern practice of tithing proves it to be the best financial investment you can make!*

FROM RAGS TO RICHES AFTER AGE 50

Not only am I grateful for my own experiences in tithing, which proved to me that it is the supreme prosperity secret of the ages, but I am grateful to the hundreds of people in every walk of life who have shared with me their tithing success stories. In modern times, just as in ancient times, people are still proving that to tithe is to invoke the magic law of increase!

A man I met while serving in my first ministry proved the prospering power of tithing in a spectacular way. He went from "rags to riches" in ten years through tithing.

At the age of 50, this man was still a failure in life. He had gone from one job to another, never quite finding his right place. He drove an old car, lived in a rented house, and wore threadbare clothes. His wife was in ill health and they spent every cent they had trying to get her healed.

They attended a lecture where they learned of tithing as the magic law of increase. This man decided to try it, reasoning that he would rather share a tenth of his income with the church than spend many times that amount for the negative and unwanted experiences of life such as he had known for 50 years. As he began tithing, expecting to be protected and prospered, he was! For the first time in his life he got a job that he liked, as a sales agent for a steel company. Next, his wife's health began to improve, so that they had less and less medical expense. Then his income began to rise as he became expert at selling his company's product.

Later, his employer passed on and the local dealership of the steel company was available. Since he was tithing, thereby expecting to be protected and prospered, this man found the faith and the courage to borrow the money to buy out this dealership. What a wonderful feeling it was to suddenly find himself owner of his own company—a lifetime dream come true—and it happened within two years from the day he began tithing!

From that point on, his success increased by leaps and bounds. Soon he was able to start an investment program for himself and his family. When buying or selling stocks, he would affirm: "IN ALL MY WAYS I ACKNOWLEDGE HIM AND HE NOW DIRECTS MY PATH." When there were losses in these investments, he would affirm: "NO MISTAKES HAVE BEEN MADE; ONLY GOOD WILL COME FROM THIS!" In one instance, he lost $20,000 in a stock transaction. Instead of becoming upset about it, he decreed that no mistakes had been made and good would still come.

Whenever a financial challenge presented itself, he continued to tithe, affirming: "VOLUNTARY, FAITHFUL TITHING OF MY GROSS INCOME ACTIVATES THE LAW OF EVER-INCREASING PROSPERITY FOR ME." The happy result was that the $20,000 he had lost was soon recovered in a much larger return than he had previously received!

Today, 12 years after beginning to tithe, this man is financially independent. He owns a beautiful home, two cars, has educated his children. He and his family travel extensively; he is active in his church, often pointing out to others who have financial difficulties the tithing law of prosperity; he plays golf and bridge extensively; enjoys his grandchildren, and has a very pleasant, happy life.

I have often heard this man say, "From the day I began to tithe, I have never hesitated to buy anything I wanted or to do anything I wished to do. I have felt that since I am now putting God first financially, I can expect to be protected, guided, and prospered in all that I undertake — and I have been."

SALESMAN BEGINS TO SELL AGAIN

When people first hear of this prosperity law, they are inclined to say, "I would love to tithe but I cannot afford it. My income just isn't big enough to include tithing now — maybe later when I am more prosperous."

When you think you cannot afford to tithe is the very time when you cannot afford not to tithe. If you have not through your human wisdom been able to be sufficiently prospered, then obviously you need the help of divine wisdom regarding your financial affairs, don't you? Consistent tithing opens the way for that guidance to come quickly. If you are in financial difficulties, having one-tenth less money will not make things any worse. So you really have nothing to lose by testing the tithing idea as the magic law of increase. You make things at least ten times easier for yourself financially when you tithe.

A salesman was finding his work difficult. He had lost enthusiasm for his product and was tired of trying to sell. He was depressed and in debt. In despair he talked with a minister. They discussed prosperity's various laws, most of which he was invoking. But when the minister asked if he was using the greatest prosperity law of all, that of tithing, he said he could not afford it. The minister then pointed out all the reasons why he should tithe, if he wished to sell again and get out of debt.

This salesman decided to try tithing a tenth of every sale he made, expecting immediate sales as a result and divine guidance concerning his indebtedness. Before leaving the minister's study, this salesman left a check for $5 as a love offering, which was a tithe of the money he expected to make from his next sale!

A few days later, he telephoned to say that the tide had turned in his financial affairs, and he was again selling. His first sale had amounted to $50, a tenth of which he had already tithed in faith, before making the sale. As this man continued to tithe from each sale, his former enthusiasm returned, clients appeared who eagerly bought his products, and the grind was taken out of selling for him. His wife also quickly found suitable, rewarding work, and she began to tithe from her gross income. Their financial affairs smoothed out, and their home life has been happier than ever before.

PROFESSIONAL MAN PROVES THIS
PROSPERITY LAW

I once knew two professional men who were partners. One tithed but the other did not. The nontither made around $20,000 a year. He worked night and day, and on weekends in an effort to make ends meet, but he could barely "get by" financially. Frequent spells of illness and unexpected mishaps in his family were always causing unexpected expense. The harder he worked, the harder he had to work. Paying the bills was a constant struggle, and collecting money from his clients was difficult, too.

His business associate made only $12,000 annually and he tithed. He and his family lived much better, had a nicer home and resided in a better neighborhood. They always seemed to have more. They certainly enjoyed life more. They did not have the illness, accidents and extra expense of the first family. This man never thought of working nights or weekends; his clients liked him and paid their accounts on time. After several years, he left his associate and went into business for himself. Soon he was making a great deal more money than his former associate had made and he was still enjoying life. By tithing he put God first in his financial affairs, and he was prospered and protected in return.

BUSINESSWOMAN SAVES PROPERTY

In loosening your purse strings, you loosen many other things that have bound you, so that you are free from the unhappy, unnecessary, unwanted experiences of life. You find that life becomes more joyous, more abounding in health and in all that makes living worthwhile.

With a heavy heart, a businesswoman talked about her various financial difficulties. She had worked night and day for years to acquire an apartment house, a farm in the country, and a restaurant. Since all of them were heavily mortgaged, she was in danger of losing them to her creditors.

When asked, "Do you practice the prosperity secret of the ages? Do you tithe?" she replied, "No, I cannot afford to tithe my money, but I do try to tithe my time to church work." She was then asked, "What is your greatest need just now — more time or more money?" "Oh, more money!" She replied. "Though I would like to have more leisure time, too."

It was suggested that she study the Bible's rich promises on tithing, which definitely state that a tenth of all income should be tithed, if one wishes to be prospered. As she studied tithing in the Bible, she realized the necessity for tithing her money if she wished definite financial returns. Tithing her time was secondary.

As she started consistently tithing a tenth of all channels of her income, she was guided to sell the farm and restaurant. Even though both were heavily mortgaged, buyers appeared almost magically, eager for these properties, and even more magically, she realized a profit from the transactions. With a sigh of relief, she used these profits toward paying off a mortgage on her apartment house, which she then redecorated. Thus she was relieved of financial stress and still had a steady income from apartment rentals, along with income from her job. She discovered that by tithing her money, her financial affairs were straightened out so that she also had more leisure time.

MARRIAGE AND PROSPERITY RESULT

It's amazing how the act of tithing improves every area of your life, including your health and happiness as well as your prosperity.

A widow once proved this beautifully. She was in debt, having trouble in her job, and was also lonely and unhappy. Convinced of the prosperity power of tithing, she tried to start tithing on two different occasions, but each time she thought about all the things she really wanted to spend that money for. It was suggested that she discontinue the actual act of tithing until she could freely give her tenth, instead of mentally holding to it and begrudging it. She was advised to continue studying the subject of tithing until she was fully convinced of its prospering power, until she felt freer in giving her tithe gift. This she did.

On the third attempt at tithing some months later, she had established sufficient faith in its prosperity power to continue tithing in the face of indebtedness and a low income. Along with the act of tithing, she continued to expand her faith by daily affirming: "I GIVE RICHLY AND I RECEIVE RICHLY NOW!"

Soon she received a gift of $1,000 from a person whom she had befriended years earlier, but who had never previously shown any appreciation for her help. With this amount she paid off her most pressing bills, and for the first time in years felt freer financially. Then as an opportunity opened in her work, she received a job transfer and pay raise which dissolved previous career dissatisfaction. As she continued to joyously persist in tithing, she happily married, though she had been widowed for twenty years. This woman now feels that it was worth all the effort she exerted in persevering beyond two fruitless attempts at tithing, since the excellent results of her third attempt have brought rich blessings into every department of her life.

MAN STOPS DRINKING WHEN HIS WIFE TITHES

A wife was having serious trouble in her marriage because her husband was drinking heavily. This woman had been advised by her doctor that she was on the verge of a nervous breakdown; she had recently undergone an operation to remove cancerous tissues from her body; their marriage was nearing divorce; and they were heavily in debt.

In desperation this woman said, "I will do anything to straighten out my life, but what can I do? I need one supreme success law that will cover everything!"

When informed that tithing was life's greatest success law, and that it works in every phase of one's life to bless, this woman replied, "I have never tried tithing because I have always had the impression that it was simply the church's way of getting money out of people. I could not see that it promised any personal benefits for me. With so many rich people in the world who can afford to support the churches, I could not see why I should make that effort, when my financial affairs are already so strained."

This woman brightened considerably when assured that *the Bible promises prosperity first to the individual who practices tithing.* Prosperity for the church just naturally follows. This woman decided to study everything she could find on the subject and to regard tithing as the road to prosperity, health, and a happier marriage.

She was soon convinced that tithing was a profitable idea. After giving her first tithe to her church, her husband's drinking began to diminish, although he knew or cared nothing about her tithing. Within several months, he had stopped drinking completely and vowed that he would never drink again. He settled down in his sales work, his income steadily increased, and they were able to begin clearing up their debts. With their increased prosperity, their marriage became harmonious, since much of their disagreement had been about money, as well as about her husband's drinking.

For a year everything went along fine. Then this wife decided that they need not tithe any longer in order to be prospered, so she stopped. Soon she was again lamenting, "I just do not understand it. My husband is drinking again. We are back in debt. Our marriage is again on the brink of divorce, and my health is again threatened." When asked if she was still tithing, she explained that she had stopped when the amount of the tithe had greatly increased and when their affairs had seemed so good, it hardly appeared necessary to continue tithing. She remarked, "I saw no reason to continue tithing for the sake of prosperity. Everything had been straightened out."

Again it was suggested that she consider resuming the tithing habit, if she wished to be habitually prospered, guided, and protected in all departments of her life. Upon re-studying the subject, she gained fresh new conviction that she should put God first financially. This time, as she resumed tithing, her husband did not immediately stop drinking. But as she persisted, an interesting thing happened: Her church announced that an outstanding minister was coming to conduct a series of special meetings. She did not mention this to her husband since he had never shown any interest in religion. However, when the meetings began, her husband announced that one of his customers had invited him to attend the first meeting and he invited his wife to go with him.

As they were dressing to attend the meeting that night, her husband's brother, who had been his steady drinking companion, dropped by with his wife, presumably for an evening of drinking. When informed of their plans for the evening, his brother asked to attend the meeting, too. Their interest in going to church at all came as a great surprise.

At the close of the meeting, when the invitation was extended to the audience to come forth for prayer help in overcoming some problem, this woman's husband went forward. His brother followed! That night they both decided to stop drinking and to become members of that church, which they did.

This woman later declared this to be the greatest miracle of their marriage. Her husband remained sincere in his spiritual faith and in his sobriety. They now attend church regularly and financially support it. This woman recently stated, "I will never stop tithing again. Twice it has proved its harmonizing power in my life." This woman found that *when we loosen our purse strings, we loosen many other things that have been binding us to unhappy experiences in life.*

Those people who find excuses for not tithing, or who tithe for a time and then stop, are robbing themselves as well as robbing God. They are inviting problems and losses for themselves where there need be none.

ALLOWANCE-GIVING OPENS WAY TO PROSPERITY

A young wife once asked, "How can I tithe when my husband does not approve? I have no income apart from his." It was suggested that she quietly tithe of the allowance her husband gave her for household expenses, for her personal use, and from whatever money that came to her in other ways.

As she did, her husband was soon promoted to a job as junior executive for his company. In this new job, he was expected to become active in religious and cultural affairs in the community. Together they began attending the church where she had previously worshipped alone. As she continued to quietly tithe from her household allowance to this church, her husband became so interested in the church that he became a member as she had already done.

Within a year, this young executive was elected a church deacon. By this time he had heard the minister preach on tithing, and suddenly he decided to tithe. At this point his wife surprised him by confessing she had been tithing consistently and that she believed it had already proved its prospering power in their lives.

When this young executive began tithing, his monthly income was between $500 and $600 a month. They have continued to tithe, and he has gone from success to greater success in his work. When he was given an overseas assignment by his company, his monthly income rose to $2,000. Both husband and wife attribute it to tithing.

WHERE YOU GIVE IS IMPORTANT

A merchant once questioned tithing as a prosperity law because he had long been tithing, but his business was no longer prosperous. He was asked, "Where do you tithe?" This man replied, "I tithe to my wife's church. I no longer attend that church because I find greater inspiration in another church which I now attend. However, my wife insists that I still tithe to her church."

It was pointed out that *one should tithe where one is receiving spiritual help and inspiration.* To tithe to an organization which does not directly help or inspire you holds little blessing either for you or for that organization, because no spiritual contact has been made between the giver and the receiver.

It was suggested that the man tithe to the church from which he was receiving guidance and inspiration; that he do this on a six-months' trial basis. As he did, he discovered that his financial affairs improved, as well as other phases of his life. Furthermore, his wife seemed to respect his tithing decision.

You may be thinking, "Yes, but I am already tithing

to the church where I receive inspiration and still I am not prosperous." Then check your attitudes to determine why you are tithing and whether you completely release your tithe after giving it. Make no mental demands upon those who receive your tithe. A gift with reservations is not a gift. It is a bribe.

There is another subtle attitude to check when tithing: Do you tithe simply because you think it is expected of you, but not freely and joyously?

I once knew a young couple who were fine church members. The husband was the Sunday School superintendent. When tithing was mentioned as the great prosperity law, this couple complained that though they tithed regularly, they were still having financial difficulties. In fact, they had been piously saying, as do many people who don't know any better, "We tithe but we do not expect to receive anything in return." They did not receive anything in return, since that was what they were decreeing.

It was pointed out that they should be tithing because they *did* expect something in return—the same prosperity and divine protection which the Lord had given Abraham as he tithed. It was pointed out that they should also expect their church to be prospered from their tithe, and that their tithe should be considered a wise financial investment for all involved. As this couple began thinking in these terms, their financial conditions improved greatly. The husband received a promotion and several pay raises over a short period of time. Other recognition has since followed.

By tithing in the right attitude, you substitute the fear that you must hold on to every penny or live in lack, for complete faith in God's power to supply your needs.

CHARITY GIVING IS NOT TITHING

Many people have the mistaken idea that giving to a needy person is tithing, but it is not. Giving to the needy is often the worst thing you can do for them, since it keeps them from developing their own prosperity consciousness. Until they do develop a prosperous state of mind, they will continue to be in need, no matter how much you do for them. The greatest thing you can offer the poor is to introduce them to prosperous thinking.

Your tithe is not properly used for yourself, relatives, friends, or charitable purposes. If one wishes to give to those channels, it should be a gift over and above the tenth which one gives directly to spiritual work. The prosperity law of tithing, as given by Jehovah to the Hebrews and as practiced by all the ancient civilizations before them, was that the tithe went always to the priests and temples, to those in the Lord's work.

A great deal of selfishness in family relationships is mistaken for true love and wisdom. Often by giving to a relative, you are keeping him from developing his own talents and abilities which would lead to his prosperity. Those who give most, if not all, to the needs of their family or others usually have small returns and often no thanks for such unwise giving. In due time, the one being helped financially comes to resent such help, since he feels obligated to the person supporting him. Innately he knows he should be developing his own abilities rather than sponging on those of another. And so he feels guilty as well as resentful.

A businessman had been sending money to his daughter and family, instead of tithing. Upon realizing that he should tithe first, he stopped sending the money to his married daughter. As he began to tithe, a health problem of long standing, for which he had spent hundreds of dollars on expensive treatment, began to clear up. Soon the treatments were no longer necessary. Meanwhile, his daughter's husband was prospered in several unforeseen ways, happy at last to have made it on his own with no further financial help from his father-in-law. Everyone had been blessed through this new financial arrangement.

Some people give only to civic, cultural, educational, or charity causes instead of to religious organizations. It is fine to give for these purposes if you feel so led, but your first tenth should go to religious causes which uplift and inspire you, or to people in religious work who are an inspiration to you. All other giving is to be commended, but is secondary to direct tithing to the Lord's work.

People sometimes try to excuse themselves from tithing by casually saying, "I do not tithe because I am a New Testament Christian and Jesus did not emphasize tithing." Although he mentioned tithing on two occasions, Jesus did not dwell much on tithing because it was a required part of temple worship and had been for hundreds of years since Old Testament times. In Jesus' time, the priests went out regularly from the temple to collect the tithes from the crops, and the Hebrews regularly brought other portions of their tithes to the priests, synagogues and the Temple. There was no question of whether the people would tithe or not; it was a spiritual requirement. Tithing is clearly a Christian teaching.

RICH RESULTS OF CONSISTENT GIVING

People sometimes say, "I do not tithe regularly but I give large amounts occasionally to God's work." *It does more good to tithe regularly smaller amounts than giving large amounts spasmodically.* Just as it is necessary to breathe out regularly in order to receive fresh air into the lungs, so it is necessary to give regularly if you wish to receive regularly.

A wealthy woman heard a lecture on tithing. Though she and her husband had given substantial donations to their church, they had never given consistently nor tithed. Even though their yearly income seemed sizeable, there was never enough money on hand to meet many private needs. Much of their money went back into their business. In spite of having several channels of income, this woman still felt financially limited.

She decided that the fault might be in her lack of consistent giving through tithing. After beginning to tithe, she felt a sense of security, satisfaction, and peace about her financial affairs for the first time. Within a few months, she received a long-distance call from the manager of her farm in another state. He stated, "For the first time in years, the farm has made some money recently. There is now $10,000 available in profits from the farm. What do you wish me to do with it?" This woman stated that previously it would have been necessary to consider the matter for some time before knowing how the money should be wisely spent. But while talking to her manager, it came to her just how the money should be reinvested in farm supplies, equipment, and seeds for the next year's crops. This guidance later proved to be the highest and best. Soon her farm was making more money than ever before.

As she continued tithing, her husband raised her private allowance. A relative sent her a check for $3,000 as a gift, stating she had decided to begin sharing her wealth with her family now, instead of leaving it in a will for them later. (Our present tax laws make it worthwhile to give gifts of money while you are living rather than leaving it in a will for others to pay heavy inheritance taxes upon later.) Since that occasion, the relative has sent her substantial sums at regular intervals, and this woman has been prospered in many ways. She no longer feels the dissatisfaction about her financial affairs which she earlier experienced.

A MILLIONAIRE CONSCIOUSNESS

The general rule in tithing in these modern times is this: You tithe on the gross amount of your personal income; and usually you tithe on the net profits from a business or corporation.[2]

Remember this exciting truth as you tithe: You are joining ranks with millionaires of all times. You are becoming attuned to that same rich consciousness which can lead to rich results for you, too!

---

2. See the author's tithing chapters in her books: *The Dynamic Laws of Prosperity*, Chapter 10; *The Dynamic Laws of Healing*, Chapter 13; *Open Your Mind to Prosperity*, Chapter 6; *Open Your Mind to Receive*, Chapter 7; *The Prospering Power of Love*, Chapter 7; *Dare to Prosper!*, Chapter 4; *The Millionaires of Genesis*, Chapter 3; *The Millionaire Moses*, Chapter 7; *The Millionaire Joshua*, Chapter 6; *The Millionaire from Nazareth*, Chapter 9; *The Prospering Power of Prayer*, Chapter 6; and her book *The Secret of Unlimited Prosperity*.

In developing your own millionaire consciousness, you may wish to paraphrase the words of Solomon, one of the world's most fabulous millionaires, and affirm often: "I HONOR THE LORD WITH MY SUBSTANCE AND WITH A TENTH OF ALL MY INCREASE. MY OWN BARNS ARE NOW BEING FILLED WITH PLENTY AND MY VATS OVERFLOW WITH NEW GOOD" (see Proverbs 3:9, 10).

It has been said that the person who takes up the practice of tithing will have at least six surprises: (1) He will be surprised at the amount of money he has to give the Lord's work. (2) He will be surprised at the wisdom and good judgment tithing gives him in using the remaining nine-tenths of his income. (3) He will be surprised at the ease with which he can meet his financial obligations. (4) He will be surprised at the deepening of his prosperity consciousness, as well as his spiritual life. (5) He will be surprised at how easily he can go from one-tenth to larger giving. (6) He will be surprised at himself for having not adopted the tithing method of prosperity sooner!

I would like to add one thing the tither should *not* be surprised about: He may find himself a millionaire!

A SPECIAL NOTE FROM THE AUTHOR

Through the generous outpouring of their tithes over the years, the readers of my books have helped me to financially establish three new churches — the most recent being a global ministry, the nondenominational *Unity Worldwide,* with headquarters in Palm Desert, California. Many thanks for your help in the past, and for all that you continue to share.

You are also invited to share your tithes with the churches of your choice — especially those which teach the truths stressed in this book. Such churches would include the metaphysical churches of Unity, Religious Science, Divine Science, Science of Mind, and other related churches, many of which are members of The International New Thought Movement. (For a list of such churches write The International New Thought Alliance, 7314 E. Stetson Drive, Scottsdale, AZ 85251.) Your support of such churches can help spread the prosperous Truth that mankind is now seeking in this New Age of metaphysical enlightenment.

HOW TO MAKE YOUR
MASTER DEMONSTRATION
RECEIVING FROM ABRAHAM

— Chapter 10 —

Another success secret known throughout the ages is that *receiving can also make you rich!*

You must receive as well as give in order to be truly successful in life. Many fine people give and give with no true understanding that they need to be just as willing to receive, in order to bring balance into their lives. You must learn to receive if you want riches.

Giving is only one-half of the success law. When you give regularly, you open the way to receive regularly, in both expected and unexpected ways. But you must be ready to receive! Otherwise, you "jam up the works" and stop your good.

I went through a period in my life where I gave, gave, gave in both tangible and intangible ways, but I did not receive as I should have. Then I began to think, "What is the truth about this situation? What is wrong?" The thought came, "You are invoking only one-half of the success law—that of giving. You must now open your mind to the other half of the success law—that of receiving."

That was a new thought to me. I had heard often about giving as a success law, but had never been informed that receiving was the other half of that law. In fact, I had the impression that I was not supposed to expect to receive; that such expectation was selfish; that it wasn't "nice" to expect to receive. And so I had remained "nice" and in lack.

What a relief it was to learn that I was supposed to receive graciously, as well as to give graciously! As I began to think about being a good receiver, it was as though I opened the gates of my mind and heart to infinite bounty. It seemed as if I had opened the long-closed passages of my soul, allowing the cramped quarters of my inner being to expand and enlarge. As I affirmed daily, "I AM RECEIVING, I AM RECEIVING NOW ALL THE GOOD GOD WANTS TO GIVE ME," my good rushed to greet me from many directions.

A SUCCESS FORMULA FOR RECEIVING

If you are one of those people who has also believed it isn't "nice" to expect to receive, though you have given generously to life, then you can know this:

All the giving you have done over the years has built up in the invisible a tremendous backlog of good for you to receive. That accumulated good has remained in the invisible simply because you have not expected to receive, and have not known how to open your mind to the idea of receiving in tangible ways.

You can now begin to receive your rich dividends which have accumulated from all your previous giving simply by saying daily to yourself: "I AM RECEIVING, I AM RECEIVING ALL THE GOOD GOD WANTS TO GIVE ME. I HAVE BEEN GIVING, GIVING, GIVING. I NOW BALANCE THAT GIVING BY BEING WILLING TO RECEIVE, RECEIVE, RECEIVE ALL THE GOOD THAT HAS BEEN ACCUMULATING FOR ME. I HAVE GIVEN RICHLY AND I AM RECEIVING RICHLY NOW!"

GET READY FOR A MASTER DEMONSTRATION

Abraham not only knew how to give, he knew how to receive.[1] As you read chapters 12 through 25 in the Book of Genesis, you discover that the Lord was constantly making Abraham rich promises about all the blessings He planned to give him. In detail, Jehovah described to Abraham these tangible and intangible gifts he was to receive. That Abraham did receive all these gifts is clearly shown through the story of his life, and toward the end it is written, "Jehovah had blessed Abraham in all things" (Genesis 24:1).

You will remember from a previous chapter that Abraham symbolizes faith and an exalted state of mind. Those same rich gifts, both tangible and intangible, that were promised Abraham are also your spiritual heritage as you reach an exalted state of mind and have faith in the goodness and bounty of God. In that state of mind, Jehovah is able to bless you in all things, too.

---

1. See the author's book *Open Your Mind to Receive*.

It is interesting, however, to note that Abraham's greatest desire was a long time in coming. As an old man, in spite of all the blessings that had been given him, he still did not have his heart's desire. He wanted a son, though it seemed an impossible dream due to his age. He could not understand why a son had not been given him, because this was one of the gifts Jehovah had often promised him.

Is there some special need in your life that has not been fulfilled? Is there some particular prayer that has not been answered? Is there some nagging desire for greater good that persists, that you have not been able to dismiss nor fulfill?

Then, like Abraham, you are ready for a master demonstration! *A master demonstration is a big result, a big prayer answered, a big dream come true.* The miracles that have happened to you have been your master demonstrations in the past. A master demonstration always includes many smaller results that you are interested in obtaining, too.

Abraham got his miracle and you can have yours! There is fascinating success symbology in how Abraham's miracle finally came about. There were certain success attitudes he and his wife had to use. Those same success attitudes are available to you. As you use them, you, too, can make your master demonstration.

ATTITUDES THAT STOP YOUR GOOD

You learn first from Abraham and Sarai what most people do when they have not made their master demonstration. At the age of 85 Abraham still longed for the son that had often been promised him. At this point, Abraham and Sarai decided that they should take matters in their own hands and to humanly try to force their demonstration. Sarai told Abraham to take her maid, Hagar, as his wife, so that a son could be born. Sarai said bitterly, "Jehovah hath restrained me from bearing" (Genesis 16:2). (It was not unusual in those days for a man to have more than one wife.)

It is this same attitude that keeps us from making our master demonstrations too. Sarai was blaming God because she had not been able to have a child. The name "Sarah" in this passage of the Bible is spelled "Sarai." That unusual spelling of the word symbolizes a negative mental attitude, for the word "Sarai" means "bitter, contentious." She was clearly in a bitter, contentious state of mind.

When you are not receiving the good that you feel you should have in life, it is because you are like Sarai. Perhaps without realizing it, you have gotten into a bitter, contentious state of mind. Like Sarai who said, "Jehovah hath restrained me from bearing," you have probably been saying, "It is not the Lord's will for me to have this blessing," or "God has kept this from me," or "God does not want me to have this."

But remember this universal truth that has been known down through the ages: *The desire for greater good in your heart is God trying to give you that good!* If God did not want you to have it, you would not have the God-given desire for it. God is a Father of lavish abundance Whose will is great good for His children, just as you wish great good for your children.

Stop ignorantly blaming your failures, your ill health, your family problems, your financial difficulties, your disappointments, your lack of good results on God. You are God's beloved child. He wants you to have everything! When you stop blaming God for your failures, you clear the way for your ships to come in; you clear the way to become a good receiver.

BITTERNESS CAUSES BARRENNESS

Jehovah had not restrained Sarai from bearing a child. Her own bitter attitudes had restrained her!

Holistic medicine teaches the power that mental attitudes have upon the body. Many a woman has not had children because of her bitter attitudes.

One such woman married while still in her teens. She and her husband later had a child, but that child died during the first year of its life. This woman then blamed God for her child's death. She became bitter toward God and said, "God took away my child. God has cursed me with barrenness." During the next 20 years, this woman and her husband longed for more children, but in spite of the best medical treatment, she had no children. Her physicians repeatedly told her that there was no physical reason for her barrenness.

This woman poured out her bitter story to a new-found friend, who replied, "God has not kept you from having children. Your own bitter attitudes have prevented it. What kind of mother would you make, as bitter as you are? Change your attitudes and you can still have children. Begin to think of God as a loving Father, not as a spiteful tyrant, and thank God every day for giving you children. You had a child once and you can have children again. Bless the soul that was given you early in your marriage, then release it to its good elsewhere, and you will make way for the children that can still be yours."

Within a year this woman, childless for 20 years, gave birth to a girl. The next year she gave birth to a boy. They have grown into healthy, happy adults who have given her grandchildren.

Along with holding bitter attitudes toward God, many people have not made their master demonstrations because of their resentful attitudes toward others. In his book *The Sermon on the Mount*,[2] Dr. Emmet Fox has explained:

> If your prayers are not being answered . . . find out if there is not some old thing about which you are very resentful. Search and see if you are not really holding a grudge against some individual, or some body of people, nation, race, social class, some religious movement of which you disapprove perhaps, a political party. If so, then you have an act of forgiveness to perform, and when this is done, you will probably make your demonstration. If you cannot forgive at present, you will have to wait for your demonstration until you can.

FEAR AND UNCERTAINTY BRING WILD RESULTS

Sarai, in her bitter state of mind, told Abraham to marry her maid Hagar. The word "Hagar" means "fear and uncertainty." When you get into a bitter state of mind (Sarai), and join your faith (Abraham) to fear and uncertainty (Hagar), you always get a dissatisfying result.

A son named Ishmael was born to Abraham and

---

2. P. 188 (New York: Harper & Row).

Hagar, but he was not the child Jehovah had promised. Ishmael was rebellious, full of conflict and opposition. The Bible describes him as "wild."

When you are in a bitter state of mind and take fearful, uncertain action in trying to force your good, you also get a wild result — a result filled with conflict, opposition, and dissatisfaction. Then, like Abraham and Sarai, you have the dissatisfying result to cope with. Yet you will still have the original problem because you will not have made your master demonstration.

Ishmael was born to Abraham and Hagar when Abraham was 86. Until Abraham was 99, nothing further happened toward his master demonstration. During this 13-year period Abraham wondered about the child of promise which Jehovah had not given to him.

This was also a period in which Abraham was forced to live with Ishmael, the wild, rebellious child that had come as a result of trying to force his good.

DELAY IS A TIME OF GROWTH

Though Abraham had a long wait during those 13 years, that delay proved to be a part of the master demonstration that was to come. It was during that period of delay that Abraham and Sarai had a chance to change their attitudes. They realized they could not force their master demonstration, that they would have to rely upon God's help to bring it to pass.

When your demonstration is delayed, it is because you are not yet ready for it! As soon as you have changed your thinking sufficiently and are ready to receive your demonstration, it will be ready for you and it will come. Nothing can stop it. Nothing has ever stopped it but your own wrong thinking. When you change, your world changes.

HOW TO CIRCUMCISE FEAR AND UNCERTAINTY

At the age of 99, Abraham was informed he could still have the child of promise, but that he would have to be circumcised. Circumcision symbolizes a cutting off of doubt, fear, uncertainty, bitterness. In success symbology, Jehovah was telling Abraham he could still have his son, if he would cut off and discard all thoughts of doubt, fear, uncertainty, and bitterness from his mind.

When Abraham told Sarai they could still have a child, she laughed; it seemed so incredible. The Lord reprimanded her by saying, "Is anything too hard for Jehovah?" (Genesis 18:14).

Here is the success formula for circumcising your mind: When doubt and fear try to say, "It can't be done," "You can't have it," "You'll never make your master demonstration," "It's too late," "You're too old," "It's too good to be true," "It's too wonderful to happen," "It's too good to last," you should reply, *"Is anything too hard for Jehovah?"* Hold to that thought and it will cut off all doubt and fear from your mind.

DEMONSTRATION COMES IN THE FULLNESS
OF TIME

Jehovah also answered Sarai when she laughed by saying, "At the set time, I will return to thee, when the season cometh round, and Sarah shall have a son" (Genesis 18:14).

It is interesting to note that in this passage the spelling of Sarai's name has changed to "Sarah," which is the usual spelling. This shows that Sarah had returned to a normal state of mind. Her bitterness was gone.

Your good can come to you when you enter into a normal state of mind. The Bible often speaks of the necessity for perfect timing in order to bring all elements of good needed to a situation to make way for a master demonstration. The promise to Abraham and Sarah was, "At the set time when the season cometh round, Sarah shall have a son."

In human terms you always want your good *right now*. But Divine Intelligence knows all the circumstances, situations, events, and personalities that are involved in your demonstration. It knows how to change and rearrange them so that at the perfect time your demonstration will come, so that it will be satisfying and right.

A demonstration that is forced and made prematurely is like a baby that is born prematurely. It usually dies, or it requires great effort to remain alive. But a demonstration that is made in the fullness of time is right for everyone involved, and all details arrange themselves accordingly.

When you are tempted to doubt whether you will ever get your heart's desires, you can cut off all doubt from your mind by saying to yourself: "IS ANYTHING TOO HARD FOR JEHOVAH? MY DEMONSTRATION WILL COME AT THE SET TIME WHEN THE SEASON COMETH ROUND. MY DEMONSTRATION WILL COME AT THE RIGHT TIME IN THE RIGHT WAY. JEHOVAH IS NEVER TOO LATE.

JEHOVAH IS ALWAYS ON TIME WITH MY GOOD!" Then keep picturing it mentally.

GREAT SECRET OF DEMONSTRATION

Learn to think a thing through rather than trying to force it through. This is the great secret for making your master demonstrations. You can have anything which you earn mentally. Your mind is your kingdom of accomplishment. You need not go outside your own thoughts to accomplish your desired good. All the good you can ever desire comes from your own conscious thinking. When you stop thinking that your good is apart or separate from you; when you start realizing that all things are at hand within your own thinking; when you realize that anything can be disposed of mentally and that all things can be created mentally; when you realize that all things can be done within your mind; then you have the secret for making your master demonstration.

You will stop trying to foolishly change other people or circumstances and events in the outer world to conform to what you want. Instead, you will get busy changing your own thinking. You will realize that no one can keep your good from you and that no one else can give it to you, until you have first claimed it mentally. You will realize that people and circumstances will change to conform to your master demonstration only after you have changed your own thinking!

Everything you wish to do, every change you wish to bring about, all the good you desire is first created within your own thinking. You do not have to beg, argue, or reason with anyone. Instead, go to work within your own thinking and deliberately choose that which you wish mentally. You thereby create your master demonstration! That was the lesson Abraham and Sarah had to learn. When they did, their demonstration came easily.

In every instance in which I have experienced a master demonstration in my life, I have always found, as did Abraham and Sarah, that it was delayed until I was ready for it mentally and emotionally; but just as soon as I was ready for it, having thought it through instead of trying to force it through, it appeared. Often I have become impatient, awaiting master demonstrations, only to discover after they were made that if they had come a moment sooner I could not have maintained them, because I would not have had the necessary understanding.

How did Abraham and Sarah finally make their master demonstration? They didn't! When they were ready mentally and emotionally, Jehovah made it for them and through them. "And Jehovah visited Sarah as He had said, and Sarah conceived and bore Abraham a son in his old age, at the set time of which God had spoken" (Genesis 21:1, 2).

When you think a thing through instead of trying to force it through, you cast the burden of demonstration upon the Lord, the law of mind action. Your good has been conceived on the mental and spiritual planes and the results will come at the right time in the right way.

TELEVISION ACTRESS MAKES HER DEMONSTRATION

The amazing thing about a master demonstration is when you think it through instead of trying to force it through, other people seem to tune in on your desire and get busy making your dream a reality for you!

This happened to a young television actress. She was

"discovered" when she sang on a television quiz show where she made a big hit. Just as her sponsors were planning to push her singing career, the quiz show scandals erupted and this show was taken off the air, along with many others.

Being a sensitive, talented person, this actress became discouraged by the unhappy turn of events. She dropped out of show business for a while. Later she went on the road playing in stock musicals and road companies of Broadway shows.

Then she began getting calls every week from a well-known television show to appear as a stooge. Since she weighs 250 pounds, she was used on the show in black-outs whenever a fat person was needed to fall in a flour barrel or receive a pie in the face for laughs.

Performing on a popular weekly television program revived her desire for that master demonstration — which was to sing instead of being a stooge on television, grateful though she was for that job.

About this time a friend of hers began reading my book *The Dynamic Laws of Prosperity*. She started thinking of this actress who she felt should be singing on television, using her true talent.

This friend devised a plan of action to bring this actress's singing ability to the attention of the television show on which she was appearing. She taped her friend singing some standard popular songs with a piano accompaniment in the background and put her songs on a long-playing record. She then took the jacket of a record album and reworked the face of it, pasting pictures of her friend involved in funny skits from shows on which she had appeared, along with a picture of the star of the show, and titled it, "Songs I Would Like to Sing on Your Show."

She took this novelty album jacket and the record-ing of her friend's singing to the producer of the show. He took one look at the jacket, laughed, put the record of her friend's singing on his turntable, was impressed and said, "We have been low on ideas for the final show of the season. Maybe we should allow all the players a chance to do something on that last show in order to show their real talents."

This friend then went home, telephoned the actress and said, "Your master demonstration is working! Let's just relax now and give thanks for it. We've done all we can to make it a reality."

For a month, nothing happened. Then came a telephone call asking this actress to meet with the other members of the cast to plan the last show of the season in which they would all appear. At the meet-ing she sang; they loved it and told her she was to sing on the last show. Elated, she rushed out, bought a special dress and new shoes for the occasion.

Then came the blow. The producer decided the show was running too long and told her that her song would be taken out, that she would not sing. In tears, this actress telephoned her friend the sad news. The friend replied, "Where is your faith? Is anything too hard for God? Let's just have faith that somehow it will still work out for you to sing. Let's just trust God, giving thanks that He makes this master demonstra-tion for you. I shall come to the show's taping expect-ing you to sing!"

Thereafter, whenever the situation came to mind, each of these people prayed, "I GIVE THANKS FOR THE PERFECT RESULT NOW. NOT MY WILL BUT THINE BE DONE!"

Next day, at the dress rehearsal, just prior to taping the show, the star attended the final rehearsal. This was the first time he had appeared since the early planning of the show. About halfway through the rehearsal, he stopped everything and said, "When is our little 250-pound actress going to sing?" "Oh," replied the producer, "she had to be cut out because the show was too long."

"What!" shouted the star of the show. "Leave out a gal with all that talent? Never! Put her back in, and take out something else." Surprisingly, they decided to cut out one number by the star himself! Of his own volition, the star of the show stepped back to make way for this unknown actress to sing on his show, which is viewed by millions!

This actress then sang the popular song, "All of Me, Why Not Take All of Me," and ended it by doing the "twist." The results were sensational.

Letters of appreciation immediately began flowing into this major network program. The producer of the show arranged for the finest theatrical agency in the country to represent this young actress, and she has signed to appear regularly on this show next season where she will have her own singing spot. Record companies are competing for her services. She has asked the friend that pushed her into all of this to be her personal manager!

Though several people aided in this master demonstration, isn't it interesting that when the crucial moment came, it was the star of the show who opened the way for this actress to sing?

Master demonstrations often have a surprise element. Sometimes just before they come to pass, it will look as if the tide has turned and the demonstration is not coming at all. This is when your faith is being tested one last time. This is when you are to

hold on declaring: "IS ANYTHING TOO HARD FOR JEHO-
VAH? MY DEMONSTRATION WILL COME AT THE RIGHT
TIME IN THE RIGHT WAY. JEHOVAH IS NEVER TOO LATE,
JEHOVAH IS ALWAYS ON TIME WITH MY GOOD!"

DEMONSTRATIONS BRING SURPRISES

When Abraham was 100 years old, the child so
long promised was born. They appropriately named
him Isaac, which means "joy" (see the next chapter).

Meanwhile, let us move on to see what happened
after Abraham made his master demonstration, since
it contains another success attitude for us. He realized
after Isaac was born that something would have to be
done about his first son, Ishmael, who was causing
much strife in the home. Although Abraham's heart
went out to this contentious, rebellious child, in order
to keep peace in the family, Abraham did what
seemed a heartless thing: He sent Ishmael and his
mother into the wilderness of Paran to live. But Jehovah promised, "As for Ishmael, behold I have blessed
him. Let it not be grievous in thy sight. I will make
him a great nation. He will become the father of
twelve princes" (Genesis 17:20).

The word "Paran" means "region of searching,
place of much digging." When people or situations
are like Ishmael, filled with contention and conflict,
they need those periods of searching, even digging,
to find themselves. Always that Higher Power is with
them in their wilderness experiences, blessing and
caring for them. As they find freedom from inner
conflicts, they then go forth to a happier life as did
Ishmael. Do not feel sorry for Ishmael. He needed to

be released and allowed a period of freedom and searching for his own emotional maturity. After he went through that period, he then happily married and became the father of twelve princes.

Many parents today need to realize the necessity for emotionally releasing their Ishmael-children who seem so filled with rebellion and hostility. A housewife had struggled for years to help her rebellious daughter. Despite all the mother's efforts to rear her daughter in the right way, her daughter was forced to marry in order to give her child a name.

At first, it seemed a heartbreaking experience for all concerned. Later, the mother said, "My daughter's husband and baby are teaching her things I tried for years to teach her. The discipline I tried unsuccessfully to give her is now being placed upon her by her husband and child. It is surprising that she now seems to be responding to it with adult understanding. Others are teaching her effortlessly what I tried hard to teach her in vain."

Emerson has written, "There are always some levelling circumstances that put down the overbearing." This daughter's wilderness period of searching and digging is proving a great lesson in maturity.

THERE ARE NO MISTAKES

From Abraham's release of Ishmael, we learn another important success attitude. Abraham and Sarah had tried to force their good through forcing the birth of Ishmael, only to learn that they had apparently made a mistake. Now they were having to completely release that mistake by sending Ishmael and

Hagar into the wilderness. From this release, great good came to everyone. Abraham and Sarah were free to rear their beloved Isaac in a harmonious, loving atmosphere free of conflict. Great good came also to Ishmael and Hagar since Jehovah protected and provided for them in the wilderness. You can be sure they were glad to leave the household of Abraham and Sarah, to be free emotionally to go their own way. The happy ending came when Ishmael eventually became the father of twelve princes.

In spite of all the mistakes in this situation, everything worked out fine for everyone. To the apparent mistakes in your life be sure to use this success attitude: Loosen those mistakes and let them go; and later, you will see they were not mistakes. Good still came from them. To apparent mistakes affirm, "NO MISTAKES HAVE BEEN MADE. ONLY GOOD SHALL COME FROM THIS." This success attitude helps take the pain out of the experience and produce the good. God's good is everywhere, even in what seem to be mistakes. Abraham proved this and you can, too.[3]

DEMONSTRATIONS REQUIRE CHANGES

We learn another powerful success secret from Abraham's release of Ishmael after the birth of his son Isaac.

When you make a master demonstration, you introduce new elements of good into your life. When something new comes into a situation, something old

---

3. See Chapter 7, "The Prospering Power of Mistakes," in the author's book *The Millionaire Joshua.*

must be taken from it. When something is given, something is always taken, too. Without constant elimination, there can be no real progress along this line.

Emerson aptly describes this great success law in his essay on *Compensation:* "Every sweet hath its sour; every evil its good; for every thing you gain, you lose something. A perfect equity adjusts its balance in all parts of life."

So when you make a master demonstration, get ready for surprises. You have received something. To balance that receiving, you will also have to give or release something. New wine does not flow easily into old wine skins. Your new good will not adjust itself to an old situation. You must be willing to let go whatever needs to go in order to make room for and maintain your new good. If you are not willing to let the old go as you accept the new, the new will not remain. It will leave you. You have to go all the way with your new good in order to retain it.

This is especially true when your new good includes people, as did Abraham's master demonstration. Emotional bonds are more subtle and tenacious than physical ones. So many of man's ills are caused by his unwise binding of persons and things to him, along with his allowing persons and things to bind him to them. In new situations, he must loosen and let go old relationships and old conditions in order to make way for the new ones. If he does not, the new relationships do not endure.

Many marriages suffer along needlessly because the husband and wife do not boldly rework old relationships with relatives and friends after marriage. They do not seem to realize the psychological as well as spiritual importance of the marriage vow, "forsaking all others." Though it seems a strong vow, it is a very necessary one to take literally if a happy, enduring marriage relationship is to follow.

SECRET OF KEEPING YOUR DEMONSTRATION

One final success secret you learn from Abraham about your master demonstration is this: After you make it, your faith is usually tested in maintaining it. But this only strengthens the demonstration, making it more secure, and so this testing is nothing to fear. However, you need to know about it, so that you will recognize the testing when it comes and not be frightened by it.

Abraham's faith was tested when Jehovah commanded him to take his beloved Isaac to the land of Moriah and there to offer him as a burnt offering. Though this would mean giving up his master demonstration, Abraham followed instructions and prepared his son for sacrifice. When he did, Jehovah informed Abraham he had only been testing him to see if he was willing to give up his son. Since he was willing, he would not have to do so.

After you make your master demonstration, you have to be willing to give it up in order to keep it. If you clutch it in fear, you may lose it. Only that which you are willing to release can you retain.

Instead of having to sacrifice his son, Abraham sacrificed a ram that had been caught in a nearby thicket. This ram symbolizes your unredeemed thoughts of fear, doubt, criticism that get caught in the thicket of your mind. After making your master demonstration, you must constantly sacrifice your "ram" thoughts. As you do, you are in an uplifted state of mind and are able to keep your desired good.

Often the most anxious time for you is when you are working and praying to make your master demonstration. But the most important time is afterwards, when you have realized your desired result. You must remain in the same uplifted frame of mind following your demonstration as you were in prior to the demonstration, in order to keep your good.

A person beset by difficulties will often apply himself with great zeal to solving his problems mentally. But that is only the beginning. If he gets too sure of himself and becomes mentally lax afterwards, his demonstration does not last.

CAREER WOMAN LOSES DEMONSTRATION

A career woman zealously worked mentally and spiritually to make her master demonstration which she felt would be to marry the right man. After beginning to work mentally on her master demonstration, she met the man. In her excitement to please and impress him, however, she stopped taking time for her daily periods of affirmation and spiritual study, as she spent every spare minute with him. She felt so assured that her master demonstration was working that she foolishly spoke of it to all her friends, telling them she planned to get married very soon.

For a number of weeks, it looked as though she would marry, but suddenly the man she hoped to marry changed his mind and left town. No marriage ever took place, though it had seemed so certain. This woman had not followed the same spiritual and mental standards to consummate this desired demonstration that she had followed to initiate it; and so it had no basis upon which to build a firm result.

This often happens when people receive a spiritual healing. They work diligently both spiritually and mentally to realize that healing, but when it comes, they let down, returning to the same negative state of mind that brought on the healing need in the first place. So their healing fades away and the old diseased condition returns.

Abraham worked steadily over a long period to change his thinking so that he could have Isaac, and he realized afterwards that he would have to remain in an uplifted state of mind if he was to keep his son. If a person of strong faith, such as Abraham, had to follow this success principle carefully, you and I can hardly expect to do less, if we wish to maintain our demonstrations.

PERMANENT SUCCESS

Abraham concluded his testing experience in a marvelous way. He named the place of testing "Jehovah-jireh," which is the sacred Hebrew term for prosperity and success (Genesis 22:14). It literally means, "The Lord now richly provides regardless of opposing circumstances." As Abraham pointed out, it also means, "In the mount of Jehovah, it shall be provided." Abraham was simply saying that Jehovah had provided him with his master demonstration; that success had come; and he was affirming that God would help him to maintain it.

Always it is in that "mount of Jehovah," in an uplifted state of mind, that your good is first provided and then maintained. When your master demonstration is being tested, you will find it all-powerful to take a cue from Abraham and sacrifice your fearful "ram" thoughts by decreeing the sacred Hebrew term for success: "JEHOVAH-JIREH, THE LORD NOW RICHLY PROVIDES REGARDLESS OF CIRCUMSTANCES."

You will find it helpful for getting into an uplifted, confident state of mind to affirm the further words of Abraham: "IN THE MOUNT OF JEHOVAH, IT SHALL BE PROVIDED," meaning, "IN AN UPLIFTED, CONFIDENT STATE OF MIND, MY GOOD IS NOW PROVIDED, PROTECTED, AND MAINTAINED."

After Abraham met his testing period in this victorious frame of mind, his demonstration was permanently assured. He and Isaac had many happy years together. As you follow through on his success attitude, your demonstrations will be assured, too. Your testing period will be over, and you will have been strengthened in maintaining your master demonstration. Your efforts can then be crowned with success.

THE SUCCESS POWER OF JOY
AND BEAUTY

JOY FROM ISAAC, BEAUTY FROM REBEKAH

— Chapter 11 —

Two things are indispensable to successful living: joy and beauty. Without these, your success will be hollow and totally dissatisfying. Beauty and joy are your special powers for success.

Most people think that *after* they are successful they can then afford beauty and joy in their lives. Meanwhile, they will grit their teeth and solemnly trudge toward their goal.

But joy and beauty are two qualities you must cultivate along the way to help you succeed. In the "before and after" pictures of success, joy and beauty are "before success" requirements, rather than those that just naturally come after. If you do not make them a required part of your "before success" equipment, you may never reach your goal. Even if you do, it can be a grim and totally dissatisfying journey, and *whatever success you attain without beauty and joy will be hard to hold.*

In the beginning man was born into an environment of beauty and joy. The soul of man instinctively craves his divine heritage of beauty and joy, and is attracted to and fed by beauty and joy wherever he finds them.

I once knew of an employer for whom no one liked to work. This solemn, serious man was a slave-driver in the true sense of the word. He was irritable, impatient, hard to please. One bookkeeper had worked for him for many years and finally had to resign because of ill health, which had doubtless resulted from being exposed to so much tension and unpleasantness on the job.

Everyone wondered what would become of this employer, since nobody coveted this bookkeeper's job. None of the local townspeople applied when the job became vacant.

Instead, an out-of-town bookkeeper took the job. She was a happy, jolly, attractive person, quite in contrast to the serious, drab, complaining person who had previously worked for this man. The new bookkeeper obviously expected to have a good time in her new job. She made her new employer the center of her day. She came in early to beautify his office and set things in order before beginning the day. She brought fresh flowers for his desk from her flower garden. She inquired about how he wanted everything done and made it a point to please him. She always had a happy comment to make, and she began the day with a smile. She often complimented him on his clothes or on some personal aspect of his day, or perhaps on his wife and family. By making things as joyous and beautiful for this man as possible, this bookkeeper slowly transformed her employer into a calm, peaceful, happy individual.

For the first time in years, the boss smiled regularly and genuinely. It was a joy to those about him to observe him so happy and relaxed. In his appreciation for this happy employee, he miraculously loosened his purse strings and gave her consistent raises. Soon she was making more money than his previous bookkeeper who had worked for him for many years. This happy state of affairs continued for some time until the bookkeeper's husband was transferred out of state, and she left her job to join him.

On her last day in the office, her boss actually cried quietly off and on all day. He held a luncheon in her honor and gave her a substantial bonus check as a going-away gift.

The next bookkeeper who came to work for this man was of the usual variety. She knew nothing of the success power of joy and beauty. This man retreated into his shell of unpleasantness. He soon regained his title of many years' standing: that of being the hardest man in town to work for.

NOTHING DISRESPECTFUL ABOUT JOY

The story of Abraham's beloved son, Isaac, and of Isaac's wife, Rebekah, indicates your special powers for success. The name Isaac means "joy, laughter, happiness," and the word Rebekah means "beauty and the soul's natural delight in beauty."

Life held few challenges for Isaac as he was the son of a millionaire. Not only did he inherit his father's riches, but he also acquired great personal wealth by his own efforts. He was a well-digger and a well-opener. Isaac has been described as a man of peace because he did not resist evil. When the Philistines demanded the well he had dug, he quietly left it to them, moved on and dug others, until they tired of pursuing a man who would not fight back (Genesis 26). He then settled down to a peaceful, prosperous life.[1]

The love story of Isaac and Rebekah is one of the most beautiful in all literature. Rebekah was a girl of spirit, the right wife for the retiring, unassertive man she married. Theirs was a marriage arranged by Abraham's servant, who according to Abraham's instructions, selected a wife for Isaac. The servant adorned Rebekah with rings and bracelets of gold after she responded to his request for water at the well. These rich gifts appealed to Rebekah's love of the beautiful. With the blessing of her family, she returned with the servant to become the wife of the young millionaire (Genesis 24).

As for the two success powers which Isaac and Rebekah symbolize: First, there is the success power of joy and laughter (Isaac). Just as Isaac was a well-opener, the power of joy opens up many powers deep within man's being, so that great good is released to come forth into his life and affairs.

There is nothing disreputable about joy and laughter, though many people seem to think so. To be sure, the hilarious type of joy can sometimes be in bad taste, but joy as a pleasant state of mind is always desirable.

---

1. See Chapter 4, *The Millionaires of Genesis.*

A troubled woman consulted a spiritual counselor about her problems and was given an affirmation on joy to use. A few days later she telephoned the counselor, stating she had stopped using the affirmation because she felt so joyous she was sure it must be disrespectful toward God!

THE ATTRACTING POWER OF JOY

Joy has an attracting power, whereas moodiness, discouragement and a negative disposition always have a repelling power. We tend to avoid gloomy, moping, whining, complaining people, though we are instinctively drawn to beautiful, pleasant people.

Joy and beauty are magnets for health, wealth, and happiness.

A woman who was overcome by grief, discouragement and debt felt she could not go on. One night she went to bed exhausted and defeated. She closed her eyes, wishing she would not have to open them again. It seemed that God and man had forsaken her. Though she did not pray a formal prayer, in her thoughts she mentally gave up and asked God to take over.

Suddenly, as if in answer to her prayer for surrender, she heard the word "joy" as if someone had spoken it out loud. The whole room seemed filled with light, although it was actually dark. Her first reaction was, "What do I have to be joyous about?" The thought came, "You are alive. Begin rejoicing for the gift of life." Then an awareness of other blessings came to her mind — the blessings of family, friends, job, and health.

In the coming days she dwelt often on the word "joy." She affirmed over and over, "JOY, JOY, JOY. MY LIFE IS FILLED WITH JOY." Things began to improve at once. Her grief was healed. Members of her family who had been out of work obtained jobs. A relative who had been gravely ill recovered. This woman was able to complete certain work assignments easily for which she was well paid. This helped to clear her indebtedness. She began to add beauty to her surroundings: a flower arrangement, a picture, a splash of color. In due time, joy overcame all her problems.

Emerson once said that no great work is ever accomplished without joy. Joy stimulates man's inner powers for success and releases them to work for him and through him.

Psychologists state that man uses only 10% of his mind power. Medical authorities state that man uses only 25% of his physical powers. This means that 90% of your mental power and 75% of your physical powers go unused. Joy can help you to release these latent powers for success, and to use them for a more wonderful, dynamic life.

THE HEALING POWER OF JOY

Some years ago a nerve specialist claimed he had found a new remedy for nerves. He advised his patients to try smiling under all circumstances. He told them to laugh whether they felt like it or not. He would have them remain in his office and practice smiling.

A business executive once heard a lecture on the healing power of joy. The speaker said, "If you can manage to smile continuously for just five minutes, you can cure any pain."

Later this executive had a sudden attack of acute

indigestion. He decided to see if joy would heal him. He went to the mirror and stood there smiling, while timing himself by his watch to be sure he held the smile for five minutes. By the end of the five minutes, he was so amused at this method that he was laughing aloud! Suddenly he thought of the acute pain he had experienced just five minutes earlier. It was gone.

Fun, laughter, joy are among the world's cheapest and best medicines. Give yourself large doses of these often. They will not only save you expensive medical bills, but they will help to make your body healthier and your life happier.

We would not need half so many hospitals, prisons, or mental institutions, if we took time in our daily schedule for fun and happy, relaxed living.

A LITTLE-KNOWN SUCCESS SECRET

People often reach a place in their progress where it seems impossible for them to attain their desires, no matter how hard they try. Close observation usually reveals that these people have tried so hard mentally and perhaps physically that they are under severe mental and emotional strain.

Invariably they have become tense and anxious, rarely relaxing. The result is that they have generated a strained, vibratory energy, which has built an invisible inharmonious wall around them, so that they are enclosed like a shell within it. This invisible shell of tension and inharmony is being radiated outward from them to others, and is repelling the very good which they have worked so hard to try to attain.

Just as soon as this invisible wall of inharmony and strained thought can be dissolved, the things these people desire are able to get through to them. Such people need to learn to relax, let go, and get into a happy, joyous, pleasant frame of mind. They should purposely "get away from it all" at regular intervals and have some fun. This breaks up the hard shell, and when they return to their normal activities, they will find that their problems have been solved and their desires have materialized.

If you have failed to attain your heart's desires though you have worked long and hard to do so both mentally and physically, this may be the reason. Dare to be joyous; dare to relax; dare to have some fun; dare to take a vacation and get away from it all. Dare to loose and let go all cares for a while. Even Jehovah enjoyed a sabbath after a period of creative effort. You can hardly afford to do less if you wish to truly succeed in life.

PROSPERING POWER OF FUN

A businesswoman recently commented that she knew this method worked for prosperity. Many years before, she and her husband had gone into business on a "shoe-string." They discovered that when their product was not selling and when their customers were not paying their bills, it was usually because she and her husband had become tense about their business affairs. Their tension was being unconsciously communicated to their customers, who were repelled by that tension.

This couple discovered that when things got tight financially, they should take whatever money was on hand and leave town for a few days to rest, relax, and have some fun. When they returned, customers would be clamoring for their product and the mail would be full of checks in payment from their charge customers.

Just by relaxing, releasing their business affairs, and getting into a pleasant frame of mind again, the tide turned for them financially.

ONE LAST SECRET ABOUT JOY

Although it isn't easy, joy that is expressed in the face of apparent defeat is the very thing that can turn defeat into victory. When meeting the great enemy host of Moabites and Ammonites, Jehoshaphat appointed singers to go before his soldiers, singing songs of praise and thanksgiving. They were victorious (II Chronicles 20:20-22). Moses gave the command, "Ye shall rejoice in all that ye put your hand unto" (Deuteronomy 12:7). A marvelous statement of joy that stirs up successful results in this: "THE JOY OF THE LORD IS A WELL-SPRING WITHIN ME, ESTABLISHING PERFECT RESULTS."

A civil-service employee heard a lecture on joy and began silently holding to the word "joy" during her work-day in a large office. Sometimes she would silently say, "I AM JOY." Her fellow workers, previously unhappy about many things, became so joyous that within a few days this woman had to stop affirming joy. The hilarity in her office was beginning to disrupt the work schedule!

True joy contains within it all power for good. If you will cultivate joy, you will find your life and affairs being arranged accordingly. But the great secret of the power of joy is this: Just getting the feeling or realization of joy is all that matters. Everything else will follow. When you can get a realization of joy; when you can stir up a warm feeling of joy from within yourself; then you have released the greatest power of heaven and earth to solve your problems, as well as bring forth new good.

Often that realization of joy will come when you are thinking of other things and least expect it. You may be in a quiet, prayerful, meditative state of mind, or you may be in the midst of a busy day. Regardless of what you are doing, when that feeling of joy wells up within you, you can know your problems are being solved. The good is at work for you. Joy is divine, and it is bringing divine results to you. It is that sublime, divine power of good you are feeling which is being translated as a joyous realization. When this happens, there is nothing more to be anxious about. Your good is at hand!

YOUR *SECOND* SUCCESS POWER: BEAUTY

In success symbology, Rebekah symbolizes the soul's natural delight in beauty. This is another of your success powers. Although Rebekah has been criticized for helping her favorite son, Jacob, cheat his brother out of his birthright, success symbology shows us why Rebekah did this. Jacob symbolizes the mental realm. Always a strong sense of beauty (Rebekah) develops as man's mental powers (Jacob) grow. So it is quite understandable that Rebekah (beauty) wanted to help Jacob (the mental realm) succeed in life, though her methods were questionable.

If you doubt this success symbology, watch it work in your own life. As you begin to think more of success and prosperity, you will become more sensitive to beauty in every form. You will actually begin to crave beauty in your world. Your soul will feed on beauty, drinking it in. You will find that the beautiful gives you a sense of peace and satisfaction that nothing else will.

When this happens you can know you are expanding your inner being to receive more good in your life. Some authorities claim that most of the things man strives to attain actually satisfy only about 2% of his outer nature. But if man spent more time in satisfying the desires of the other 98% of his inner nature, then the outer needs would also be fulfilled.

Just as you absorb the light of the sun and the freshness of the air, make it a point to absorb beauty in every form that pleases your soul. As you drink in the beauty of nature; as you bask in the beauty of rich furnishings and attractive surroundings; as you revel in the beauty of elegant clothes, fine literature, art, and music; as you absorb the beauty of illumined, uplifted thoughts; you are feeding that all-important 98% of your inner being. You can be sure that both your inner and outer needs are being satisfied.

As you experience beauty in the forms that satisfy you most, you are laying hold of life, health, strength, power, wisdom, and wealth. You are stirring up the qualities of life, love, wisdom, power and substance that are within you. As you learn to feed your inner being with more beauty in these pleasant ways, you will have to work less hard in outer ways. The riches of your inner being will begin to provide for the needs of your outer world as well.

HOW TO MAKE A START

A famous actress was once asked how she stayed so young, though she was actually past 70. Her reply was that she remained youthful by looking at beauty, appreciating beauty, thinking about beauty.

You can have more beauty in your world if you will begin right where you are now to add whatever touches of beauty are possible. Then dwell much upon the beauty you have added. As you do, beauty will multiply in your life, because beauty attracts beauty. Other people will begin to give you beauty. It will come in many ways. The important thing is to make a start. Also, as you dwell more on beauty and do all that is possible to produce it in your world, you will become more successful and prosperous.

PERSONAL APPEARANCE IMPORTANT TO SUCCESS

I once lectured on the importance of creating a beautiful atmosphere if one was to succeed in life. I cited the example of regularly eating by candlelight while using one's good china, silver and linens, even if the menu were only "pork and beans." After the lecture, a man approached my husband and skeptically asked, "You surely don't go along with your wife's theory that eating by candlelight helps a person succeed in life, do you?" When my husband announced that he did indeed favor this method, the man's surprised expression suggested that he might, after all, consider the idea. This man may have been a great success already but his appearance made one hardly think so.

Another businessman who was considering a new business venture went to a counselor for prayers for guidance in the matter. In his new work he would meet prominent business people, and though he had a fine knowledge of his field of work, he did not present a good appearance. He was in dire need of a haircut, a shoe shine, and a clean suit. The counselor, not wishing to offend the man by speaking of his appearance, instead spoke of the power of a prosperous appearance as a key to business success, along with the power of affirmative prayer and success attitudes.

When the businessman appeared again, he was freshly groomed, wearing a new suit and exuding an air of confidence and success. Within a short time he was successfully established in his new work, which now takes him all over the world. His prosperous appearance has helped him to meet the challenges of his international job confidently and successfully.

BEAUTY IS NECESSARY TO SPIRITUALITY

Beauty is not only necessary to your success but also to your spirituality. Jehovah pointed out the importance of beautiful clothes and beautiful surroundings as a reflection of one's spirituality. Whenever you want to feed your mind on the idea of elegant clothes and rich surroundings, examine Chapters 24-40 in the Book of Exodus. There you find the specific instructions Jehovah gave for the priests' garments to be made of fine linens of brilliant colors and worn with emeralds, diamonds, and other precious stones set in gold. Jehovah said that these garments were to be made for "glory and beauty" (Exodus 28:2). Further-more, they were to be made by "skilled workmen" (Exodus 28:6) equivalent to our modern designers and tailors. These beautiful clothes were later described as "garments of glory." As a rich child of a loving Father, you also qualify as a priest of God, entitled to wear beautiful clothes that enrich your soul.[2]

Even the tabernacle that was moved from one place to another in the wilderness was richly furnished. You find in Exodus lavish descriptions concerning the pure gold candlesticks, the curtains of fine linens overlaid in gold and silver.

In the beginning a rich, beautiful universe was created for man and that beautiful universe is still his. A loving Creator expects man to reflect his innate spirituality through appreciating and reflecting beauty in every possible way. Isaiah, one of the most power-ful of the prophets, realized this and tried to point it out to the people of his time. Isaiah belonged to the aristocratic class in Jerusalem and he may have been a member of the royal family. He constantly made rich affirmations to his followers describing beauty and joy: "I WILL GREATLY REJOICE IN JEHOVAH, MY SOUL SHALL BE JOYFUL IN MY GOD; FOR HE HATH CLOTHED ME WITH THE GARMENTS OF SALVATION. HE HATH COVERED ME WITH THE ROBE OF RIGHTEOUSNESS." (Isaiah 61:10). This is a marvelous prayer to use to invoke the success power of beauty and joy.

---

2. See Chapter 7 of the author's book *The Millionaire Moses*.

BEAUTY IS NECESSARY TO HEALTH

Beauty is also necessary for your health. When you are trying to get free of aches and pains, that is the time to wear your brightest, lightest-colored clothes. The body seems to respond to bright, light colors which suggest life, health, vitality.

Color healing is an ancient science that is now being rediscovered. It was practiced in the healing temples of ancient Egypt, India, and China. Experiments have recently been made in some of our modern hospitals to learn the effect of color on a patient's recovery. Particularly in mental hospitals is color therapy known to be effective.

A woman who had suffered for months with various aches and pains found that neither medical nor metaphysical treatment seemed to help, until it was suggested that she stop wearing the dark clothes which she had worn for so long. As she put on light, bright clothes, her body seemed to rejoice in being clothed in beauty, and her aches and pains faded away. She also looked many years younger as she clothed herself in beauty. This also helped her to mentally accept a perfect healing.

When you feel you cannot go on, dress in your best clothes, get a new hairdo or fresh haircut, and put your best foot forward. This helps you to relax and release your problems.

Often without realizing it, we try so hard to solve our problems that we actually clutch them to us mentally and emotionally, and we find that they cannot be solved. An atmosphere of joy and beauty helps us to relax and release them so that they can be dissolved and we can be rid of them.

Hospitals in the ancient Arab world were built in beautiful surroundings, amid spacious gardens. Not only were the hospital rooms large, bright, and beautiful, but music was played to soothe pain. Healing through music is another ancient science now being rediscovered. *That which adds joy and beauty to your life also adds prosperity, healing, and happy experiences.*

A MYSTICAL PROSPERITY FORMULA

There is an ancient mystical formula for putting your best foot forward for success that has always fascinated me: When you have done the best you could, seemingly to no avail, put on your best clothes and sit down to wait for the heavenly guest who is to pass over your threshold that day.

A businessman heard of this occult success formula at a time when he was wondering how to meet a pressing financial need. Having fruitlessly explored various avenues of financial help, he was considering the only one left, that of selling some valuable stocks to meet this need. Since he did not wish to do this, he decided to try this mystical success formula by putting on his best suit, looking as a rich and prosperous as possible, and sitting quietly in his office on a certain day, doing nothing, until he got strong guidance about the financial matter.

As he did this, within an hour a telephone call from his stockbroker reported that a certain stock, which previously had appeared almost worthless, had taken a sharp rise, and he would reap a rich profit if he wished to sell it immediately. Since this was not the valuable stock he had previously dreaded having to sell, he happily let it go. As he did he silently gave thanks that his heavenly guest had visited the stock market first before passing over his threshold that day!

GIVE SOMETHING BEAUTIFUL

Another way to use the success power of beauty is this: when you are depressed and things do not seem to be going your way, *give something beautiful to someone else!* It can be a beautiful object you have on hand which you wish to share; or it can be a gift which you specifically purchase for someone else.

Resolve now to begin giving, giving, giving as you have never given before. *When you think you cannot afford to give is the very time when you cannot afford not to give.*

Share your time, talents, substance. Give of your friendship and love. Give kind words of praise and appreciation. Say often to those nearest you. "I love you and I think you're wonderful." Say to the down-hearted, "You can succeed. You have what it takes!" Do not forget to give yourself words of praise and blessing, too. Self-condemnation causes more failure and ill health than anyone realizes.

Write notes, send cards for all occasions, give flowers, candy, books, records, and other lovely gifts. These acts make you feel rich and they enrich the lives of the receivers. It takes so little to make people happy; often it is the little acts of kindness which cost the least that can mean the most to others.

When your own problems have not been solved or your own needs have not been met, give something beautiful to someone else. As you do, you open the way for your own problems to disappear.

THE MAGIC OF GIVING

A man in the real estate business heard a lecture on the success power of giving something beautiful. This man had for many months tried to rent some business property. The Christmas season came and it still had not been rented. During the holidays it was brought to his attention that expensive repairs would have to be made on his unrented property.

This man's first reaction was, "With this additional expense, I cannot afford to give anything this Christmas." Realizing that he wished to receive divine guidance concerning the rental of his property, he decided to keep all channels to his good open by giving.

As though he had no extra expense, he then went forth into the Christmas shopping throngs and happily purchased gifts for friends and relatives in a greater degree than ever before. He did not give stintingly, but appropriately and joyously. With the purchase of each beautiful gift, he felt richer.

One night, just prior to Christmas, as his wife was wrapping his many gifts in beautiful holiday paper, a knock was heard at the door. It proved to be not a renter but a prospective buyer for his property. The next night, a second prospective buyer visited him. This man soon saw that although he had attempted to rent this property for months, nothing had happened until he had first entered into the spirit of joyous giving. As soon as he gave, buyers appeared. The sale of this property proved to be the happy solution to his financial distress.

The Wise Men of old knew the great secret of giving beauty. It was doubtless one of the secrets of their wealth. They traveled far with camels and servants, attired in rich, colorful clothes, adorned in jeweled turbans. They came bearing the richest of gifts for the unknown child: gold, frankincense, and myrrh. It is interesting to note that they did not first go, seek out the babe and verify His divine identity before procuring rich gifts for Him. Instead they came bearing the rich gifts in the faith that He was the Messiah and that their prayers had been answered. They gave first! (Matthew 2:11).

A wealthy lady was driven by her chauffeur over 100 miles weekly to attend a prayer group I once conducted. Always this woman came in laden with gifts for everyone in the prayer group. Often her gifts consisted of lovely flowers grown in her garden which her servants prepared as individual corsages for all the ladies in the prayer group. Sometimes her gifts were books or other items of beauty and inspiration which brought joy to the recipients. We all learned much about the success power of giving from that lady. It is little wonder she was so happy and so rich.

BE A GOOD RECEIVER OF BEAUTY

Along with the importance of giving beauty, it is also necessary to be a good recipient of the beauty which others wish to share with you. Perhaps you have had the disappointing experience, as have I, of trying to help someone in need by giving them something, only to find that either they did not acknowledge the gift, or they seemed quite unappreciative of it. *Lack of gratitude is the reason many people remain in poverty and ill health.* Often they are inclined to grab everything given them and then to be critical of their gifts, not even bothering to say, "Thank you."

Always express thanks for the kindnesses extended you, whether you can actually use the gift or not. If you cannot use it, quietly pass it on to someone who can, but express thanks to the giver and be grateful that someone cared enough to add beauty to your life. The thought of the love and generosity that accompanies a gift is priceless, regardless of the value or appropriateness of the gift itself.

YOUR SUCCESS POWERS OF JOY AND BEAUTY

As you reflect upon the success attitudes of Isaac and Rebekah, remind yourself often of your success powers of joy and beauty. Joy is a magnet for all good things of the universe to hasten to you, while depression is a magnet that causes trouble to fly to you. *There is absolutely no problem-solving power in a depressed state of mind.* All depression can be dissolved as you dwell much upon the idea of "joy, joy, joy."

Beauty is also a physical, mental, and spiritual necessity to your well-being. When your problems have not been solved, look about you to see how you can add beauty to your world. Not only should you be willing to give beauty, but be willing to receive it, too. Absorb beauty in every form. To do so first uplifts and inspires you, then opens the way for greater health, wealth and happiness to come to you than you have previously known!

PLAN YOUR WAY TO SUCCESS

THE POWER OF PLANNING FROM ESAU AND JACOB

— Chapter 12 —

What do you want to accomplish and experience during the next week, month, or the next five years? What are you doing about those dreams?

If you have just been living from day to day, taking life as it comes, then you have been pouring large portions of your potential success down the drain of failure, and you have been living a mediocre life. You have also been missing the exciting adventure that comes from planning your way to success.

Here is one of life's greatest success secrets: *You have the power to plan your way to success! When you do plan your way to success, you organize all the powers of heaven and earth to help make your plan a reality.*

If you just rock along with the tide of daily events, you automatically attune yourself to unnecessary and unwanted experiences. You live on the surface of life, exposing yourself to the disappointments, delays, frustrations, pain, financial difficulties and inharmonies that always follow surface thinking and surface living.

There is nothing new about planning your way to success. Great men of all times have dared to do so. Over and over in the face of insurmountable obstacles, they have succeeded while others without a plan have failed. What they planned for they achieved. You can plan for success and achieve it, too!

FAMOUS MASTER PLANNERS OF HISTORY

Much of the phenomenal success of Franklin D. Roosevelt could be attributed to a success plan. Twenty years before he became President, a master plan for his success was worked out, not by Roosevelt, but by a friend named Louis Howe. He became so convinced of Roosevelt's potential as a great leader that he mapped out a timetable for the future success of F. D. R. He even began to address him as "Mr. President." He refused to become disturbed about his success plans for Roosevelt even when the latter became ill. Instead he continued to work on his master plan.

Twenty years later when Roosevelt became President, Louis Howe opened a bottle of sherry he had purchased many years earlier, which he had been keeping for a celebration when his friend was elected to the highest office in the land. On that day, Louis Howe had the satisfaction of witnessing an achievement for which he had been planning for 20 years.

Perhaps you are thinking, "Yes, but it was a lot easier for Roosevelt to achieve his goals than for the average person, because he had wealth and influence to assist him."

A master plan for success works even if you have nothing more than a definite plan. If you can conceive what you wish to accomplish, you should work out a timetable for your success, hold to that expectation, and quietly get busy working toward it. Your master plan will draw to you whatever else is needed to make your life as you wish it to be. That is the magnetic power of a master plan.

We find this was also true in the case of Adolph Hitler, who used the master plan idea destructively. In the 1920's he was unknown. He had no money, no friends, no influence, nor was he trained for any skilled work. But he did have a plan which he began to invoke while in jail as he wrote the book *Mein Kampf,* in which he outlined his master plan.

A recent biographer has said that World War II might have been avoided had the proper authorities taken seriously Hitler's master plan as outlined in his book. Because he was an unknown, with nothing but a jail record and some fantastic ideas, it hardly seemed reasonable to believe him. But his master plan worked anyway—to the destruction of millions of people.

One of the most famous people of the twentieth century who planned his way to success was Winston Churchill. Early in his career he decided he wanted to prepare for public life, but he was a political unknown. He succeeded in getting some English newspapers to allow him to write for them from the trouble spots of the world. His vivid on-the-scene newspaper accounts attracted a large following, and he became popular with British readers. He then ran for various political offices. Each time he was defeated for an office, he would just run for another one!

Robert Lewis Taylor wrote in his book, *Winston Churchill: A Biography of a Great Man,* that the most mystifying aspects of the elections was Churchill's attitude when he lost. His manner was no different from those who had won! After one election in which Winston Churchill had lost, he turned to the winner and said, "I don't think the world has heard the last of either of us." This remark, coming from a man who had just been defeated, confused the winner so much that he rushed out to recheck the election returns to be sure that *he* and not Churchill had really won. The biographer wrote of Churchill, "He was a master planner."

YOUR TWIN POWERS FOR SUCCESS

The earliest master planner in the Bible was Jacob, the son of Isaac and Rebekah. As he planned his way to success, like his father and grandfather, he became a millionaire.

Historians have often described Jacob as a shrewd individual, stressing his faults and mistakes with merciless severity. To be sure, Jacob was no saint, but he became a great man, the father of the 12 tribes of

Israel. As he struggled to overcome his faults, as he was patient in disappointment, he turned to God for guidance in his extreme experiences. Jehovah never reprimanded him for his shrewdness, which was a spiritual gift. Instead Jehovah helped him to learn how to use it rightly and he went on to outstanding success. We can learn several important success attitudes from Jacob.

Like so many people who are eager to get ahead in life, Jacob first tried to force his good to him when he stole his brother Esau's birthright. Actually they were twins, but since Esau was slightly older, under the Hebrew law he was heir to his father's material riches, as well as his spiritual blessings. The word Esau means "one swept away" or "one who rushes forward wildly and impulsively." Esau symbolizes man's physical nature.

The word Jacob means "supplanter," symbolizing man's mental nature. Jacob was holding Esau's heel when they were born, showing that the mental is directly connected with the physical and attempts to hold it in check at all times, even from the time of birth.

Jacob need not have cheated to get the rich spiritual blessings his father intended for Esau. The mental realm (Jacob) is always the connecting link between the spiritual and the physical (Esau) phases of man. Had Jacob been more patient he would have eventually received a spiritual blessing. Esau, in his physical approach, as one who rushes around wildly and impulsively, as one who is easily swept away by appearances, could not have fully appreciated that spiritual blessing, and it doubtless would have been passed to Jacob anyway.

You are like Esau when you are swept away by the challenges that face you, when you rush around impulsively trying to make things right on the physical, visible plane of life only. If you handle challenges from the physical level of life alone, you are often cheated out of your birthright of good, just as was Esau.

Instead, resolve to use more fully your mental powers to claim your birthright of good. Begin to supplant your surface methods by working things out on the mental plan of life first.

However, do not underestimate the importance of Esau, who quietly went his way after Jacob took his birthright. Esau became rich, he had many possessions, and he was the head of a race. Don't forget that Esau and Jacob were twins. The physical is just as important in your success as is the mental, and you should constantly bless and care for your body, as well as for your mind.

I know of several people who upon learning of the power of thought, decided the body was not important. In their zeal to become mental and spiritual saints they became very pious and self-righteous; they criticized and denied the body its rightful functions in life. In each instance, instead of becoming mental giants, they became nervous wrecks with both mind and body affected.

When cheated of its rightful place in man's development, the body rebels. Mental hospitals bear witness to the fact that a neglected body will destroy the channels through which the mind is meant to function perfectly in man. The physical cannot be ignored. It must have its place in the fully developed person. Bless your body often, praise it, appreciate it and give thanks for it. Such an attitude heals fatigue, often heals serious disease, and makes way for the mind to work more effectively through the body to produce complete good in man's world. That mental and spiritual giant, the apostle Paul, emphasized the importance of the body when he said, "Know ye not that your body is a temple of the Holy Spirit which is in you, which ye have from God? . . . Glorify God therefore in your body" (I Corinthians 6:19, 20).

The importance of the mind and body working together is shown by the fact that years later the twin brothers, Esau and Jacob, were reunited. It was a happy occasion and a time of great rejoicing for them. Your physical and mental powers are your twin powers for success, too. When you use both for planning your way to success, the results can be happy and fruitful.

MASTER PLANNER BECOMES MILLIONAIRE

After Jacob took the birthright from Esau, he was forced to leave home. This proved to be a tremendous blessing because it gave Jacob an opportunity to develop his mental powers and to become a success on his own. As he made his way to a new land to seek his fortune, Jehovah did not reprimand him for what he had done, but made him a promise, similar to the rich promises He had made earlier to Jacob's father and grandfather: "The land whereon thou liest, to thee will I give it. . . . And behold I am with thee, and will keep thee whithersoever thou goest, and will bring thee again into this land; for I will not leave thee" (Genesis 28:13, 15).

In return for these rich promises, Jacob made a success covenant with God which proved to be his master plan for success: "If God will be with me, and will keep me in this way that I go, and will give me bread to eat, and raiment to put on, so that I come again to my father's house in peace, and Jehovah will be my God. . . . Of all that Thou shalt give me I will surely give the tenth unto Thee" (Genesis 28:20–22).

In this success covenant, Jacob clearly indicated what he would do and what he expected a loving Father to do toward his master plan for success. Jacob boldly asked for definite prosperity, protection, and reconciliation with his family. That Jacob received these blessings is clearly shown through later events. He was not only given bread to eat and clothes to wear, but he became a wealthy man. One of his sons, Joseph, became the prime minister of Egypt. Years later when Jacob decided to return from Haran to the land of his birth, he was reconciled with his brother Esau as he had decreed in his success covenant.

Even as did Jacob, you can make a success covenant with God as a powerful invoking of the master plan idea.[1] The marvelous thing to realize is that you and I have access to the same rich promises for a good life which the Lord made to Jacob and to his father and grandfather before him. Knowing our rich heritage, we should not hesitate to get busy claiming it by planning our way to success!

---

1. See chapter on "The Prospering Power of a Success Covenant" in the author's book *The Millionaires of Genesis*.

FIRST: A SIMPLE SUCCESS PLAN

There are six simple methods you can use to plan your way to success. Perhaps the easiest way to invoke a master plan for success is to sit down quietly and write out your desires for success for the day, the week, the month, or the coming year. I suggest that you write down your long-range desires for success for the coming year on one list, and then regularly write down your desires for the current day, week, or month on a separate list which you view daily.

The ancients knew the power of doing this. They found that by putting in writing how you want your life to be, you reach past all fear and uncertainty into a higher realm of accomplishment. *Through your definite written words, you dissolve all obstacles and barriers on the visible and invisible planes of life. Your written words go out into the ethers of the universe to work through people, circumstances, and events to open the way for your desired good to become a reality.*

By writing down your desires, you are getting definite in planning your success, and you make contact with the friendly visible and invisible forces all about you that wish to help your dreams come true. Your written words move on the spiritual ethers, above time, space, and circumstances, to produce successful results for you.

At one period in my life the words I constantly wrote down describing my desire for a more successful life were these: "I CLEARLY SEE THE PROSPERITY OF MY NEW LIFE NOW. MY LIFE IS FREE, GLAD, POWERFUL. SOME BLESSED GOOD IS COMING TO ME NOW. RIGHT PEOPLE,

RIGHT PLACE, RIGHT POSSESSIONS, RIGHT PROSPERITY APPEAR NOW." This definite description for success seemed to move out into the ethers and bring my good to me.

HOW THIS SUCCESS PLAN WORKS

A woman in her 40's, happily married and the mother of several children, was also a talented musician. She had played piano and organ professionally and had written several songs that she hoped to see published. She had dreamed of one day having a musical comedy she had written produced on Broadway. Concentrating on her marriage, she had stifled her dreams, thinking she should be satisfied being a happy wife and mother.

One day she learned of the power of planning your way to success, the first step being to write out your desires for immediate fulfillment. As she made lists of her desires, interesting things began to happen.

First: She wrote a song that had been scheduled for recording by a young singer for a recording company, but an unhappy situation had arisen between her and the singer's manager. After writing out her desires for this situation to be harmoniously settled and for her song to be recorded as originally scheduled, this housewife received a telephone call from the singer's manager. They met, ironed out their differences to everyone's satisfaction, and her song was soon recorded and sold briskly.

Second: Weeks earlier she had sent some jingles to a radio station, but had received no response. The day after writing out her desires, she had a call from the station. Not just one, but *ten* radio stations were interested in buying her jingles!

Third: After she listed her desires for the perfect expression of her musical talents, the producer of a summer stock company telephoned and offered her a summer job playing the piano in one of his shows out of state. She did not accept the job because she did not wish to be away from her husband and children, but this offer showed her the power of writing down her desires.

Fourth: A few days later another producer telephoned asking her to play the piano for his summer stock company which was just 20 minutes from her home!

Fifth: She had made a master recording of another song she had written and sent it out to many recording studios. When she had about given up on having that recording accepted, but had nevertheless listed it as a desire, a friend heard about her record and suggested a studio to whom she should submit it. She did, and they immediately bought her song.

Sixth: Some time previously she had written a script for a Broadway musical, but had never believed it could really be produced. After writing down her desires for acceptance of her script, she realized that a famous Broadway star was the type needed to play the leading role in her musical. She wrote to him, describing her play and asking him to consider reading the script. By return mail, he asked to see the script, which he is now considering.

All these events are preliminary steps to a successful career for this musician-housewife, but their fruition make her realize that her dreams already may be coming true.

WHY THIS SUCCESS PLAN DID NOT WORK

A young businesswoman decided to plan her way to success by listing her desires a month at a time. However, at the end of the first month, when checking her list, she realized that only three items on her list had come to pass during the month. As she studied the list closer, she realized why. Of a number of things she had listed for the month, only three of those desires had been *specific*. The others on the list had been vague, general, indefinite. The three about which she had been definite had come to pass, but the others had not.

In contrast, a schoolteacher worked on her list of success plans for several months. Finally, when 27 out of 30 items listed had come to pass, she showed me her list. It is little wonder she had been so successful. Her list revealed that she had been definite in what she wrote down about each desire. There was nothing vague, general, or half-hearted about her list. Each item was specific and clearly to the point.

WHY YOU CAN CHOOSE SUCCESS

The reason why you can plan your way to success is this: When you list your desires, make a success covenant, or work out a master plan for success, you are basically doing one important thing. You are choosing what you want instead of worrying about that which you do not want. *The word "choose" is a magic word to the mind.*

Your mind constantly works through what you choose. When you choose what you want, you feed your mind the mental equivalent of whatever it is you have chosen, and your mind gets busy trying to produce your choice as a result. The magic word which describes a real power known to the mind is the word "choice."

All things are done by choice. When you make a choice, you open the way to results. If this sounds too simple, just try it. Experience will convince you that your practice of choosing produces results. Things always happen after decisions are made. Make a mental habit of deliberate, bold, direct choosing of what you want. This causes a decision to be made in your thinking, and results always follow a strong decision. Your mental choice produces results, but it is up to you to make that mental choice first.

SECOND: ANOTHER TYPE OF SUCCESS PLAN

Along with list-making, another way to invoke your master plan is to write out in detail how you want a situation to be, in contrast to what it now appears to be. This is taking the list-making idea a step further, and it works.

I recall once using this method regarding a speaking engagement that I had accepted months before. As the time drew near to speak to a women's club, I grew apprehensive because of various reports I received concerning the unresponsiveness and supposed sophistication of the group. Most of them were reported to be wealthy, bored, cynical, women who were seeking entertainment rather than inspiration in their club work. It was even predicted that, since I was in religious work, I would not be well received by the group and should cancel the engagement.

But after further reflection, I felt that it was by divine appointment that the invitation had come to me, that perhaps those women instinctively wanted to hear the words of inspiration I would give them. I decided to take control of the situation mentally by writing out a description of how I wanted that experience to be. Among other words, I wrote down this description of my forthcoming speaking engagement: "GOD'S LOVE GOES BEFORE ME MAKING EASY AND SUCCESSFUL MY WAY. I LOVE THESE WOMEN AND THEY LOVE ME. GOD'S LOVE GIVES ME WORDS OF GUIDANCE, INSTRUCTION, AND CLEAR INSPIRATION FOR THEM, WHICH THEY LOVINGLY RECEIVE AND APPLY IN THEIR OWN LIFE EXPERIENCES. THIS IS A HAPPY EXPERIENCE FOR ALL CONCERNED, AND ONLY HAPPY RESULTS COME FROM IT FOR ALL OF US."

The result was that I have never fulfilled a more congenial speaking engagement. It took place in a lovely ballroom enhanced by flowers, music, and beautifully attired women. They did not appear bored, cynical, or unfriendly. The attractive lady who introduced me confided that she was a reader of mine, as did others in the group. As for their reception to my talk, the ladies listened intently, laughed often, and were quite responsive. (Several who were having serious problems made appointments and counseled with me later.) At the conclusion of the lecture, a lady from my home state, whom I had not seen in years, greeted me and reminded me she was a friend of my mother and had known me as a child. It was an entirely delightful experience.

FROM BOOKKEEPER TO COMPANY PRESIDENT

A man who had worked as a bookkeeper for a bakery for many years learned of the power of planning his way to success, and decided to try it. He wrote down a detailed description of the way he would like his life to be as president of his own bakery.

A remarkable thing happened only two weeks after he had written down his description of his desired success. He was approached by several people in the bakery business who said they wished to form a bakery corporation in which they would furnish the capital, but which he would manage. He would be listed as president of the company, would shoulder all responsibility for its operation, and would be given the opportunity to buy into the company as he prospered.

Today this man is a successful company president who flies around the country in his private plane, lecturing to business groups on the principles of success. It all began the day he wrote out a detailed description of the success he wished to experience.

THIRD: THE POWER OF A SUCCESS COVENANT

Another way to plan your way to success is by following the exact method that Jacob followed: that of making a definite success covenant with God in which you describe the success you will trust God to help you achieve, and in which you describe what you will do for God in appreciation. In a business agreement there is always a party of the first part and a party of the second part. Each party covenants what he will do and what he expects the other party to do. Jacob covenanted to show his appreciation to God through tithing: "Of all that Thou shalt give me I will surely give the tenth unto Thee" (Genesis 28:22).

The late Dick Cutting, a well-known actor, once wrote an article entitled, "My Free-Lance Contract with God," which appeared in the Unity publications. Mr. Cutting was a movie and television actor, whom you may have seen in early television ads playing the part of "Manners, the butler." He appeared as the little butler dressed in derby-striped pants, red vest, starched shirt, neat bow tie, carrying an umbrella. He was shown as a tiny man bringing to his hostess's attention a certain brand of table napkin. Mr. Cutting also appeared in such movies as "Magnificent Obsession," in which he played Dr. Dodge.

In his article, he recalled that he was out of work when he made his success covenant. In his covenant, he asked God to be his agent, employer, manager, and source of all his supply. In return, he covenanted to tithe a tenth of all channels of income to God's work. Of this part of his success covenant, he wrote: "A happiness-maker in my contractual dealings with God is tithing. It is a glorious feeling to give part of my manifest supply back to God so that He can use it in His wondrous ways to help others. It is an excellent system for keeping His supply flowing through me."

Concerning the power of a success covenant, he wrote, "Relying upon God as my employer has provided me with many acting jobs, some of which came when I least expected them."

He once was being considered for a part that he very much wanted to play. The character was rich in human qualities, and the role would have paid well, taking him on tour to several foreign countries. The director and writer were charming people. Everything looked promising. He worked hard in auditions and gave many readings for the client.

He then waited several months for the decision. Finally it came: the part was given to someone else. Knowing he had made a success covenant with God, this actor thought, "One door has closed, but another is even now opening." Then it came: a part that took Mr. Cutting and his wife on a long paid vacation to a beautiful section of the United States. Instead of one movie in that area, Mr. Cutting made two!

After that came an excellent spot in a television commercial that earned him residuals for months. If he had been away from the United States making the film for which he was turned down, he could not have capitalized on the bigger opportunities that came his way.

Concerning the power of making a success covenant with God, Dick Cutting concluded: "God knew what was best for me, as He always does. . . . God leads us from one good thing to another, when we let Him."

FOURTH: USE A FIVE-YEAR PLAN FOR SUCCESS

Along with (1) writing down your desires; (2) writing out a detailed description of how you want things to be; and (3) making a success covenant with God; there is still another method that you've doubtless heard about: (4) the five-year plan.

A salesman recently told the story of a former employer who is now a very prosperous man. This salesman was profoundly impressed with his former boss's apparent sudden prosperity and finally summoned the courage to ask his secret.

His former boss stated that two years before he had taken a trip to the southwestern part of the United States to consult with some oil men who were interested in his type of business. These oil men asked to see plans for his company for the next year and for the next five years. In amazement he confessed that he had no written plans. They then asked him to talk with their accounting department, who questioned him about his financial affairs.

These oil men then agreed to invest in his business provided he would go home, hire accountants to work out a five-year plan for his business success, and then seriously work toward that goal. This man followed their advice. His business, backed by these oil men, has since greatly prospered. In fact, he has become the owner of two other companies in a short length of time, now flies his own private plane, and today is a highly successful executive. He is no longer just "rocking along" trying to keep the financial wolf away from the door, and all because of definite, long-range plans.

It is good to have a long-term success plan such as the five-year plan. (As is brought out in Chapter 14, Joseph saved the ancient world from starvation because of a 14-year success plan.) But it is also wise to have a short-term success plan which is included in the larger plan, because *the mind thinks best in terms of immediate results.* In this way your mind does not delay working for your success. When it has immediate goals, and also is aware of the bigger goals, the mind gains extra incentive for bringing forth quick results, along with working steadily toward the bigger ones. The mind loves to dwell upon present and continuing results.

KEEP QUIET ABOUT SUCCESS PLANS

Perhaps you are wondering what to do if you try to plan your way to success and your plans don't work out. Always when you begin to work with a master plan, if you are truly sincere and consistent, and if your original plan does not work out, enough *will* happen along the way to convince you of the power of master planning. You will then be able to rework your desires so that more of your master plan will work.

All of the success techniques given in this book are like anything else. Practice makes perfect. The more you work with success attitudes, the more they work for you.

When your plans have not worked out, it is often because you have talked about them and dissipated their power for producing results. *Always keep quiet about your success plans.* Don't try to get someone else's approval. Don't try to convince anyone else that you are right. The doubts of others can dissipate your dream. If you keep quiet about your dreams and keep believing in them, the same Power that gave you those dreams will give you the opportunities and the means for making them come true, at the right time, under the right circumstances.

A businessman had been in financial difficulties for some time. He heard about the master plan success method, and he devised a plan for his business that covered a five-year period. For months and months, he worked on his master plan, but nothing happened. During conversations with a friend who had introduced him to the master plan idea, he realized why his plan was not working. He had been trying to convince his wife and mother-in-law that at last he was going to attain success. They didn't believe him and bluntly said so. Their doubting, critical attitudes were neutralizing his efforts.

He saw that it was not necessary for him to convince anyone of his planned success. Instead, as he quietly invoked his master plan, saying nothing, the successful results did their own convincing.

FIFTH: THE DIVINE PLAN IS THE SUBLIME PLAN

If you do not know what the master plan for your life should be; if you have no particularly strong desires or ambitions; then there is a sure method that will reveal the master plan for your success.

In recent times some world leaders have talked about the "grand design" for their country's progress. There is a "grand design" for your progress, too. There is a place in life you can fill which no one else can. There is something wonderful and satisfying which you are to do. The grand design for your life includes the right people, rewarding activities, perfect development and expression of your talents and abilities, true prosperity, and soul-satisfying success. In this grand design for your life there is no limitation; only health, wealth, happiness, and perfect self-expression are God's plan for you.[2]

---

2. See chapter entitled "Prosperity through the Divine Plan" in the author's book *Open Your Mind to Prosperity*.

You can become aware of and begin tuning in on the grand design of your life by thinking often about the "divine plan." There is a divine plan for your life, and that plan is the sublime plan. For the revelation of this divine plan to you, especially for awareness of the next step in it, affirm often: "THE DIVINE PLAN OF MY LIFE IS THE SUBLIME PLAN FOR MY LIFE. THE DIVINE PLAN OF MY LIFE INCLUDES HEALTH, WEALTH, HAPPINESS AND PERFECT SELF-EXPRESSION. THE DIVINE PLAN NOW UNFOLDS FOR ME, THROUGH ME, AND ROUND ABOUT ME IN GOD'S OWN WONDERFUL WAY. I NOW RELEASE EVERYTHING THAT IS NOT A PART OF THE DIVINE PLAN OF MY LIFE. I NOW ACCEPT AND FOLLOW THE DIVINE PLAN OF MY LIFE AS IT IS REVEALED TO ME STEP BY STEP."

SPECIAL CLUES FOR SUCCESS

SPECIFIC SUCCESS ATTITUDES FROM JACOB

— Chapter 13 —

After you plan your way to success, there are several definite success attitudes you can use to help your master plan come true. Jacob's attitudes and actions after he made his success covenant give you these special clues for success.

When Jacob journeyed toward the land of Haran to work for his uncle Laban, he seemed, from one standpoint, to have every strike against him: he had been forced to leave home; his brother had threatened to kill him; he was past 40; and he had nothing of tangible value to help him succeed.

But from another standpoint, Jacob had everything necessary for success although his assets were intangible. As he prepared to make his journey, his father gave him a blessing appropriate for a future million-

aire: "God Almighty bless thee, and make thee fruitful . . . and give thee the blessing of Abraham, that
thou mayest inherit the land of thy sojournings, which
God gave unto Abraham" (Genesis 28:3, 4).

Along with this rich blessing decreeing his success,
Jacob also held in mind his master plan for success
which he had made with Jehovah after leaving home.
Thus he started for the new land equipped with little
of tangible value, yet he possessed the basic inner
ingredients that were to bring him great rewards.

YOUR *FIRST* SUCCESS CLUE

This applies to you, too. You may not have any
tangible assets as you plan your way to success, but
remember that you have the same intangible assets
for success as did Jacob, and they are more than
sufficient to help you reach your goal. You have the
rich blessing of a loving Father, who wishes you to
prosper and succeed. That heritage for success is fit
for a millionaire! You also have your master plan for
success. *If these are all you have, then they are all
you need.* That is your *first* special clue for success.

SECOND: THINK ABOUT SUBSTANCE

After making his success covenant, Jacob journeyed
to Paddan-aram in the land of Haran where he went
to work for his uncle Laban. The word Haran means
"exalted, uplifted," and the word Paddan-aram symbolizes "substance" and success. Jacob attained an
exalted state of mind as he began to think about the

success he expected to achieve in this new land. He doubtless thought much about the invisible substance of the universe out of which his success could be formed through rich ideas and actions.

Your *second* special clue to success is this: After making your success covenant, you can also reach an exalted state of mind by expecting to succeed, by concentrating on your future success. If you have nothing tangible to help you immediately bring about that goal, then dwell upon the idea of "substance" out of which all riches come. The ancients knew the power of thinking about substance, thereby drawing success and prosperity to them.

Scientists tell us that substance is that which stands under and supports every visible object you see in the world about you. If you do not have enough money, perhaps the divine equivalent of money is trying to come to you. As you think about substance, you open the way for substance to manifest in whatever prosperous way is best for you at the moment.

You can mold invisible substance into visible results by affirming often: "DIVINE SUBSTANCE IS THE ONE AND ONLY REALITY IN MY LIFE, AND I AM SATISFIED WITH DIVINE SUBSTANCE NOW." For your more definite needs affirm: "DIVINE SUBSTANCE APPROPRIATELY MANIFESTS FOR ME HERE AND NOW." When it seems that your good is being withheld, dissipated, or taken from you, declare: "DIVINE SUBSTANCE CANNOT BE DIMINISHED. DIVINE SUBSTANCE CANNOT BE EXHAUSTED. DIVINE SUBSTANCE CANNOT BE WITHHELD FROM ME. DIVINE SUBSTANCE CANNOT BE TAKEN FROM ME. DIVINE SUBSTANCE IS EVERYWHERE PRESENT AND I WISELY USE IT NOW. DIVINE SUBSTANCE IS THE ONE AND ONLY REALITY IN MY LIFE AND AFFAIRS, AND DIVINE SUBSTANCE DOES NOT FAIL TO APPROPRIATELY MANIFEST FOR ME NOW. THE PERFECT

RESULTS OF DIVINE SUBSTANCE NOW APPEAR IN RICH, APPROPRIATE FORM."

AMAZING RESULTS OF CALLING ON SUBSTANCE

In the book *The Dynamic Laws of Prosperity,* I related several amazing stories of people who turned failure into success through affirming substance. Since I did not give the affirmations they used to attain their results, here I wish to review those stories and to point out that they used the affirmations on substance given above.

When his stock market transactions were especially low, a businessman began to call on substance. In the next two months, he made more money on the stock market than he had made during the past year.

As the owner of a cleaning plant began to call on substance, his business increased $400 per week over his previous income, even though three other cleaning plants in the same area closed down during this period.

A housewife who received an annual income from a relative's estate had not received her yearly check. At first she was fearful that it had been a bad year and that perhaps she would receive nothing. As she began to affirm substance as the only reality in her financial affairs, the check arrived late, but it was for three times the amount received the year before!

While another housewife decreed substance, her husband received the best job he has ever had in the space program. Furthermore, his new employer insisted that his starting salary would be $100 more per month than he was asking.

DOCTOR PROSPERED BY CALLING ON SUBSTANCE

A doctor proved the success power of affirming substance. As he began to decree that divine substance was the one and only reality in his financial affairs during a period of economic slump, an insurance company employed him to treat its salesmen, his fees to be paid promptly by the company. As he affirmed that substance could not be withheld from him, many of his previously non-paying patients began to pay long overdue bills!

As he affirmed that substance was manifesting for him in rich, appropriate form, another interesting thing happened: Two years previously he had attempted to purchase a piece of business property, but the owner had asked twice the amount the doctor felt led to pay. So he dismissed the matter from his mind, thinking that if the property was his by divine right, he should be able to purchase it at the lower price.

After he began affirming that substance was appropriately manifesting for him, the owner of the property came to him and stated that he now wished to sell the business property. Having no other buyers, he was ready to sell it at half the amount he had been asking for the last two years—exactly the figure the doctor had felt led to pay.

You should constantly think of and appreciate substance because it contains every element of good: life, love, wisdom, power, unlimited good. It waits upon man to form it as he will. Substance appears in your world as results according to your thoughts and words. How often you have molded tangible things, conditions, and experiences that you did not want, because you molded substance through your thoughts of disease, inharmony, old age, and failure. Now you can begin to mold substance as successful results by thinking in terms of success, as did Jacob. The foregoing statements on substance will help you open all channels to your success.

THE AUTHOR'S EXPERIENCES WITH SUBSTANCE

In my own experience, I have proven to my complete satisfaction the power that is generated by giving substance my conscious thought. In one instance, while I sat in my church study completing some writing assignments that were due, I suddenly realized how hungry I was; but there seemed to be no time to prepare food. So I affirmed: "DIVINE SUBSTANCE IS THE ONE AND ONLY REALITY, AND DIVINE SUBSTANCE DOES NOT FAIL TO PROVIDE RICH, APPROPRIATE RESULTS FOR ME NOW."

I then went back to my writing. Within a few minutes, I received a telephone call from a lady who had recently moved into the neighborhood, whom I had not met. She had seen the light on in my study and realized I was working late. She wondered if I would consider sharing a meal she had already cooked; she said that if I would, she would send it over to me on a tray, while it was still warm. Within a few minutes from the time I made my affirmation, I was enjoying a complete meal in my study, provided and prepared by someone I had never seen before.

In another instance, I was thinking of new clothes. I had in mind a particular type of dress with matching jacket that was currently in fashion, but I had no money with which to purchase it just then. Within a few days after affirming substance as the one and only reality in the matter, a friend gave me the type of dress and jacket I desired, which were more beautiful than those I had been able to visualize.

In still another instance, when my son was in need of certain items of clothing, I began to affirm that substance was appropriately providing for him. A friend telephoned late that night to say that she had a box of boy's clothing that she wanted to give to him. She even mentioned specific items of clothing that she had on hand in abundance, and they proved to be the very items that he longed for.

Never discount the power of substance. It underlies everything in your world and it is controlled by your ideas about it. Whether it is life, love, wisdom, power, or more financial good that you want, give substance your whole-hearted attention and appreciation. It will become your obedient servant, only too happy to work with you, for you, round about you — and it will provide for you in every way.

It is little wonder that Jacob became a millionaire. He knew the secret of calling on substance to meet his needs. Immediately after going to work for his uncle in Paddan-aram, when he had no tangible assets, he began calling on substance. It brought riches to both him and his uncle. It can do the same for you!

THIRD: MEET DISAPPOINTMENT CONSTRUCTIVELY

It is a good thing that Jacob got into an exalted state of mind, dwelled much upon substance, and expected to succeed when he went to work for his uncle, because he had many challenges to meet. He could not have met them victoriously had he not been in an exalted state of mind, expecting to succeed regardless of circumstances.

Jacob agreed to work without pay for seven years in order to make Laban's daughter, Rachel, his wife. At the end of the required seven years, in spite of the fact that Jacob's work for Laban had made his uncle an exceedingly prosperous man, Laban tricked Jacob into marrying Rachel's older sister, Leah.

Though this seemed unjust, we see here the law of sowing and reaping at work. Jacob had earlier been influenced by his mother into cheating his brother, Esau, out of his birthright. He was now being cheated in return. The third important clue for success to remember here is that Jacob met this disappointment constructively and then went forward to success. He realized that he was now reaping what he had earlier sown. He did not resist this sad experience because he knew he had brought it on himself. Instead he persistently worked another seven years for Rachel.

When you meet a disappointing experience constructively, you always go forward to greater good! When you are cheated, when it seems your good has been withheld from you, it may be that like Jacob, you cheated or withheld someone else's good from them in the past. An old score is now being settled. Instead of whining, "This is a terrible injustice, I have been cheated," say to yourself, "I have paid for past mistakes through this present disappointment, I meet this disappointing experience constructively and I now go forward to success." Do not waste time and energy fighting the present disappointment; if you do, you will lose sight of your success goal and you will mire down into failure.

FOURTH: PERSIST TO SUCCESS

Persistence is your *fourth* special clue for success. Jacob was determined to succeed. He knew his uncle could not cheat him out of his success indefinitely, and he proved it. He agreed to work another seven years for Rachel, which he did uncomplainingly. Emerson has written: "Good has its price, and if it came without that price, it has no root and the next wind will blow it away. I no longer wish a good I do not earn."

Remind yourself often of this great clue for success when yours is slow in coming: "EVERY DAY IN EVERY WAY I AM GROWING MORE PROSPEROUS, SUCCESSFUL, VICTORIOUS. I AM MADE FOR PEACE, HEALTH, PLENTY. I AM MADE FOR SUCCESS. I AM NOW EXPERIENCING SUCCESS IN EVER-INCREASING DEGREES OF GOOD. FOR THIS I PRAISE AND GIVE THANKS."

This is a delightful mental process to which your mind will quickly respond. Stop thinking of the failures and mistakes of yourself or others, and start concentrating on every phase of success that has been or is now evident. *The mind is strengthened, uplifted, and invigorated by thoughts and words of success; but it seems to shrivel and weaken when assailed by thoughts and words of failure and poverty.* The mind delights in helping a prosperous thinker become more successful.

As you build your mental, emotional, and spiritual foundations for success, speak in terms of your good rather than in terms of apparent problems. Speak of your blessings rather than of your challenges. Emphasize the good in your life, knowing that as you do, it will increase.

Persist in doing these things step by step, day by day. Perhaps your mind has been steeped in thought habits of loss, lack, and limitation. If so, it may take time and patient effort to clear your thinking of the negative in order to make way for success. Perseverance is your key to victory at this point.

CHARM AND PERSISTENCE LEAD TO SUCCESS

Recently a lady who manages a charm and modeling school proved the power of persistence to bring success out of apparent failure. A local rehabilitation center asked her to offer courses to two blind girls who were preparing themselves for jobs in the business world.

From the start the instructor noticed that one of the blind girls fitted easily into the pattern of ordinary class behavior. She was quiet, cooperative, and able to follow instructions with little difficulty. Since she seemed by nature a positive, ambitious person, she made good progress and was obviously benefited by the course. When she finished her charm studies, she was quickly employed as a switchboard operator. Her employers soon reported that they were pleased with her work and her happy, confident outlook on life, despite her handicap.

With the second blind girl it was quite a different story. Her husband was also blind, and they had several children which made it imperative that she find work to supplement the family income. Yet in the charm classes she frequently disturbed the other students by her talkative and sometimes boisterous behavior. She tried to dominate the discussions, and insisted upon talking endlessly about her handicap. The instructor tried to convince her that others in the classes, and fellow workers later in the business world, would not think of her as handicapped if she would cease referring to her blindness.

The instructor arranged to talk with this girl's husband, who helpfully offered various reasons for her unseemly behavior. He admitted that he had been very critical of her, especially when he would come home from work to find the house in disarray, the children neglected, and dinner unprepared. At the instructor's suggestion, the husband agreed to try a more positive approach, to praise and compliment her, and to help her to regain interest in being a competent wife and mother again. It was a new technique, and it proved to be a pleasant experiment for all concerned.

The charm school instructor obtained some inspirational books printed in Braille for this girl to read. As she studied the mental and spiritual methods for successful living, she began to respond to the classes in grooming, make-up, and fashions. She calmed down, improved her voice technique, and radiated a new sense of poise and self-assurance. As her appearance and attitude in the classes improved, a corresponding change took place in her home life. On completing the charm course, she found a part-time job which filled her needs nicely.

Because they saw the remarkable improvement made by this problem student during the charm course, the rehabilitation center officials asked the charm school instructor to accept a number of other blind girls for similar training. As a result of her persistence through difficulties to eventual success with one student, this instructor saw her school enrollment increase greatly, with more and more blind students coming to her for help.

FIFTH: PICTURING, JACOB'S NEXT SUCCESS SECRET

Although Jacob had worked hard to help Laban prosper, had married his two daughters, and had strived to provide adequately for his own family, still Laban did not reward Jacob for his 14 years of service.

Having once been deceived by his father-in-law, Jacob came to realize that he could trust him no longer. After working for many fruitless years, Jacob asked to be released so that he could return with his family to his homeland. Laban did not want him to leave because he depended upon Jacob's valuable services. He made a bargain with Jacob. He promised him that all spotted, ring-streaked, and speckled animals born thereafter to the flock would belong to Jacob, so that he might start his own herd. It sounded like a fair bargain and a step toward success for Jacob.

But soon it became apparent that Laban had no intention of sharing his wealth with the son-in-law who had made him rich. Laban secretly ordered the spotted female animals removed from the flock, leaving only plain ones whose progeny presumably would all be plain-colored.

Upon learning of Laban's trickery, Jacob realized he must now take deliberate steps to create his own prosperity. He took fresh poplar rods and peeled white streaks in them. When the strong, healthy herds were ready to conceive, Jacob placed these streaked rods in the gutters around the watering troughs where the herds came to drink. The flocks conceived before these rods, and they brought forth young that were ring-streaked, speckled, and spotted.

The imaging power of the mind brought to Jacob his own good when he was being cheated. Deliberate use of the picturing power of the mind accounts for the rapid increase in Jacob's possessions. He previously had used this picturing power to greatly increase Laban's flocks, and he now used it to increase his own.

This is your *fifth* special clue for success: When it seems your success is being withheld from you after you have honestly worked to achieve it, instead of fighting, arguing, or trying to reason with anyone to make it come to pass, quietly get busy picturing the results you desire. Then say to yourself: "MY GOOD CANNOT BE WITHHELD FROM ME. MY GOOD CANNOT BE TAKEN FROM ME. MY GOOD NOW COMES TO ME IN GOD'S OWN WONDERFUL WAY!"

Just as Jacob knew he could increase his flocks by using the picturing power of the mind, so can you picture your good and have that good quietly come to you, regardless of what others about you are saying or doing.

The success power of imaging is so important that you find it repeatedly mentioned in Biblical stories. In Genesis alone, Abraham, Jacob, and Joseph used this success power. As pointed out earlier, it was also one of the steps in the creation story. Imaging was a well-known technique for success among the ancients.

A PICTURED DREAM COME TRUE

A businessman wished to consummate a business deal which included the services of two business associates. It had previously been impossible to close this deal, because these two associates were estranged. He realized that argument or persuasion would not work to bring them together, so he quietly began to think of the two men, deliberately picturing them as reconciled, happy, and friendly again. Through a series of surprising events that unfolded, after he began holding this mental picture, the two men were brought together and reconciled. The business deal was completed with benefit to all involved.

SIXTH: BE READY FOR THE NEXT STEP

As Jacob continued to image success, both he and Laban continued to increase their wealth, though Laban seemed jealous of Jacob's prosperity. Finally Jacob had a dream in which Jehovah told him he should return to his native land. There he would be free of Laban's jealousy, and able to enjoy a good life with his family.

Laban's hostility toward Jacob's increasing prosperity proved to be a blessing in disguise. It caused Jacob to release his present place of service, which had its dissatisfying aspects, and to go forward to complete success in his own land.

This is your *sixth* special clue for success: You will find that your success is progressive. When you have reached certain stages in your growth, others around you may become hostile to your success. Often you will find that, like Jacob, you have completed the phase of your success due from that experience. The dissatisfying aspects of it are a means of "kicking you upstairs."

You have outgrown the present experience and are ready to move on into new circumstances. There you will be more independent and able to expand rapidly into your good, without restraints or interference by others.

I have found that when I have extracted the good from an experience, it often becomes dissatisfying in every way. All doors to further opportunity or advancement close to me there. This helps me to realize I have outgrown that situation, have learned all it had to teach me, and am restless to go on to new good elsewhere. Such divine dissatisfaction arising into any experience is good, because it gives us the courage and incentive needed to launch forth into new and untried experiences elsewhere.

The Indian philosopher Tagore might have been describing this phase through which we all pass on the way to our Promised Land when he wrote, "I cast my own shadow upon my path because I have a lamp that has not been lighted." When this happens to you, dare to go forth to new experiences, so that you may develop greater talents that are trying to be born. Dare to get your lamps of success fully lighted!

SEVENTH: HOW TO OVERCOME FEAR

Jacob dared to get new lamps lighted by journeying home to face new experiences. In order to live peacefully in his native land, he first had to be reconciled with his brother, Esau.

He sent word to Esau that he was on his way home. He also sent gifts. In return he learned that Esau was coming to meet him accompanied by 400 armed men. Upon hearing this, Jacob feared that his brother, remembering his past mistakes, still planned to make good his threat of many years to kill him.

The manner in which Jacob met his fears reveals your *seventh* clue for success. He sent his family ahead while he remained alone at the ford of Jabbok. The word Jabbok means "to wrestle," and there Jacob wrestled with an angel until the break of day. This angel symbolizes our own higher self with which we often wrestle when we are trying to overcome fear and solve our problems.

When a great problem looms before you, as did Jacob's uncertain meeting with his previously hostile brother, it is good to wrestle in your own thinking with the thought of good, declaring that only good shall come from the experience. In wrestling with the angel, Jacob's thigh was thrown out of joint. The thigh symbolizes your human will which is often "thrown out of joint" and dislocated when you try to force your own human way.[1] This can result in injured pride or wounded self-esteem. At such times, instead of insisting that the problem must be resolved according to your opinions, declare: "NOT MY WILL BUT THINE BE DONE. SUCCESS APPEARS AND THE GOOD BREAKS FORTH NOW IN GOD'S OWN WONDERFUL WAY." All fear and all human will can then subside, and you will be able to go out and meet that experience victoriously.

You may often have to wrestle with your ideas of success until the breaking forth of good in your affairs. Like Jacob, you *should* wrestle with your ideas of success, continuing to hold onto them until the dawning of greater good in your life.

In any challenging situation, it is always darkest just before the dawn. At such times, like Jacob, you can declare to your ideas of success and victory: "I WILL NOT LET THEE GO, EXCEPT THOU BLESS ME" (Genesis 32:26). As success breaks forth, you will no longer have to wrestle with it because you can see it working for you.

EIGHTH: RECONCILIATION BRINGS SUCCESS

It is interesting to note that after Jacob wrestled with the angel, his name was changed to Israel, meaning "prince of God." When he had cleared away all thoughts of fear, he sent forth gifts to his brother,

---

1. Read about the relationship of willfulness to the thigh in Chapter 12 of the author's book *The Healing Secrets of the Ages*.

then confidently went forth to meet him, and they were happily reconciled. This is your *eighth* special clue to success. *Nothing is fearsome when you meet it as a prince of God!* Say to your challenges: "THIS SITUATION CANNOT OVERWHELM ME, BECAUSE I MEET IT VICTORIOUSLY AS A PRINCE OF GOD."

Jacob's master plan for success had now been completely fulfilled. God had been with him, protecting him and guiding him in all types of experiences. Through it all, he had been prospered beyond his greatest expectations. He had been given 12 sons who became heads of the 12 tribes of Israel. He had been reconciled with his family and was able to live happily in the land of his birth.

NINTH: LIFE FORGIVES AND REWARDS

When you persist toward success, like Jacob your present success supplants and replaces all previous failures. This is your *last* special clue to success: Life forgives you of your past mistakes, as Esau forgave Jacob. Life becomes rewarding and satisfying for you. Indeed, you become a prince of God!

HOW TO OVERCOME INJUSTICE
SPECIFIC SUCCESS ATTITUDES FROM JOSEPH

— Chapter 14 —

In all the mail I have received from many parts of the world, I recall very few letters in which the writers stated they had had a completely happy life. Hundreds of letters have come from people who feel that their present problems are the result of unjust experiences of the past.

One unhappy woman once stated that all her problems of ill health, financial lack and personal unhappiness stemmed from the fact that she had been born prematurely 50 years ago! A former business executive who is now "down and out" financially and also suffering from severe health problems feels his troubles began when he was jilted by his fiancee who married another man many years ago. An unsuccessful salesman wrote that for years he has been trying to sell all types of products but to no avail. He then related with great resentment in the next paragraph of his letter how a relative married a multi-millionairess and has never had to work a day since. This salesman has for many years considered this a great injustice and indignantly wrote, "My philosophy of success is earn it, don't marry it."

If you feel you have been unjustly treated in life, then *join the club!* There are millions of people all over the world who are members of this sad fraternity. There is no extra membership fee for joining "Injustice International." You have already paid the price in blood, sweat, and tears. Not that your membership in this club will do you any good. In fact, to continue as a member may do you actual harm.

Many people live in a vicious circle of ill health, family problems, and financial troubles because they feel they have been unjustly abused and cheated out of their good, either in the past or present. As they continue to dwell on these unjust experiences, injustice continues to multiply in their present affairs.

The wise thing would be to consider how you can get out of this club rather than partaking of its "benefits" any longer.

Joseph in Egypt shows you how. Joseph symbolizes the imaging, increasing power of the mind. Egypt symbolizes any state of injustice in which you find yourself. It is through using your imagination justly that you are able to rise out of that injustice victoriously, as did Joseph.

FIRST: UNJUST EXPERIENCES CAN BE STEPS TO SUCCESS

The story of Joseph, as found in Chapters 37-50 of the Book of Genesis, is one of the finest success stories of all times. Joseph the dreamer became a millionaire and saved the ancient world from starvation as he developed his imagination to perceive only good from his unjust experiences. Nowhere in the life of Joseph do you find that he reacted negatively to any of the trials he experienced.

Joseph might be described as the first truly positive thinker of the Old Testament, because he constantly dwelled upon and claimed the goodness of God in every experience.

Many people nowadays consider it a modern concept that God is good, completely good, and only good. But there is nothing new about this viewpoint. Joseph knew that God was good, and he proved the success power of holding to this concept of God in the midst of prolonged injustice and hard experiences of every kind.

If you should feel that you have had a hard life filled with all kinds of unjust experiences, it will make you feel better to read the life of Joseph. He had to meet jealousy, injustice, slavery, deceit, imprisonment, and privation, but he never allowed these negative experiences to get him down. *He made every unjust experience a stepping stone to success and so can you!* This is your *first* success secret from Joseph.

SECOND: FROM INJUSTICE TO SUCCESS

If ever there was anyone who had a right to an injustice complex, it was Joseph. Joseph, as the favorite son of his father, Jacob, was given a coat of many colors. This made his brothers jealous. At the age of 17, Joseph had a dream in which his brothers' sheaves were bowing down to Joseph's sheaf. In another dream, the sun, moon, and stars were honoring Joseph. These dreams were symbolic of the success Joseph was to achieve later as prime minister of Egypt.

Joseph made the innocent mistake of telling his dreams to his jealous brothers, who resented his grandiose claims. They then sold him to some merchants for 20 pieces of silver, and he was taken to Egypt as a slave.

In Egypt Joseph was sold to Potiphar, an officer of King Pharaoh. For a time things went well for Joseph, as an overseer of Potiphar's affairs. But a period of temptation, suffering, and bondage began for Joseph when Potiphar's wife falsely accused him of committing adultery with her. He was imprisoned without trial.

But Joseph would not be kept down. He mastered his dungeon experience and soon he was placed in charge of the other prisoners. When King Pharaoh became displeased with his chief baker and butler, they were sent to prison and placed in Joseph's care. They told Joseph of their strange dreams, which he interpreted. As Joseph predicted, the chief baker was hanged by order of the king; but the chief butler was restored to his job at the royal palace.

The chief butler promised Joseph that when he was restored to favor, he would tell Pharaoh about Joseph's ability to interpret dreams, but he did not. For another two years Joseph languished in prison, completely forgotten. During this period he might have become very discouraged and bitter toward the chief butler for his lack of gratitude, but he did not. *Joseph intuitively knew that there is a universal law of justice that always comes forth in due season to make all things right when it is quietly recognized.*

One day Pharaoh had a dream that the magicians and wise men of Egypt were unable to interpret. It was then that the chief butler remembered Joseph, who was hastily brought out of the dungeon. Joseph easily interpreted the king's dream in which he predicted seven prosperous years and seven lean years for Egypt. At this point, Joseph's troubles were over. The success he had imaged since he was 17 was now within his reach.

One might say that Joseph was an "overnight success." He had awakened that morning in a dungeon where he had languished for several years, but by nightfall he was prime minister of all Egypt, second in command to King Pharaoh of the most powerful empire of that age.

Joseph proved that any picture firmly held in mind is bound to come forth in its own time and way. He proved that the longer your success is in coming, the bigger it will be when it arrives, provided you quietly hold to the thought of success every step of the way. This is your *second* success secret from Joseph.

THIRD: A SUCCESS FORMULA FOR INJUSTICE

On the day Joseph became prime minister of Egypt, King Pharaoh took his signet ring from his finger and gave it to Joseph. He arrayed him in fine clothes and put a gold chain around his neck which indicated his high office. He also had Joseph ride in the second chariot. To make his success complete, Pharaoh then gave Joseph a wife. At the time of his sudden rise to success, Joseph was 30 years old. It had been 13 years since his brothers had sold him into slavery. He immediately began touring the land as prime minister, directing grain to be gathered and stored. During those seven prosperous years, his two sons were born.

Certain success attitudes are revealed in the name of his sons. He named the first son Manasseh, which means "forgetfulness." His reason for thus naming his son was, "God hath made me forget my toil and my father's house" (Genesis 41:51).

This is a powerful success attitude. Joseph knew that to dwell upon hard experiences of the past would impair his present success. Like Paul, he was forgetting the things that were behind so that he could press forward to present success (see Philippians 3:13, 14).

You may feel that you have every human right to be bitter about the past, but your human rights to bitterness will not heal the past nor help you succeed in the present. Much ill health is caused by allowing destructive emotions to lock the mind in a vise of supposed injustice. When you entertain feelings of resentment and bitterness, your health is certain to be damaged. Such acid emotions can keep success from you too. Joseph knew this and refused to allow himself to become embittered, for he knew that *bitterness is a luxury none of us can afford.* This is your *third* success secret from Joseph.

BITTERNESS CAN MAKE YOU SICK

A retired businesswoman had been ill for months. Her physician said her system was filled with poison, which drugs had not dissolved. After prolonged treatment, her ill health persisted. Finally her doctor told her there was no physical reason for her illness, and that he was not certain how to diagnose her case.

When a friend called her one day, the sick woman spoke of the uncertainty as to the cause of her illness. The friend replied, "I do not know what your health problem is, but I know what will cure it. When there is a health problem of long standing, which medical treatment has not been able to heal, there is a need for releasing thoughts of injustice and bitterness from the past and present. Bitterness produces poison in the mind and body."

These words met with a deep response within the sick woman. She realized that she was filled with thoughts of injustice from long ago. She then poured out a story of bitterness and resentment which she had retained in her memory for many years. Some years previously, she had been divorced by a "worthless husband" who left her with a small son to support. The responsibility of rearing a child alone gave her a feeling of injustice, about which she was still very indignant. As she told this part of her story, she described in venomous terms just what she still thought of her former husband.

Her bitter story continued as she told how unjust and unfeeling her brother had been, when she had turned to him for financial help after the divorce. He had done little for her and her son, and for many years had ignored them completely, although he had become a millionaire. She felt that any effort to try to mend an old misunderstanding between them would make it appear that she was "after his money," but the bitter memory of unjust treatment from him lingered.

After she struggled for years to rear and educate him, her son had become a fine business executive. He had provided his mother with a lovely little home, a car, and a generous monthly allowance. Although she was very proud of her son, she hated his wife who, because of previous unpleasantness, would not allow her to visit in their home.

Although this woman was now living in comfort, instead of counting her current blessings, she was still dwelling on the hard experiences of the past. Her bitterness was not hurting her former husband, her millionaire brother, or her son's wife. They were all busy and happy. Instead her bitterness had poisoned her own mind and body. She was a sick, miserable, unhappy woman who was unable to enjoy her lovely home or drive her nice car. Her main activity was to remain at home nursing resentments about the past.

The friend, who had pointed out that feelings of bitterness and injustice produce poison in the mind and body, suggested that this woman release the past and daily count her present blessings. It was also suggested that she make plans to visit soon with someone she enjoyed, assuring her that as she did, her mind and body would improve.

Though it was difficult to turn her attention from the past to the present, she did so. The next time the friend heard from her was by a postcard she mailed from a distant city, saying that she had decided to visit an old friend and that it was proving to be a happy experience. Furthermore, her health had improved considerably during her brief visit.

As this woman continued to concentrate on her present blessings, forgiving and releasing the injustice from the past, her ailments faded away. The bitterness in her dissolved, too. This sick, embittered woman soon became a normal, healthy individual again.

Just as Joseph wisely declared, "God hath made me
forget my toil and my father's house," this woman
found it wise and life-giving to forget the unhappy
experiences of the past.

FOURTH: BE FRUITFUL IN THE MIDST
OF AFFLICTION

Joseph named his second son Ephraim, which means
"very fruitful," "productive," because he said, "God
hath made me fruitful in the land of my affliction"
(Genesis 41:52). Joseph knew that only as he named
his past experiences "good" could he be successful in
the present.

When he affirmed, "GOD HATH MADE ME FRUITFUL
IN THE LAND OF MY AFFLICTION," he was saying, "ONLY
GOOD RESULTS CAME FROM ALL MY TRYING EXPERIENCES,
AND ONLY GOOD RESULTS SHALL COME TO ME HERE AND
NOW." Many people ruin their lives by nursing the
hurts of unjust experiences. If, like Joseph, they
would forgive and call those unjust experiences good,
they would be surprised at the success that would still
come to them.

Like Joseph, you can become successful in the place
of your affliction if you will decree concerning it:
"GOD MEANT THIS FOR GOOD AND I INSIST UPON THE
GOOD FROM THIS EXPERIENCE. I SHALL BECOME VERY
SUCCESSFUL BECAUSE OF THIS EXPERIENCE."

During the seven lean years, when Joseph's brothers
journeyed to Egypt to buy grain, he recognized them.
When they came a second time he revealed his true
identity saying, "I am Joseph your brother, whom ye

sold into Egypt." He then explained how he felt about what had seemed a most unjust experience: "God did send me before you to preserve life . . . And God sent me before you to preserve you . . . And to save you by a great deliverance. So it was not you that sent me but God . . . God hath made me lord of all Egypt" (Genesis 45:4-9).

Joseph clearly pointed out that he believed his unjust experiences had actually been part of a divine plan for the preservation of life, for the deliverance of many out of famine and starvation. Despite injustice, his divine destiny to become prime minister of Egypt was fulfilled.

If you will examine the unjust experiences in your life, you will see where a divine plan was at work in the midst of them. Something good resulted from them. People often develop their inner powers and abilities when they have to face extreme experiences, which they would never develop if they coasted along on the surface of life.

Joseph later arranged for his whole family to come to Egypt to live. After his father Jacob's death, his brothers feared revenge. But Joseph again reassured them, "Fear not . . . As for you, ye meant evil against me, but God meant it for good" (Genesis 50:19, 20).

When other people seem determined to wrong you, decree: "YOU MAY MEAN THIS FOR EVIL, BUT GOD MEANS IT FOR GOOD." And for past grievances affirm: "GOD MEANT IT FOR GOOD!" In that way, you will still tune in on the good from any distressing experience.

It is through this *fourth* success attitude, illustrated by Joseph, that you can become prime minister of your world. When you dare to be fruitful in the midst of affliction, you, too, reap rich rewards.

FIFTH: LOVE AND JUSTICE
NEUTRALIZE INJUSTICE

A woman once telephoned me about an unjust experience she and her husband were facing. She angrily described how a business acquaintance was trying to cheat them out of their good in a financial transaction. When her husband took their foreign car to the only dealer in town who repaired such cars, they were told that parts would have to be ordered from Europe.

Weeks went by before the parts arrived and the car was repaired. When this woman and her husband went down to pick up the car, they became indignant about the amount of the repair bill, and refused to pay it. Thus the car remained with the dealer for several more weeks, while they consulted an attorney. He investigated and suggested that they pay the bill, saying it was not exorbitant under the circumstances.

For weeks this woman had been making strong, condemnatory statements about the injustice they had endured. They finally paid the bill and picked up the car.

But before long the car was in need of repairs again! Since there was only one dealer in the area who could repair it, they were again facing the same man. History repeated itself: He examined the car and stated he would have to order more parts from Europe. Again there was delay. Again they questioned the repair bill.

At this point, the woman telephoned me wanting to know what to do. I suggested that she clear the air of negative feelings by clearing her own mind of the belief in injustice. It was pointed out that until her belief in injustice was resolved in this situation, she would continue to have trouble. Stolidly she began affirming: "THE DIVINE LAW OF LOVE AND JUSTICE IS DOING ITS PERFECT WORK IN THIS SITUATION NOW, FOR THE HIGHEST GOOD OF ALL CONCERNED."

She had become so upset about this experience that it had made her sick. As she began to use statements affirming love and justice, she calmed down and began to feel better. When she had gained a sense of peace and harmony about the situation, and had cleared her mind of ill feeling toward the dealer who had repaired the car, she went back to his shop, greeted him in a friendly manner, and was amazed when he told her he had decided to charge her less than the original figure quoted. The matter was concluded harmoniously. As she continued to affirm divine love and justice for the entire situation, her car gave no further trouble.

But six months later this woman again contacted me. This time she was as upset and angry as before. She stated that a great injustice had been done to her husband in a business transaction. The apparent injustice had disturbed her so much that she became ill, went to bed, and was treated by several doctors. The last doctor had been able to help her, but she had a relapse and went back to bed when she saw his bill. Not only was she bitter about the earlier injustice that had made her ill, but *now* she was sick about the medical bill and felt the doctor had been equally unfair. Injustice had multiplied for her.

Again she was given the same statement to use: "THE DIVINE LAW OF LOVE AND JUSTICE IS DOING ITS PERFECT WORK IN THIS SITUATION NOW, FOR THE HIGHEST GOOD OF ALL CONCERNED." It was pointed out that this was the same affirmation that had been given her for previous grievances. She now understood that she was paying a high price for her resentful attitude. Because of her repeated declarations of injustice, she had attracted more unjust experiences to her. Since she felt she was constantly being wronged, her decrees had made it appear so.

It was suggested that there were probably bitter experiences in the past which she had not forgiven or released; that she should search her memory and get busy forgiving such experiences; that only as she was able to overcome her belief in injustice would her life be free of it.

For many months this woman daily affirmed that the divine law of love and justice was at work in her life. She has had no more unjust experiences. She is a happier, more secure person who now realizes that it was her own attitude that attracted these unjust experiences to her. She knows that as long as she keeps her thinking straight, injustice cannot touch her. Thoughts of love and justice can neutralize injustice in your life too. This is your *fifth* success secret from Joseph.

SIXTH: SHOCKS CAN BRING GROWTH

Resolve now that you will release any injustice complex you may now have, so that you will be free from this day forward from unfair treatment. Joseph clung to the thought of God's goodness during 13 years of cruel, searing experiences. It seemed that both God and man had deserted Joseph, but he refused to believe it. His faith paid off in a big way.

The ideas that have helped me the most when I have seemed beset by unjust experiences have been these by James Allen in his book *As A Man Thinketh:*[1]

> Suffering is always the effect of wrong thought in some direction. It is an indication that the individual is out of harmony with himself. . . . A man only begins to be a man when he ceases to whine and revile and commences to search for the hidden justice which regulates his life. As a man adapts himself to that hidden justice, he ceases to accuse others as the cause of his condition, and builds himself up in strong and noble thoughts. He ceases to kick against circumstances, but begins to use them as aids to his more rapid progress.

When I quoted this passage in a lecture, a lady in the audience got so upset by these words that she rushed home and went to bed. It was a shock for her to realize that her own thoughts had caused so much injustice in her life. It was also a shock to learn that she would have to give up her false beliefs that other people and outside conditions had caused her unjust experiences.

But as Emerson points out, our growth sometimes comes in shocks. It proved true for that lady. After she recovered from the shocking truth about injustice and started putting the blame for injustice where it belonged—squarely upon her own attitudes—she was able to begin straightening out her thinking and her life. She arose from her bed of pained thinking and went forth to a much healthier, happier, more prosperous life. Our growth can come in shocks, too. This is your *sixth* success secret from Joseph.

---

1. Published by DeVorss & Co., Marina del Rey, CA 90294.

SEVENTH: CALLING ON HIDDEN JUSTICE
MAKES THINGS RIGHT

Instead of holding unjust thoughts about your life or the lives of others, begin now to declare that there has been and now is a "hidden justice" coming forth from what seems to be unfair experiences. This will help you to balance your own thinking. As you right yourself, you will find all things and people in your sphere becoming right, getting into proper perspective. They may move out of your life, or you may leave theirs. If not, desirable changes will come in present conditions.

A businessman was in an automobile accident. It seemed a most unjust experience. He was riding in a taxi to a business appointment, when the taxi driver ran through a traffic light and crashed into another car. This man was injured and out of work for several months. His medical bills piled up, and he had to borrow money on which to live.

When the case opened in court, the judge stated that the insurance company was not liable for anything more than his medical expense. The man was asking for additional funds to take care of the time he had been away from work, as well as for paying the medical bills. The court awarded him only one-third of the amount he requested, which barely paid his bills and did not pay for lost time from work.

Since he was not (to all appearances) responsible for the accident, it seemed an unfair settlement. But this man knew better. In reality he knew he had attracted that accident and unjust court settlement to himself. During the morning preceding the accident, he had attended a business session where remarks by the leader of the meeting incensed him so that he angrily left the room. He then returned to his office, vented his anger there, called in an associate and for an hour loudly criticized the leader of the meeting. (This was not the first time he had so acted, for he had been criticizing this business leader for months.) It was later that day that he took the taxi which had the accident.

This man was a student of the mind. He knew that he could not be wronged, cheated, or taken advantage of by anyone but his own unjust thoughts. He knew he had to clear up all thought of injustice or further wrongs would stalk his path.

Instead of brooding about the matter, he took full responsibility in his own thinking for all the injustice that had come to him. He then began clearing it up by decreeing that the divine law of love and justice would still do its perfect work for him; that his hidden justice was now revealed.

For several months well-meaning relatives and friends insisted that he appeal the court decision. Instead, he continued to affirm that the hidden justice was revealed. As he did, justice came to him in another way. Upon returning to work after the accident, he received a promotion he had long hoped for, went on to a higher paying job, and within a short time had received in income the additional sum he had hoped to receive as the court settlement! Nothing had been lost. His good came, but not in the way he had expected.

Don't hold on to unjust experiences. Affirm that the hidden law of justice is still at work, coming to you in God's own wonderful way. Then release the unjust experience. Stop talking about it. Stop thinking about it. Let it go completely. That opens the way for the hidden justice to reveal itself to you, often in ways that will surprise you, through new and un-foreseen channels. This is your *seventh* success secret from Joseph.

DO NOT FEEL SORRY FOR OTHERS

Charles Fillmore has written in his book *The Twelve Powers of Man:* [2]

> Many persons doubt that there is an infinite law of justice working in all things. Let them now take heart and know that this law has not worked in their affairs previously because they have not called it into activity. When we call our inner forces into action, the universal law begins its great work in us, and all the laws both great and small fall into line and work for us.

Begin now to "call" the divine law of justice into action by proclaiming: "THERE IS A HIDDEN JUSTICE AT WORK IN MY LIFE AND AFFAIRS, AND IT BECOMES VISIBLE NOW."

Begin to "call" the divine law of justice into action for other people, who seem to be at the mercy of unjust experiences. Declare for them, "THERE IS A HIDDEN JUSTICE AT WORK IN YOUR LIFE, AND IT BECOMES VISIBLE NOW."

We often waste a lot of time feeling sorry for other people. This never helps them or solves anything. When you see someone who seems to be a victim of injustice, you can begin to help him to think right,

---

2. Published by Unity School of Christianity, Unity Village, MO 64065.

if he is receptive to right thought. In any event, you can begin to think right about him by decreeing love and justice, and by calling on the hidden justice in the situation to appear.

It is especially good to remember that you can call the law of justice into action for other people, when they seem unable to invoke it for themselves.

This is especially true where children are concerned, for they seem defenseless against apparent injustice at the hands of others. When you observe this, remind yourself of the great truth stated in an earlier chapter: the soul of man is created in the image and likeness of God and has been given dominion over every phase of life. The soul of man has the power to choose the circumstances into which it will be born in order to grow, unfold, and develop certain talents and abilities.

When you find a child growing up amid injustice, you can know that before birth his soul chose those circumstances through which to evolve, and ultimately to fulfill its divine destiny. You can know that such a one is a strong soul who will often go on to a better adult life than will youngsters around him who are meeting less strenuous challenges. How true it is that "out of the mud comes the lily." As you read the biographies of great people who have made splendid contributions to mankind, you often find a history of apparent injustice in their early lives. Instead of feeling sorry for children amid injustice, affirm: "THE HIDDEN LAW OF JUSTICE IS AT WORK FOR YOU, MAKING ALL THINGS RIGHT."

In like manner, when you hear of a person dying an "untimely" death, it seems unjust, especially if a spouse and young children are left behind. But the soul decides when it will leave this world and under what circumstances, so there is truly no injustice. Always the power of choice has been exercised, though perhaps subconsciously. The soul is fulfilling its divine destiny in some way you cannot humanly see or understand. Man is like an iceberg. In reality we see only a small part of his entire being.

COLLEGE STUDENT PROVES JUSTICE

A college student felt that she was being discriminated against by a professor because of her race. She felt that he was unduly critical of her work. She became especially disturbed when, at the beginning of a term, she was again assigned the same professor who had given her failing grades previously. She felt that it was grossly unfair to be required to take the same course under the same professor again.

She talked with a counselor who suggested that she use this experience to prove that the only injustice in this situation stemmed from her own unjust attitudes. She was advised that as she cleared up her attitudes of injustice toward the professor, the situation would be resolved.

Reluctantly this student began affirming: "THE DIVINE LAW OF LOVE AND JUSTICE IS NOW WORKING PERFECTLY THROUGH ME TOWARD ALL PEOPLE, AND THROUGH ALL PEOPLE TOWARD ME." Gradually her attitude improved; so did her grades and her relationship with this professor. In due time she realized that her thinking was really the source of her difficulties. At the end of the term she passed the course in good standing, and all ill feeling had faded away. This student had proved the words of Emerson: *It is impossible to be cheated by anyone but yourself!*

JUSTICE IN STATE SENATE

A lady senator seemed to meet injustice on every hand in her first term of service in her State Senate. It was a frightening experience. As she tried to introduce legislation that seemed important, a veteran senator who resented her presence warned her that he would use his power to defeat her bill. Though she worked hard and gained the approval of many, it seemed this man's insidious actions would win out.

However, a young doctor who was interested in the passage of her bill learned of the prejudicial measures which the senior senator was trying to take against this lady. He heard this senior senator boast that his influence would kill any bill this woman sponsored. The doctor had several friends who agreed to join him in affirming daily for this lady legislator: "THE DIVINE LAW OF LOVE AND JUSTICE IS NOW WORKING PERFECTLY THROUGH YOU TOWARD ALL PEOPLE, AND THROUGH ALL PEOPLE TOWARD YOU."

When this lady's bill came before the Senate for approval, the elder senator rose and said, "I do not approve this bill and I intend to defeat it. As you all know, I have the seniority, the influence and the power to do it. This bill shall not be passed." Usually such claims by this senator brought the results he desired.

But this time some of the younger legislators conferred among themselves. They decided to change their vote in favor of this bill, believing that no piece of legislation should be defeated merely because of spite. The bill was passed by an overwhelming majority!

EIGHTH: JUSTICE WORKS IN MYSTERIOUS WAYS

If you think you are being unjustly treated by relatives, friends, employers, or by your government, invoke the activity of divine justice. This is the most enduring reform which you can apply to the situation. When you are in doubt as to the right thing to do in seeking justice in your affairs, ask that the eternal spirit of justice come forth into the situation and reveal to you that which is your own good. *Then accept the results that come, whether they are what you personally expected or not.* Justice works in mysterious and surprising ways. This is your *eighth* success secret from Joseph.

Conversely, if you are tempted to criticize and judge others, declare: "I NO LONGER CONDEMN OR FIND FAULT WITH OTHERS. NEITHER DO I BELITTLE OR CONDEMN MYSELF."

When you affirm divine justice for yourself and others, you become more loving. You refrain from all manner of criticism. You keep your eye fixed on the good. Your mind thinks more clearly. You develop a more kindly disposition. In fact, a wonderful renewal of your whole being takes place.[3]

---

3. See Chapter 4, "Your Healing Power of Judgment," in *The Healing Secrets of the Ages.*

NINTH: JOSEPH'S BASIC SUCCESS SECRET

The *basic* success secret we learn from Joseph[4] was that he met and conquered his hardships because he insisted that God's goodness was present in every situation. Furthermore, Joseph would not accept defeat. Instead, he trained his imagination to see only the good and he reaped a rich harvest of goodness. He refused to hold a grudge against anything or anybody, since he realized that such a grudge would withhold success from him.

Affirm divine justice for all your life experiences. As you do, your life will take on a magic touch. It will no longer seem dull or meaningless. You will experience health, happiness and true success. For this purpose affirm often: "I USE MY IMAGINATION TO SEE ONLY THE GOOD, AND I REAP A RICH HARVEST OF GOODNESS." This might have been Joseph's victory prayer. It can surely be yours!

---

4. See chapter on "The First Billionaire, Joseph" in the author's book *The Millionaires of Genesis.*

SEX IS A SUCCESS POWER

GENESIS' FINAL SUCCESS SECRET FOR YOU

— Chapter 15 —

Let us get down to the plain facts about sex. When you realize the true nature of sex in its three phases, you will find yourself better able to understand and control one of your greatest powers for health, wealth, and happiness.

In this enlightened age, much emphasis is being placed upon the life force within man commonly known as sex. Everywhere you look, sex is present in some form. In the mineral world, you observe sex as chemical affinity. In the animal world, you see sex as the desire for procreation. In the world of man, *sex is basically the desire for self-expression, the desire to create and to share in every phase of life.*

Many popular songs, books, movies, and television programs are based on a sexual theme. Newspaper columns and books offer advice to the love-lorn and sexually frustrated. A few decades ago, sex was considered a taboo subject in polite society. With the relaxed standards and freer attitudes of today, the glorification of loose morals leads many people to believe that the Ten Commandments have gone out of style.

However, there is a reason for the increasing interest in sex. *The subject of sex is foremost in the mind of man because sex is a natural, normal phase of his being that demands expression on all levels of life. Sexual desire is always with you in some form because it is the life force that fills you from birth to death.* Your family relationships—maternal, paternal, and filial—and your friendships and associations with others outside your family, are all phases of sex activity. You cannot escape sex in some form.

SEX IS NOT SINFUL

In the past, religious leaders have either remained non-committal or loudly condemned sex, and some have shunned the subject completely. Many people have been confused by theological comments about sex as the "original sin," or that man was "conceived in sin." However, as pointed out in Chapter 4, the only sin mentioned in the Genesis creation story is that of Adam and Eve partaking of the belief in evil.

As for man being conceived in sin, *God created man in His own divine image,* as stated unmistakably in the first chapter of Genesis. The second chapter of Genesis describes how God took His highest creation and gave him life: "Jehovah God formed man of the dust of the ground and breathed into his nostrils the breath of life, and man became a living soul" (Genesis 2:7).

As explained earlier, the term "dust of the ground" seems to have confused many people; it simply means that man was fashioned out of the universal radiant substance from which everything upon earth is formed. Scientists describe this radiant substance in exalted terms, declaring that it is filled with light, energy and every degree of good that man could ever desire. This term "dust of the ground" definitely does not suggest that mankind was conceived in sin. Man was conceived and created by God Himself, without sin or stain.

God would hardly have created Eve for Adam if sex were a forbidden phase of man's being. Instead, the Bible indicates that God created Eve for Adam to give his life meaning and balance: "It is not good that man should be alone. I will make him a help meet for him" (Genesis 2:18).

The only forbidding (and forbidden!) thing about sex is man's gross misunderstanding and consequent misuse of this great life force. God meant it to be a high and holy phase of man's being, and we should remember that the word "holy" means "whole, balanced, integrated." The Bible does not ignore the subject of sex. It plainly gives many examples of how sex, when rightly expressed, leads to a happy way of life. The curse which Jehovah God placed on Adam and Eve, causing them to leave the Garden of Eden, is meant to indicate that sex unwisely expressed leads to bondage and unhappiness. As stated in Chapter 4, man can return to Eden whenever he gets back into an Eden (pleasant, harmonious) state of mind. This applies to the sexual phases as well as to other aspects of this life.

You may find it confusing as you read the Book of Genesis to realize that some Bible patriarchs (such as Abraham and Jacob) had more than one wife. These men lived many years before Moses—centuries before God gave man the Ten Commandments, which stipulated higher standards of conduct. In those ancient days, it was believed that marriage within one's own family and the taking of more than one wife were divinely approved practices, so that the Hebrews would not have to marry into "heathen" races. It was also practiced to encourage God's people to grow in numbers, as He had promised they would.

SEX IS THREEFOLD

You should not suppress or feel guilty about your deep desires and longings, but you should learn how to properly direct them. There are many ways you can express sex because it is threefold. Sex is (1) physical, (2) mental-emotional, and (3) spiritual. Realizing this, you will find that there are many ways you can properly direct your sex drive into these three phases of your being.

Physically, sex is the basis of your bodily energy and drive, your health and vitality. *Mentally and emotionally,* the life force expressing through you is your deep feelings, your talents and abilities, your intellectual and emotional urgings. It is your mental access to ideas and your emotional ability to produce satisfying results by using those ideas.

Spiritually, the life force expressed through you is your passion for the Truth about God, man, and the universe. When you "hunger and thirst after righteousness," that is your life force coming alive in your spiritual nature. Your prayer power and intuitive ability, your spiritual insight and understanding, your desire to know more of God and His goodness, to express it in your own life and to share it with others — these are your spiritual outlets for the life force within you. People who go about doing good individually and in organized groups are expressing the life force on the spiritual level.

Sex is far more than just physical desire. It is the creative desire for worthwhile self-expression in every aspect of life. When this tremendous sexual desire is not channeled constructively, it becomes bottled up and suppressed so that destructive results usually follow, such as mental disorders, nervousness, frustration, emotional imbalance, drug and alcohol addiction, and other ills. Immoral relationships and undue preoccupation with the subject of sex are the result of misunderstood, misdirected sexual desire.

Conversely, much of the beauty and convenience we find about us are the result of man's deep sexual desire to create, to express, and to share on the physical, mental-emotional, and spiritual levels of life. Art, music, literature, the inspiration of religious zeal, and the wonders of scientific research are just a few of the important expressions of the life force in man which have contributed to the advancement and increasing satisfaction of the race.

SEX IS MORE THAN PHYSICAL

The grand secret about sex is that it can be trans-muted and directed through your thoughts, attitudes, and actions to benefit every phase of your world!

Thus, do not deprecate sex. Appreciate it in its threefold nature and make it work for you. You can become its master instead of its slave.

At times you may have found sexual desire welling up in your physical nature as powerful longing and desire. You probably sought to gratify that desire on the physical level, which gave you relief. At other times you may have discovered that physical expression of sex was not enough to bring relief. The discontent, the restlessness, the vague inner longings continued to haunt you.

Often people have said, "I found the act of sex disappointing, after I had been led to believe it was the supreme experience of life." Such disillusionment comes because the sexual desire within you wishes more than just physical release to bring true satisfaction. It also desires expression through the mental-emotional and spiritual phases of your being. Erich Fromm has explained in his book *The Art of Loving:*[1] "Sexual desire aims at fusion, and is by no means only a physical appetite, the relief of a painful tension."

Because of this deeper emotional and spiritual desire for expression, illicit sexual relationships are dissatisfying and usually frustrating. They cannot provide the deeper meaning or the secure feeling of loving

---

1. Published by Harper & Row.

and being loved on the highest level, because shady sexual relationships have a built-in guarantee for only temporary thrills and lasting self-condemnation.

HOW TO SATISFY YOUR DEEPER LONGINGS

How do you satisfy your deeper sex longings? It is much easier and simpler than most people realize.

A woman felt that her husband was making undue sexual demands upon her and that he was also dissipating himself physically, risking his health and affecting his potential business success. A little conversation revealed that her husband was greatly dissatisfied with a new job he had taken. He felt unsure of himself in this new field, after having been eminently successful in another type of work.

It was pointed out to this wife that her husband's attention might have been unduly centered on physical sex satisfaction simply because he was not finding mental and emotional satisfaction in his new work. His lack of mental and emotional sexual release had perhaps caused the life force within him to become dammed up, goading him to seek overactive release on the physical level.

It was suggested that this lady give her husband as much mental and emotional support as possible by sincerely praising his ability to make good in his new work. She was told that this would help her husband to begin properly expressing the life force within him on the mental and emotional levels again; and as that happened, their sexual relationship could then become normal.

She followed these suggestions. Her praise of her husband's abilities helped him to dissolve feelings of inferiority and insecurity that the challenge of his new work at first presented. Not only did their sexual relationship return to normal but her husband became successful in his new job. Also, their marriage took on a new glow of mutual appreciation as she continued to express sincere praise, patience, and kindness.

YOU CAN DIRECT PHYSICAL DESIRE

Perhaps you are thinking, "Yes, but just how do I know which way to direct my deep longings and desires, when those periods of restlessness and discontent come?" Realize that Divine Intelligence pervades the universe and you. Affirm at such times: "DIVINE INTELLIGENCE NOW DIRECTS MY DESIRES CONSTRUCTIVELY FOR MY GREATER HEALTH, WEALTH, HAPPINESS, AND FOR TRUE FULFILLMENT." Divine Intelligence loves to work for you. It is your obedient servant that awaits your recognition and command. Scientists state that you live in a sea of intelligence which is moved upon by your thoughts.

You might also find it a source of satisfaction and peace to affirm: "WITH GOD'S HELP, I AM DIVINELY SATISFIED IN MIND, BODY, FINANCIAL AFFAIRS AND IN MY RELATIONSHIPS NOW." Do not be afraid to turn to your loving Father about your sexual desires, because your Creator gave you those desires in the first place to motivate you toward greater self-expression and fulfillment. God knows all about sex, so do not cut yourself off from your best source of help during your restless periods.

At such times, the life force within you feels stifled because it is seeking more than just physical expression, which is also appropriate at the proper time. Perhaps some new talents or latent abilities are trying to come forth through you.

Many married women who do not need to work, and many retired people, too, continue to work, since it gives satisfaction and emotional release to their talents and abilities.

A businessman was intensely disturbed about his deep desires which caused his mind suddenly to become strongly preoccupied with the allures of sex. His relations with his wife had not dispelled his mental and emotional fascination with the subject.

In this connection, Joshua Loth Liebman has written in his book, *Peace of Mind*.[2]

> All of us have amoral fantasies and unmoral dreams. They are part of our mortal equipment. To deny their existence is impossible; to bury these thoughts and fantasies in the subcellar of our minds is to invite explosions of guilt, aggressions, and even physical pain.

This man's amoral fantasies soon became an obsession with him. He became frightened, and thought he was "losing his mind."

In this state of anguish and turmoil he came to me for counseling. He stated that he was very successful in his work, active in community affairs, that he had

---

2. Published by Harper & Row.

a happy home life, and was one of the pillars of his church. Upon questioning him, it was revealed that, as a business executive, he was under severe mental strain daily. When I asked about his recreational activities, he declared that he had little time for diversion, but that he read at home in the evenings, listened to music, and relaxed mentally. It was evident that perhaps he needed more physical release to balance his unusual mental activity.

This executive followed the suggestion that he should become more active physically during his leisure hours. He resumed his habit from college days of playing golf and tennis. He joined a bowling team and began doing some outdoor gardening. In a number of ways he externalized his energies and gave more attention to the physical plane of life.

When the subject of sex tried to assert itself in his thinking, he began saying silently, "PEACE, BE STILL." When guilt feelings about his intense sexual thoughts tried to crush him, he learned to overcome them by frequently reading the 51st Psalm: "CREATE IN ME A CLEAN HEART, O GOD, AND RENEW A RIGHT SPIRIT WITHIN ME. IN THE INWARD PARTS MAKE ME TO KNOW WISDOM." In these ways he was able to re-direct his thinking and his desires. The life force within this man found physical and spiritual direction, as well as mental-emotional balance.

SEX IS MENTAL

People with active, keen minds often need to consciously direct their deep desires to both the physical and spiritual levels of life, as did this man, in order

to balance their highly developed mental-emotional
natures.

The life force within you is filled with intelligence.
It knows when you need to think more of your physical being and to express more on that level. It knows
when you need to express within yourself more on
the mental and emotional levels; and it knows when
you should be giving more attention to your spiritual
development. Furthermore, the life force within you
has many ways of sending you warning signals about
how to direct your desires.

Rhythm is the law of the universe and is needed
by each person for a well-integrated life. Often if you
are not aware of the level on which your desires should
be expressed, the innate intelligence within you will
balance and integrate those desires through your subconscious actions. You will simply do whatever is best
at the moment to bring balance without consciously
realizing it. But at times, when those desires need
a special change of pace for balance, if you do not
subconsciously respond to them, they may react quite
dramatically in order to get your attention, and urge
a drastic change needed for balance.

A young unmarried man once found that his mind
suddenly became very confused. After months of
intense concentration in his work, he found himself
intellectually exhausted. He did not care for most
physical sports. Realizing that he must externalize
his attention more toward the physical plane of life,
he began daily sitting quietly out-of-doors, observing
nature and enjoying the sunshine and fresh air. In
this simple way, as he began directing his attention
outward, his mind began to clear. It was several
weeks before he was able to resume the mental work,

but he had found this a simple way to bring physical and mental balance again.

GET RID OF EXTREME NOTIONS ABOUT SEX

Many people have extreme notions about sex. Some believe it is wonderful to glorify the physical expressions of sex, as depicted in most movies and novels nowadays. Others take the stern puritanical view that sex is evil, and that the body should be denied. Both viewpoints obviously need to be balanced. Sensuality, over-indulgence, or perversion of the natural forces in man are clearly not normal or healthy, and neither is asceticism. To deny the body its natural functions does not make a person wise or holy, and it certainly does not lead to a satisfying way of life. There is no more reason for seeking life-fulfillment through asceticism than there is in trying to find satisfaction in over-indulgence. Both extremes are abnormal and usually bring abnormal results.

A woman once bragged that she had not allowed her husband to have sexual relations with her for over ten years. She thought she was being "very spiritual." She seemed shocked when told that her ascetic habits obviously had warped her attitudes toward marriage and toward life in general. Her body was afflicted by ill health, and she was extremely nervous. Her rigidly ascetic attitude toward her husband probably arose from her deepseated fear of sex.

It was suggested that she consult a doctor. When she did, he bluntly told her that her husband should have "thrown her out" years ago! He then talked to her about readjusting her concept of sex as being normal and right, rather than as "sinful and harmful." He pointed out that she should enjoy all her senses, for that was why God gave them to her. He informed her that moderation, not total suppression, was the answer to her ills, and his advice proved true.

After another lady had studied occultism, she became convinced that she should cease all sexual contact with her husband. Some months later she began to realize that her extreme ideas of being "holy" had driven her husband into several affairs with other women, as well as to alcoholism. She finally saw that there was nothing holy, balanced, or satisfying about a marriage that produced such unhappy results. When she resumed normal relations with her husband, the other women soon faded out of his life.

This lady was startled to learn that the Bible does not say there is anything wrong with sex, but simply describes the many problems that the wrong use of sex can cause. Jehovah God gave clear decrees to Moses concerning the moral behavior of the Hebrews. In the Book of Leviticus, unchastity, adultery, and incest are specifically prohibited. In the New Testament, the apostle Paul gave definite instructions on sex to the early Christians in his First Epistle to the Corinthians. There he discusses wedlock, the behavior of the married, the unmarried, the virgins and the widows.

This lady also learned that attraction between men and women is essential to their balanced development, as well as to the expression of their talents on all three levels of life. Generation, the bearing of children, is a divine urge for man's self-expression. The need for reproduction is not the only reason behind the force that draws men and women together. God put desire in man and woman so that the world should be preserved and enriched by their union, just as He implanted in each form of life the desire for its counterpart.

Each male has qualities of body, mind, and spirit that complement qualities in the female. Likewise, a woman's feminine qualities need to be harmonized with her mate's masculine attributes to assure a richer, more balanced life. Divine Love and Wisdom generate the physical magnetism that draws men and women together and that holds them together. Biologists refer to this basic attraction as the law of gender, by which all Nature seeks to unite male and female elements for balanced integration. Sexual desire between male and female is a natural yearning for fulfillment through mating and true union. A prominent religious leader has described sex as "solace for the soul."

SUBLIMATION CAN PRODUCE SUBLIME RESULTS

Conservation and right use of the life force as sexual expression are important for a happy marriage. Excessive use of the physical drive in man can lead to ill health, emotional imbalance, intellectual lassitude, and even to prostration and death.

A young couple often boasted to their friends that they had had sexual relations every night for years. It certainly seemed plausible—the wife looked at least ten years older than she actually was, and her husband died prematurely at the age of 36.

Are you unmarried and wondering how to express your sexual desires in a satisfying way? Medical authorities have observed that, while the weak, nervous individual may become unbalanced when his or her sexual appetite is curbed, the strong person is made still stronger by sex conservation! The life force needs to be conserved, not suppressed, in order to properly be released through your mental and emotional nature as talents and abilities.

A keen, alert mind that is being used constructively is a marvelous channel for the life force, and it can accomplish tremendous work without undue effort. Thus to refrain from physical sex expression does not mean that one is sexless or devoid of sex appeal.

Dr. Alexis Carrel has written in his book, *Man The Unknown:*[3]

> The testicle, more than any other gland, exerts a profound influence upon the strength and quality of the mind. In general, great poets, artists, and saints, as well as conquerors, are strongly sexed. The removal of the genital glands, even in adult individuals, produces some modifications of the mental states. . . . Inspiration seems to depend on a certain condition of the sexual glands.

If your life situation is such that sex activity is not a part of it, do not feel that you are being left out in expressing life's basic force. You can know that the lack of physical sex activity is leading you to greater expression of your innate talents on the mental and emotional planes of life. As you get busy deliberately developing your talents mentally and emotionally, they will lead you to greater prosperity, happiness, and a deep sense of fulfillment. This can lead to a

---

3. Published by Harper & Row.

happy, well-adjusted life that may eventually include marriage and physical fulfillment.

Man has been prone to believe that physical sex expression is the only satisfying outlet for his genera-tive powers, but sexual energy is also brain energy and emotional go-power. *Many outstanding achieve-ments have been made by men and women who turned their passion into intellectual and artistic efforts.* This fact should be of special interest to those who find that personal choice or other circumstances have shaped for them an unmarried state.

MANY PEOPLE ARE AFRAID OF SUBLIMATION

If you are disturbed by the idea of sublimation, realize that the word "sublimate" and the word "sub-lime" have a common root meaning!

A business woman, who was widowed, insisted upon having an affair with a married man. For sev-eral years this affair continued, offering only tempo-rary physical relief for this woman, attended by emo-tional turmoil and confusion. She became very ner-vous and her financial affairs were so disorganized that she almost went bankrupt, though prior to this affair she had been quite successful in her work.

She firmly believed that this unsavory affair was needed for her physical comfort. It terminated only with the death of her lover, and she was left to mourn in painful silence while his wife inherited his fortune and soon happily remarried. All that this business woman could hope to collect from this experience was her wits. She was then forced to face her dire financial situation.

What a pathetically high price this woman paid for so little satisfaction! During the years of her illicit relationship, had she dared to sublimate her sexual desire into emotional drive for business success, she doubtless would have retained her previously fine health and financial security. Perhaps she would also have happily married.

Sublimation is nothing to fear. It can lead to the development of talents, powers, abilities you never dreamed you possessed. It can also lead to a happy, balanced way of life that includes marriage and sexual fulfillment.

DISSIPATION LEADS TO FAILURE

There are simple ways that people regularly dissipate the life force. Scattered thinking, scattered emotions, scattered actions all lead to a scattering of the life force that depletes you of physical energy needed for success; it depletes your mental energy required for an intelligent course of action for progress; it depletes your precious emotional drive essential for putting that plan to work, and for persevering until success is achieved.

When a person refuses to practice sexual sublimation and transmutation, even temporarily, he often meets with emotional disappointment and financial failure.

The easiest way for a person who finds himself (or herself) in an unmarried state, but who strongly desires marital happiness, is to begin conserving his physical forces and activating his intellectual and spiritual abilities. This very process will develop within him that "certain something" or "inner glow" that will radiate from him unconsciously as a magnetic quality. It will attract to him the right people and situations that can add to his personal happiness and success. This is true sublimation and it can lead to sublime results.

KINDNESS IS SEX IN EXPRESSION

You often need the emotional expression of sex more than the physical! All mankind needs the emotional expressions of sex, such as sincere praise, kindness, patience, courtesy, good will. Indeed, the world seems crowded with married people who have physical access to sex and yet who are still unhappy. Often the emotional aspects of sex, expressed as simple kindness, are lacking in these marriages. Usually when these emotional aspects of sex are freely expressed, the marriages are happier and more secure on all levels. But when this aspect of sex is left out of the marriage, it can be the cause for all kinds of trouble.

HOW TO RE-ESTABLISH SEX IN MARRIAGE

As a wife persistently offered praise and kindness to her philandering husband, his wayward actions changed, and their marital rift began to heal. He had not been intimate with his wife for several years, and he still hesitated to do so.

Finally one night his wife felt she could no longer be deprived. She wanted to assure her husband of her deep love for him in spite of past events, which she realized had been partly her fault. In making physical and emotional preparation, she dressed especially for her husband, and quietly waited for his return from a late business meeting. As she waited, she quietly formed the mental picture of him as a loving husband in every way.

She visualized her husband as the ardent lover he had been to her on their honeymoon. She pictured herself as the loving, attractive, understanding wife she had once been to him. Over and over she declared softly to herself: "OURS IS A HAPPY, SATISFYING, WELL-ADJUSTED MARRIAGE OF TRUE AND LASTING FULFILLMENT."

When her husband came home, he seemed to be subconsciously attuned to her feelings. After several years of coldness, their marital relationship was happily and satisfyingly resumed. In fact, they later had several children.

Another housewife, whose husband had not made love to her in five years, solved the problem by directing her attention to the spiritual plane of life. She began to daily pray: "I GIVE THANKS THAT DIVINE LOVE IS DOING ITS PERFECT WORK IN MY MARRIAGE NOW." As she affirmed divine love, her husband's indifference was replaced with kindness and a new interest in her, and he resumed their sexual relationship. Their marriage has never been happier.

Whether married or unmarried, it is good to know that a basic universal law is the law of polarity that ever seeks expression through man. Within you are both masculine and feminine characteristics that need to be developed in order to give you a well-integrated personality. Until you begin achieving this polarity or balanced expression of love and wisdom within yourself, there will be little satisfaction or happiness from your relationship with others. For this purpose, affirm: "LET DIVINE LOVE AND WISDOM BE BALANCED IN ME. LET DIVINE LOVE AND WISDOM EXPRESS BALANCE THROUGH ME NOW."

If you feel that this thing called love is lacking in your life, begin to realize that you can deliberately arouse love from within yourself. As you do, it will subconsciously flow out from you in mysterious and happy ways to attract to you whatever responses of love you are ready for. *When you develop your innate love faculty sufficiently, there will be no need to reach out and try to force love to come to you.* Instead, love will spontaneously come rushing to you, magnetically attracted by your own inner radiation.

WHAT ABOUT FRIGIDITY AND IMPOTENCE?

While there are people who seem to concentrate on the physical experience of sex, others show little interest in it, their cool indifference earning some women the label, "sexually frigid." Many a wife has frozen up in the face of what she feels are excessive demands by her husband. But quite frequently such a wife has exaggerated her husband's ardor in her mind, and by secretly resenting him, has subconsciously only activated his attention more and more. Some people are more responsive to the mental-emotional phases of sex, which give them the same warm glow and sense of fulfillment that others find through physical sex.

Often people find themselves as marriage partners to the opposite type, in order for each to give the other the balance between the physical and mental realms that is needed for a well-integrated personality and way of life.

Resistance to sex isn't the answer. Graceful adjustment in which one thinks of the other's needs can help bring balance and harmony in the relationship. Imperious demands by the husband or frigid indifference by the wife are unhealthy extremes which must be brought into balance. In such situations it is good to affirm: "DIVINE ORDER, HARMONY AND PERFECT ADJUSTMENT ARE NOW ESTABLISHED AND MAINTAINED IN OUR MARRIAGE."

Husbands would often find their supposedly frigid wives more physically responsive to sex if they gave them the emotional stimulation of praise, kindness, courtesy and consideration on a daily consistent basis, not just in connection with the physical act of sex.

Male impotency is often considered a medical problem affected by hormonal changes, or as a side effect from the use of certain medications. It has been reported that emotional abuse of past or present, whether physical or verbal, as well as drug abuse, can cause either frigidity in women or impotency in men. Both medical and chiropractic professionals, as well as psychologists, psychiatrists and other therapists have reported favorable results in treating these problems.

SEX IS SPIRITUAL POWER

Just as sex is physical and mental-emotional, sex is also spiritual. There are times when you need to deliberately direct your attention to its spiritual phases for your balance, serenity, and well-being.

When you want to be alone, when you need to be quiet and meditative, when you seek to absorb uplifting words from the Bible or other inspirational literature—at such times your spiritual nature is trying to get your attention, so that it may fill you with new life, new hope, new inspiration, new peace.

When you have your quiet times of prayer and inspirational study, meditating upon some spiritual word of power, you often feel a warm stirring of life within you. It tranquilizes and harmonizes your whole being. If your body has been fatigued or in pain, often that energizing life dissolves the pain and fatigue. If your mind has been confused or fearful, that soothing life can calm and clear your thinking. If your emotions have been irritated, that quickening life can pour a healing balm upon them. Depression and discouragement fade away. Along with giving you peace of mind and a sense of deep inner joy, that vital life surge will reveal to you wonderful new ideas which you can use to bring great success to your world. Dr. Alexis Carrel might have been describing this process when he wrote in *Man the Unknown:* "Man integrates himself by meditation just as by action."

What is that warm life within you? It is the life force which is always with you from birth to death. On the *physical* plane we have described it as sex. On the *mental-emotional* plane we have described it as talent and ability. On the *spiritual* plane, it is your prayer and healing power. It is the God-power coming alive within you.

When the life force wells up within you in your quiet times, realize that it is your divine instrument for good. You are making contact with the greatest power on earth — the living power of God within and around you. When you contact and release this life force, wonderful things happen. And in the process, you prove to your own satisfaction that sex *is* a success power that can pervade every phase of your life!

Conclusion . . . .

REMEMBER—YOU CAN
HAVE EVERYTHING!

One of the greatest success attitudes I have shared with you in this book is the promise, "You can have everything." In countless ways the success secrets of Genesis convey to you that message, from the lavish creation story to the astonishing success story of Joseph.

I shall never forget the fascination which those four words held for me when I first saw them years ago in an inspirational article. I was so thrilled with the slogan "You can have everything" that I clipped it from the article and taped it in a place where I could view it daily. Whenever I was doubtful as to whether desired good was coming to me, I would reassure myself by reading over and over those confident words. I held fast to those words for years. Gradually they have transformed my life.

SUCCESS ON ALL LEVELS OF LIFE

In closing, I wish to share with you one last success story related to me by a reader from Nevada:

So many wonderful things have happened to me and mine since I began studying *The Prosperity Secrets of the Ages.* I can only list here the most dramatic results I have obtained:

1. I was unemployed at the time I began to study this book. I affirmed for a good position with a salary of $15,000 or more per year. *Result:* I had my choice of two jobs! The one I chose pays $15,000 plus a commission. Total income last year as an Employer Consultant and Negotiator of Labor Contracts for Employees' Associations was in excess of $20,000, and it will be far more this year.

2. I gave a copy of *The Prosperity Secrets of the Ages* to a friend who was unemployed and unhappily involved with a married man. *Result:* She got a job within a week. A few months later she married a fine, successful businessman and is presently expecting her first child. She no longer has to work.

3. I affirmed an annual $50,000 increase in revenue for the organization for whom I work. *Result:* $20,000 has been replaced in lost membership, and an additional $30,000 revenue has been scheduled.

4. Part of my responsibility in my job is that of labor negotiator (an unusual job for a woman). It fell my lot to go up against the largest and most powerful union leader in this state, and one of the most powerful in the United States. I had never negotiated on my own before. No one believed I had a chance. My own board of trustees was about to desert me. In the middle of my negotiations, the director gave notice of quitting and the whole staff also threatened to quit. (This was not related to my

negotiations, however.) In addition, the attorneys retained for my organization (because of imagined wrongs) notified the board president they would withdraw their services if I were kept on.

I made appropriate affirmations continuously throughout that two-month period. *Results:*

(a) Complete success in my negotiations! I have become famous for my courage and skill at handling the whole business.

(b) The president of the board gave me his complete confidence . . . and stood between me and the forces who were threatening me . . . and he fired the attorneys.

(c) Two more attorneys came to my assistance at no cost to my organization.

(d) The whole board of directors now agrees that my negotiations have established a precedent that has improved the labor relations climate for the entire state.

(e) More beneficial results are happening daily. We have a new managing director who is very compatible with the staff and me.

5. My 16-year-old daughter has learned the value of speaking forth prosperity affirmations daily, and is on her way to a wonderful way of life. She has quadrupled her income through affirmations used from *The Prosperity Secrets of the Ages.* She was earning $30-$35 per week. She is now earning this and more per day.

6. The employers whom I represent have individually given me very generous gifts. I have started one employer on the way to success through giving him *The Prosperity Secrets of the Ages.*

7. I owned a second deed of trust that had been delinquent for two years. I affirmed "light" and prosperity for the person who owed me. *Result:* He paid me off in full just before Christmas.

8. Lost objects have been found.

9. I had been affirming I would soon be a size ten again. After using an affirmation, one of my clients made me a present of a weight reducing program which begins tomorrow.

Just as predicted in this book, my funds seem to buy more and last longer now. It is a good feeling to have a balance left over after paying one's bills on time. Furthermore, my tithes are ten times what they were only a few months ago! All of these experiences have proved to me that it is true: *I can have everything. And so can you!*

THE AUTHOR'S FINAL MESSAGE

I find it significant that the "Book of Beginnings" —Genesis—begins and ends in an atmosphere of lavish abundance. I trust that as you use its "success attitudes" herein described, you shall experience the peace, health and plenty that are yours by divine right. It's true: "You, too, can have everything!"

CATHERINE PONDER

SPECIAL NOTE: Suggested for your further study is the author's companion book, *The Millionaires of Genesis.*

ABOUT THE AUTHOR

Catherine Ponder is considered one of America's foremost inspirational authors. She has written more than a dozen books, which include such best sellers as *The Dynamic Laws of Prosperity,* and her "Millionaires of the Bible" series.

She is minister of the nondenominational Unity faith—long known as "the pioneer of positive thinking"—and Dr. Ponder has been described by some as "the Norman Vincent Peale among lady ministers." She has served in Unity churches since 1956, and heads a global ministry in Palm Desert, California.

She is listed in *Who's Who in Religion* and *Who's Who in the World.*

A SPECIAL NOTE FROM THE AUTHOR

Through the generous outpouring of their tithes over the years, the readers of my books have helped me to financially establish three new churches — the most recent being a global ministry, the nondenominational *Unity Church Worldwide*, with headquarters in Palm Desert, California. Many thanks for your help in the past, and for all that you continue to share.

You are also invited to share your tithes with the churches of your choice — especially those which teach the truths stressed in this book. Such churches would include the metaphysical churches of Unity, Religious Science, Divine Science, Science of Mind, and other related churches, many of which are members of The International New Thought Movement. (For a list of such churches write The International New Thought Alliance, 5003 E. Broadway Road, Mesa, Arizona 85206.) Your support of such churches can help spread the prosperous Truth that mankind is now seeking in this New Age of metaphysical enlightenment.

NOTES